Hartner

No. 2627
$23.95

TURBO PASCAL PROGRAMMING
with applications

Dr. Leon A. Wortman

TAB BOOKS Inc.

Blue Ridge Summit, PA 17214

Turbo Pascal, Turbo-87, and TurboBCD are trademarks of Borland International, Inc.
TTIDY is a trademark of Major Software.
Spinwriter is a trademark of NEC.
IBM is a trademark of International Business Machines.
WordStar is a trademark of MicroPro International.

FIRST EDITION
FIRST PRINTING

Library of Congress Cataloging in Publication Data

Wortman, Leon A.
Turbo Pascal programming with applications.

Includes index.
1. PASCAL (Computer program language)   2. Turbo
Pascal (Computer program)   I. Title.
QA76.3.P2W68   1985   005.13′3   85-22292
ISBN 0-8306-0227-5
ISBN 0-8306-0127-9 (pbk.)

Contents

Disclaimer

The contents of this book represent descriptions, explanations and examples of programs intended to be compiled and executed with the Turbo Pascal compiler copyrighted and published by Borland International. This book is intended for educational and entertainment purposes. No warranty of the book's contents and programs in any specific or general application is made by the author or by the publisher of this book. The reader or the user of the materials contained in it is solely responsible for the applicability.

Acknowledgments

I am especially grateful to Phillipe Kahn and his excited, enthusiastic, and high-spirited team at Borland International. They've broken the pattern that was appearing to become the software industry's mold: high prices, doubtful quality controls, incomprehensible documentation, and nonexistent or grudgingly given customer support. Borland's business methods are proving that, if all else should fail, one should try integrity. And, they aren't even faced with "failure," but with continuing success.

My debt is also acknowledged to Thomas O. Sidebottom, one of the most talented "multilingual" programmers in Silicon Valley. As my living tutor, he patiently helped me climb out of a BASIC programming rut to a gratifying level of skill with Pascal.

Introduction . . .
Get Ready!

Were you one of those who noted an especially important event in November 1983? At that time a small and unknown company in Scotts Valley, California, started shipping version 1.0 of a new compiler for the relatively old and well-known Pascal programming language. The company called its product Turbo Pascal. Borland International, the company, still calls it by that name, but now the company is much bigger and is very well-known worldwide.

Pascal, the programming language, was originally created as a language particularly well suited to teaching computer programming in the classroom. Pascal may never have been intended for use in writing complete applications programs. If that was so, however, many of us weren't aware of it and began to extend the use of Pascal outside the classroom and into applications and utilities of all sorts, simple and complex.

During the past several years a number of variations of what is generally referred to as the standard or generic Pascal have been created. Each of the variations may follow the general structure of the standard or generic Pascal; however, each usually incorporates significant modifications in the syntax and may subtract or add predefined procedures and functions that will be recognized only by the applicable compiler, which may be equally nonstandard or nongeneric.

With rare exceptions, Pascal compilers had or have common failings. They are slow in doing their jobs of converting the Pascal source code to executable code. Their error-trapping methods may be inadequate, and the error-messages may be ambiguous or vague. But, slow as it may be, the compiling process is a necessity. To a busy programmer eager to see the compiler process his source code and execute it, the waiting time can become boring, irritating, time consuming, and terribly frustrating.

Thus, when Turbo Pascal, Version 1.0, arrived on the scene on November 15, 1983, many who have been working with other Pascal compilers eagerly risked the relatively small purchase price of $49.95 to sample and test the claims for speed made for Turbo Pascal by its publisher. Version 1.0 was soon updated to version 2.0, and at the same time, Turbo-87 with support for the 8087 math coprocessor was introduced. Borland began shipments of Turbo Pascal Version 3.0 in 1985.

Also in 1985, Borland introduced TurboBCD, with special numeric and string field-formatting features for business applications. Thus, in less than two years after the release of version 1.0, there were three varieties of Borland's Turbo Pascal compilers.

The rest is history; it is a model for a success story.

Borland International is still in Scotts Valley. Its reputation, physical size, and dollar volume have gone well beyond the original expectations of Phillipe Kahn, its founder. Borland's pricing and value delivered have irrevocably changed marketing practices among software developers.

Versions 1.0 and 2.0 astonished everyone with their speed, their interactive editors, their powerful syntax (very close to the"standard") and built-in functions, their outstanding compiler and I/O error-trapping, and their ease of operation. Turbo Pascal reduced compilation time from minutes to seconds! Amazing and delighting its users, Version 3.0 compiler source code at a speed more than twice as fast as Version 2.0, which was ten or more times faster than other popular Pascal compilers.

At first, the mistrusting ones among us may have thought of Turbo Pascal as a tinkerer's toy, a cheap way to hack at or play around with Pascal. Turbo Pascal has, however, earned its rightful place among the important, indispensable tools for the development of serious applications programs.

The following facts are provided for users or programmers interested in the logistics concerning the preparation of the materials in this book.

The code was written with the editor built into the Turbo Pascal compiler. The code was formatted (made to look tidy and easy for humans to read) with an excellent and inexpensive utility program called TTIDY written and supplied by Major Software, Los Altos, California. The text for the chapters was written with WordStar 3.31 and checked for spelling with CorrectStar; both programs are published by MicroPro International. The code was compiled with Turbo Pascal, Version 3.0, and tested on genuine IBM-brand PC, XT, and AT systems, and a XT look-alike imported from Taiwan. The code was printed with a NEC Spinwriter, Model 7710, equipped with an Elite-12 thimble. The printouts were used as artwork for production-printing.

The intention of this book is to provide some ready-made code and some not completely ready-made code you can customize and enjoy. At the same time, the heavily commented code provides you with a tutorial, a learning vehicle for some of the features that makeTurbo Pascal exciting to work with. This book is not intended to and does not take you from "zero to 60" as a Pascal programmer. No one book seems able to do that. This one provides a good beginning for some and additional knowledge for others who may already have some experience with Pascal or even with Turbo Pascal. You have to experience the phenomenon of Turbo Pascal. Its power and speed are among the indescribable and satisfying things one encounters in a high-level programming language.

With this introduction, I extend cordial invitations to use and profit from this book to those who have already discovered the remarkable capabilities of Turbo Pascal and want more source code to work with—and to those who are still using other Pascal compilers (and may be still waiting for the compilers to finish their multiple passes). I believe you are about to have a generous learning experience and a very good time!

WHAT THE PROGRAMS DO

The following pages give you a brief introduction to the purpose of each program in the book.

CNTWORDS and CNTWRD (Chapter 3) are word counting programs for text files.

HISTO (Chapter 4) enables you to create histograms for your data entries.

CONTRIB (Chapter 5) helps you determine whether or not a specific product contributes to the profitability of your operations, and lets you know how much it contributes to your profits or losses.

DAYSCRED (Chapter 6) enables you to calculate the effects on your cash flow of typical collection periods for accounts receivable; you can determine how long it takes, on the average, to collect your accounts receivable, which is a measure of merit worth tracking.

CHKBOOK (Chapter 7) has merit whether or not you believe you can keep your checking account records up to date without using a computer. In this case, the code's the thing that's important!

DEPREC (Chapter 8) is useful if you have capital assets (such as your computer); it will allow you to make a rapid calculation of three different methods for depreciation that will satisfy your needs, and of course, the IRS.

INVSTVAL (Chapter 9) can benefit you if you made a cash investment a while back. You know the original and the current market value. Now you want to know how much it has changed as a percentage of the original value. Would you have done better investing it elsewhere or putting it in a long-term deposit-account in the bank where it will earn interest?

MORTLOAN (Chapter 10) creates tables of data for a mortgage or a loan; it calculates, displays, and prints the periodic payments and separates and adds up the progressive interest and principal amounts.

NETWORTH (Chapter 11) calculates your material net worth—the difference between everything you own and what you owe. At the same time you will learn about writing string arrays in Turbo Pascal.

AUTORPT and TRIPRPT (Chapter 12) generate reports of expenses incurred during trips (business or pleasure); these reports are essential in business when you ask your employer for reimbursement and when you must meet the strict record-keeping requirements of the IRS.

SETPRNTR (Chapter 13) offers a menu to send configuration codes to your printer; when you choose a letter, the printer is instantly set to the mode you want. You can easily modify the code to match your specific printer.

TIMETRND (Chapter 14) prepares a moving averages table to help you evaluate the direction a business has been moving in with respect to time; it provides a valuable tool for forecasting sales and budgets.

LINEPLOT (Chapter 15) is an application valuable to anyone in engineering, manufacturing, operations, marketing, and sales who must plot a series of equidistant data points on a graph.

METRICS (Chapter 16) allows you to choose from a menu of 24 metric-to-English and English-to-metric conversions. Precision formulas are built into the program and provide instant data.

SORTLIST (Chapter 17) enables you to sort text and alphanumeric data according to the ASCII collating sequence; this tested code can be used as the basis for writing procedures for your own programs.

APPRAISL (Chapter 18) enables you to appraise the merits of a manager, a supervisor or any employee, and print a report of the appraisal.

BRKEVEN (Chapter 19) asks you to enter the fixed costs, the variable costs, and the selling price of a product or a service; when you select the range and increments to be calculated, the program instantly computes the break-even point (the point at which there is neither loss nor profit) in quantity. The program then generates and prints a comprehensive table of data.

REPCOMM (Chapter 20) generates a master record of sales revenues and commissions earned, paid out, and still owed to sales representatives; it also prints a detailed summary report.

SALESRPT (Chapter 21) computes and prints a table of sales data, including individual performances, averages, and the amounts by which each individual's performance is above or below the average level.

MINICALC (Chapter 22) imitates a four-function calculator; it can be customized to your specific needs.

PRNTEST1 AND PRNTEST2 (Chapter 23) are two versions of a printing program that puts your printer through its paces; both versions of the program are valuable for benchmarking your printer's character and graphics printing quality.

COPYIT (Chapter 24) enables you to copy a file to another disk or to the same disk using the same or any other "legal" filename, and to make a hard copy of a file by sending it to LST, the printer.

PRINTIT1 and PRINTIT2 (Chapter 25) are two programs for listing (printing) ASCII files; they provide examples of error handling under Turbo Pascal.

START, UPDATE, and LISTALL (Chapter 26) are three programs that together form a study of the structure of a fundamental database program.

DATAFILE (Chapter 27) includes the START, UPDATE, and LISTALL programs, which are converted to procedures and revised to form an integrated database program with comprehensive error handling.

DATAFIL1 (Chapter 28) incorporates the lessons about menus, forward procedures, error handling, and displaying and printing information from previous chapters. DATAFIL1 is an enhanced and useful database manager that can be used for creating and maintaining a name, address, and phone number directory.

Chapter 1

Get Set!

Here we go, off into the land of the mystical (or mythical) Frank Borland, the red-suspendered hybrid mountain man and leprechaun. Is he a continental elf or an American hillbilly? He may be real or imaginary. Few of us care. We just enjoy his harmless sense of humor and mustachioed visage peeking out at us as though he were thinking, "I know a bug that you don't know!"

It's reasonable to assume there are "bugs" somewhere in the Turbo Pascal compiler. If there are, however, you won't be bothered by any of them as you work and play your way through this book of programs and tutorials. The programs in each of the chapters have been compiled with Turbo Pascal, Version 3.0; then they were repeatedly run and tested. The tutorials were checked out by language experts, programmers, and business people. There's no pain left; you can only gain.

The intention of this book is to enhance your pleasure in working with Turbo Pascal. I make several assumptions about the readers of this book. You have some knowledge and experience, however minor, with entering source code through an editor and in using a compiler to process the code to a COM or an EXE file, the form in which it can be executed.

I assume you may have had some prior experience with the so-called standard Pascal or one of the near-standard Pascal compilers, or even with Turbo Pascal. This book is intended entirely for the Turbo Pascal compiler, which has some important syntactical differences (as well as similarities) as far as standard Pascal is concerned. I will not spend time and space identifying these similarities or differences. They are not important at this time.

What is important right now? You should have the documentation for Turbo Pascal, Version 3.0, and the Turbo Pascal disk itself. This book's contents, too, are important to you, and you are urged to use it in close conjunction with the easy-to-read Turbo Pascal documentation.

The Turbo Pascal documentation contains the syntax and rules of procedure. The documentation comes with the disk; you cannot get the disk without the documentation, so there is no point in wasting your time here by duplicating everything that has already been said so well. There is, however, always room for a book that can help you improve your programming fluency and skills, and add to your library of utilities, programs, and procedures. This book can do those things for you.

Each subsequent chapter in this book contains the complete source code for a program in Turbo Pascal. The code is at the end of each chapter and is preceded by a twofold tutorial: (1) what the program is and does after it has been compiled and executed, and (2) notes concerning features of the code that are especially interesting or important to learn so you can more easily apply them to other programs you may want to write. The code itself contains numerous comments, providing an additional source of tutorial material.

With care and attention to the programs' details you will be able to extract clauses, statements, procedures, and functions that can very well become the foundation for your own library of *utilities* (timesaving programmer's tools that, with very little revising, can be used over and over again in program after program).

Although each chapter and its program can stand alone, I am sure you recognize that many of the programs are less comprehensive and powerful than a commercially-released program usually is. Some of the chapters' programs are designed to trap human errors. Others are not as well-protected against human error. Because of this, they offer you an opportunity to practice and to learn how to add to, revise, and enhance source code. You are encouraged to "borrow" any program's functions or procedures and to insert them appropriately into another program to enhance its operation.

The "omissions" you may detect in the source code given in this book are deliberate. Some of the programs may even *crash* because of a human error, such as the entering a letter of the alphabet when a numeral was expected. If you do make a program crash because this kind of error was not trapped, consider it an opportunity to learn how to add an I/O-error trap. Examples are used in some of the programs in this book and are also detailed in the Turbo Pascal documentation.

Rest assured that error traps and other such niceties are known to us. Some have been used quite deliberately in several of the programs. Omitting them from a commercial program not intended for user-modification may deserve your wrath and your demand for a "bug-free" update or a refund; however, the "bugs" (if that's what you choose to call them) you may find in the programs in this book are there for you to eliminate with any one or more of your favorite Turbo Pascal constructions.

Chapter 2

And Go!

Let's start with a few short programs that illustrate and explain a few of the programming techniques you will be using throughout this book. For example, Turbo Pascal has a built-in function to clear the screen. It is equivalent to the PC-DOS and BASIC command CLS. Thus, when you see this line of code:

```
ClrScr ;
```

you will recognize instantly that it is there to clear the screen and make it ready for the next instruction. (Don't forget the semicolon that comes after ClrScr with no other code or characters, other than a space, separating the two.) Note that the space is not essential. It's a matter of personal choice. Some programmers always put one space between the end of a statement and the terminating semicolon character; other do not. Both are technically correct. Neither one performs better than the other because the compiler ignores such empty spaces. The space is included before the semicolon in the code listings you will see in this book.

Another valuable function built-into the IBM-PC versions of Turbo Pascal and used very often is:

```
Delay(n) ;
```

This does exactly what the word *delay* means. It delays the start of the action

3

called by the line of code following the Delay(n) ; statement. The time-length or duration of the delay is in milliseconds represented by the letter n enclosed in parentheses. Thus, the statement Delay (1000) ; delays the start of the next action or delays the termination of the previous action for 1 second. Delay(1500) represents a duration of 1.5 seconds. Delay(2000) causes a delay that is 2 seconds in duration,and so on.

Here is the code for a short program that illustrates the use of the Delay function:

```
{ This short program provides an illustration of a delay loop. }
{ Note: Turbo Pascal has a built-in function called "DELAY".   }
{ Whenever possible, use DELAY(n) ... (n) is expressed in       }
{ milliseconds, or DELAY(1000) is a 1000-millisecond or a       }
{ 1-second delay.                                               }

PROGRAM Delay ;

  VAR
     { We'll only deal with whole seconds. }
     DelayLength : Integer ;

  BEGIN
     { Delay }
     ClrScr ;
     { Display the request at the screen.                              }
     Write('Enter the length of the delay in seconds: ') ;
     { Wait for the number of seconds to be entered at the keyboard.   }
     ReadLn(DelayLength) ;
     { Use the 'delay' function with built-in 1000-millisecond timing. }
     { To arrive at the correct timing in seconds, multiply by 1000.   }
     Delay(DelayLength * 1000) ;
     { Display the final statement. }
     WriteLn('The ',DelayLength,' second(s) delay has been completed.')
  END.
  { Delay }
```

In a run of the Delay program, the screen is cleared and you are asked to enter the length of the delay in seconds. ReadLn waits for keyboard entry and assigns it to the variable DelayLength. The Delay function deals with milliseconds, so to convert the number assigned as a value to Delaylength to seconds, the program must multiply DelayLength by 1000. A delay of the appropriate duration then occurs and the last WriteLn argument displays a confirming statement. This short program can be used to test and arrive at the value for Delay(n) appropriate to the application in which it will be used.

There are two kinds of delimiters used to incorporate comments in the source code: (1) surround the comment with left and right curly brackets; as in { a comment must be placed inside the brackets }; or (2) surround the comment with a matching set of left and right parentheses with an asterisk following the opening or left parentheses with an asterisk directly preceding the right or closing parentheses, as in (* a comment must be placed inside the delimiters *).

The compiler watches for a matched set of delimiters and signals a compile-time error if they are not matched left and right. Either type, but not both types, of delimiters can be used to enclose a single comment. Which should you use? Whichever looks better to you at the time. Both can be used at will within the same program, as long as they are not mismatched. For example, { this is a comment *) or (* this is a comment } will be declared as errors and will stop the compiler's action.

Human errors made at the keyboard can be caught and signaled via a screen display through the use of various error traps. Here is an illustration of error trapping in conjunction with a password program that can be used to keep unwanted or unauthorized persons from accessing private data or security information without absolute knowledge of the very specific password. The source code is given here in PASSWORD.PAS, and it has been heavily commented to guide you through its actions:

```
PROGRAM PassWord ;

  CONST
    StrLength = 20 ;                { Passwords can be up to 20 characters long. }

  VAR
    Decoded_Input : STRING [StrLength] ;    { Decoded user input.                 }
    Password : STRING [StrLength] ;         { Put the real password here.         }
    User_Says : STRING [StrLength] ;        { Put the user's response here.       }
    I,TOP : Integer ;                       { Whole numbers are required.         }
    Right_On : Boolean ;                    { TRUE or FALSE conditions.           }

  BEGIN
    { the main part of PassWord }
    ClrScr ;
    Password := 'private' ;                 { This is the password. }
    { To make the password work, you  }
    { must type the letters in reverse }
    { order.  To change the password,  }
    { change the password 'private'    }
    { to the desired new one.          }

    REPEAT
        { Keep repeating the request UNTIL the }
        { entry is correct, or it's no go.     }
    Write('Enter the password: ') ;
        { Get the user's entry for the password. }
    ReadLn(User_Says) ;

        { Set Top to equal how long the string is, and }
        { set the length of Decoded_Input equal to Top. }
    Top := Length(User_Says) ;
```

```
      Decoded_Input[0] := Chr(Top) ;

          { The program reverses the typed order of the  }
          { characters of User_Says by moving each of the }
          { characters to its corresponding position at   }
          { the end of the string Decoded_Input.          }
      FOR I := 1 TO Top DO
        Decoded_Input[Top - I + 1] := User_Says[I] ;

          { Right_On is TRUE if Decoded_Input and Password }
          { are the same; otherwise Right_On is FALSE.     }
      Right_On := Decoded_Input = Password ;

        { If the user doesn't enter the correct password, }
        { display a message and continue.                 }
    IF ( NOT Right_On) THEN
      BEGIN
        WriteLn ;
        WriteLn('The password entered is not correct. Try again.') ;
             { To stop the program here, on a separate line add }
             { the reserved word HALT and a semicolon (;).       }
        WriteLn
      END ;
  UNTIL (Right_On) ;

    { If the password is entered correctly, }
    { this confirming message is displayed. }
    WriteLn ;
    WriteLn('The password is correct!') ;
    WriteLn('You are inside the program...') ;
    { Note: the rest of the program would follow from this point. }
END.
{ PassWord }
```

As shown above, note that BEGIN must always have a matching END. And REPEAT must be matched with UNTIL. Also, the word DO must follow a FOR statement when the argument contains more than one line of compilable code. DO is followed by a BEGIN statement and, of course, the argument must conclude with an END. For easy reading and checking with the unaided eye, the column-indentations are formatted to line up a BEGIN with its matching END and a REPEAT statement with its matching UNTIL.

I will illustrate an option to either display or print information. In Turbo Pascal, the default path is to the CONsole, which is the screen-display of your monitor. The following line of code within a program steers the output of the statement to the screen:

```
WriteLn('This would be seen on the monitor.') ;
```

This line is the same as:

```
WriteLn(CON,'This would be seen on the monitor.') ;
```

You can use uppercase, lowercase, or a mixture for CON. Choose which-ever you prefer, but try to be consistent in using it. My personal preference is for solid caps. To my eyes they seem to stand out better and reduce confu-sion with other calls to devices. If another style suits you better, do use it.

Turbo Pascal makes it very easy for you to steer the same statement to the printer instead of the console, as in this example:

```
WriteLn(LST,'This would be sent to the printer.') ;
```

You can use both statements to send almost simultaneously to the screen and to the printer:

```
WriteLn(CON,'This would be seen on the monitor.') ;

WriteLn(LST,'This would be sent to the printer.') ;
```

So, generally speaking, use CON to send to the display and LST to send to the printer. There are conditions under which the keywords ASSIGN and REWRITE must be used. I deal with those cases in other programs and chapters later in this book. Note that the standard INPUT and OUTPUT do not have to be declared. When they are omitted, the compiler assumes they exist.

Here is a short program I call PRNDEMO.PAS. It compiles to become the executable file PRNDEMO.COM:

```
{ Program to demonstrate directing information }
{ to the printer or to the screen.             }

PROGRAM PrnDemo ;

  VAR
    Print_It : Text ;                  { This sends to the printer.   }
    Ch : Char ;                        { User's response stored here. }

  BEGIN
    { PrnDemo }
    ClrScr ;
    REPEAT
      Write('Do you want a screen-display or a printout? (S or P): ') ;
      Read(Kbd,Ch) ;       { This form of "Read" eliminates the <CR> key. }
    UNTIL (Ch = 'S') OR (Ch = 's') OR (Ch = 'P') OR (Ch = 'p') ;
    IF (Ch = 'S') OR (Ch = 's') THEN
      BEGIN   { Without a WriteLn-director, `S' defaults to the screen. }
        WriteLn ;
        WriteLn('This is the first line at the screen.') ;
```

```
            WriteLn('This is the second line at the screen.') ;
            WriteLn('This is the third and last line at the screen.') ;
         END
      ELSE
            { If 'P' (Printer) was selected, send to the printer.        }
         BEGIN
            { To redirect the output to the printer, the path to the     }
            { printer must be opened.  It can be done with the directive }
            { `LST'.  To send to the printer, specify `LST' rather than  }
            { to the default, which is the monitor's screen or `CON'.    }
         WriteLn(LST) ;   { LST sends output to the printer.             }
         WriteLn(LST,'This is the first line at the printer.') ;
         WriteLn(LST,'This is the second line at the printer.') ;
         WriteLn(LST,'This is the third and last line at the printer.')
         END                 { Note for every BEGIN there's a matching END. }
   END.
   { PrnDemo }
```

Another of Turbo Pascal's features enables you to use a sort of shorthand for some elements of code. Note the UNTIL statement and the line following it in PRNDEMO.PAS:

```
      UNTIL (Ch = 'S') OR (Ch = 's') OR (Ch = 'P') OR (Ch = 'p') ;
      IF (Ch = 'S') OR (Ch = 's') THEN
        .
        .
        .
```

```
Those two lines of code can also be written briefly as:
```

```
      UNTIL Ch IN ['S','s','P','p'] ;
      IF Ch IN ['S','s'] THEN
        .
        .
        .
```

As far as the user is concerned, both styles are identical in operation. One requires a bit less code than the other. Again, use whichever you prefer. I use both at will in this book merely to demonstrate flexibility in this area of Turbo Pascal. It is, however, prudent to learn to use one method well and then use it consistently in the programs you write.

One more item of interest before you get into writing code for complete programs is simple error-trapping. For this example, I will demonstrate range-checking. The program asks you to select (type) a number in the range of 1 to 12. If the number that is entered is less than 1 or more than 12, the program traps the error and displays a message on the screen. If the number entered is within the range of 1 to 12, the program accepts the entry and continues to its next programmed action. The example is called ERRTRAP.PAS:

```pascal
{ Demonstration of IF..THEN..ELSE used }
{ in trapping an out-of-range error.   }

PROGRAM ErrTrap ;

  VAR
     { We'll deal with real numbers. }
     Number : Real ;

  BEGIN
    { ErrTrap }
    ClrScr ;
     { The user is asked to pick a number in a given range. }
    Write('Select a number in the range of 1 to 12: ') ;
     { The user enters a number. }
    ReadLn(Number) ;
     { The program tests the user's entry. }
    IF (Number < 1) OR (Number > 12) THEN
          { If the user enters a number smaller than 1   }
          { or greater than 12, the trap is sprung and   }
          { a message is displayed in the first WriteLn. }
      BEGIN
        WriteLn ;
          { Number:4:2 formats the display of the }
          { real-number entry to two places.      }
        WriteLn('Your selection of ',Number:4:2,
                ' is out of the range of 1 to 12.') ;
        WriteLn('Sorry about that!') ;
      END
          { On the other hand, if it is in the   }
          { range of 1 to 12, the program jumps  }
          { past the first statement to the 'else'. }
    ELSE
      BEGIN
        WriteLn ;
        WriteLn('Your selection of ',Number:4:2,
                ' is in the range of 1 to 12.') ;
        WriteLn('You can continue with the program.') ;
      END
          { Additional PROCEDURES that continue }
          { the program could be placed here.   }
  END.
  { ErrTrap }
```

Chapter 3

Counting Words of Text

The code for a program that counts the number of words in a text file provides an excellent exercise in the use of a programming language. At the same time, the program is quite useful to people who must write a stipulated amount of copy—a certain number of words—to fit a specific allocation of space. The "words" may be for a report limited to a stated maximum number of words, a column written for the company's or club's newsletter, or whatever.

Code that counts words is often written as a programmer's exercise. Such programs can be found in many programming languages and in program-teaching texts. To enable you to learn while generating a utility with value, this chapter gives you two word-counting programs, CNTWORDS and CNTWRD. One is a variation of the other in its performance; as far as word counting is concerned, both produce the same results.

How many times have you run into situations like the following? The boss says to you, "Write a brief report . . . oh, say, about 250 words summarizing the situation as you see it . . . in your own words."

The advertising agency needs a paragraph of copy, "50 succinct words" that describe the high-technology product your department has just designed and marketing wants to advertise. An editor wants the public relations department to give him a 300-word update.

The tech writer has to fill 2.5 pages, estimated at about 625 words of double-spaced text, in order to balance the documentation.

The sales manager insists that all weekly reports, excluding data, be held to 300 words maximum. Perhaps he also insists that the reports be no shorter than 200 words, to avoid the cryptic styles that are often adopted by those who hate to write.

The editor of your professional association's newsletter has asked you to write a short piece: "Oh, about 225 words; half a column."

The old-fashioned time-consuming grunt work—write, stop, do a printout, manually count the words, redo, add words, cut words—all this hassle can now be put forever behind you with the CNTWRD and CNTWORDS programs. With either of the two programs, the problem of knowing how much you have written is simplified. And, because you have rid yourself of the onerous chore of manually counting the words, your style shows a noticeable improvement. Whatever the requirement, if your task includes counting words, CNTWRD and CNTWORDS can do it for you in a matter of seconds, and you don't even have to do a hard-copy printout!

HOW DO YOU COUNT WORDS?

Before I review the specific source code for the programs, I first ask the question, how do you count words? Do you really count words when you scan the page with point of your pencil? No—you are really counting the *space between words*.

As you know, every written word is preceded by a space. Whether there is one space or many spaces (such as when you hit the TAB key and enter a multiple number of sequential spaces), you count the separation between individual words as a quantity of 1. This is the key to the fundamentals of the scheme for writing a word counting program in any language.

Some languages are better suited to running certain routines and procedures than others. BASIC is well suited to calling and reading DATA statements. Pascal is not. But, Pascal is better suited than BASIC to reading, looking into, examining, analyzing, and reporting on a text file that is external to the program and that is identified by a unique name. And Turbo Pascal is exceptionally well-suited to the purpose.

The source code is heavily commented so that you can comprehend its structure and process. Equally important, you will be able to go back to it any time and not wonder "Why in the name of inspiration did I write the code that way? What does this particular command mean and what does that function really do?"

Actually it is not necessary to use comment delimiters at the start and end of each physical line that contains comments. One at the start and one at the end of the individual comment—provided no source or program code is included—are all that is required.

Remember that the programs CNTWRD and CNTWORDS are actually doing the counting task the same way we count words. They count spaces and tabs, determining that a space or tab followed by a character marks the start of a word; thus, the word count is incremented by one for each occurrence. When they can find no more word starts in the text they are examining, the End Of File (EOF) is reached and the WHILE (not EOF(f)) DO loop is exited. The total word-count, which is the final value for COUNT in the programs' code, is displayed on the screen. The program sounds a BEEP, closes the file, and ends.

CODE LISTING FOR CNTWORDS

```
{ This is a word counting program.  It counts }
{ a sequence of characters contained in a     }
{ text file.  Spaces and Tabs indicate the    }
{ end and start of words.  After the text has  }
{ been examined by this program, the total     }
{ COUNT of WORDS found in the text is shown     }
{ on the screen.  Thus, the user is able to    }
{ determine whether or not a required          }
{ wordcount has been achieved in the text.     }

PROGRAM CntWords ;              { Identify the program; a Pascal requirement. }

  VAR                    { Define and assign values to the VARiables.  }
     Ch,Space,Tab,Beep : Char ;
     Count : Integer ;
     F : Text ;
     FileName : STRING [14] ;      { The maximum number of letters is 14. }
     WordFound : Boolean ;

  BEGIN
     { The main part of the program BEGINs here by clearing the screen. }
     ClrScr ;                       { Call the clear-the-screen function. }
     GotoXY(5,10) ;                 { Send the cursor to col 5, row 10.   }
     LowVideo ;                     { Display video in low intensity.     }
     { Display the opening instruction. }
     Write('ENTER THE NAME OF THE TEXT FILE TO BE COUNTED: ') ;
     HighVideo ;                    { Display video in high intensity.    }
     { Wait for the name of the text file to be }
     { entered at the keyboard; then respond.   }
     ReadLn(FileName) ;
     Assign(F,FileName) ;
     {$I-}    { Prepare for IO errors, such as a nonexistant FileName. }
     Reset(F) ;
     {$I+}
     IF IOresult <> 0 THEN       { We can't find the file; an IO error? }
       BEGIN
         GotoXY(10,12) ;       { Start the next line at col 10, row 12. }
         WriteLn('Do you have the correct filename?  I can''t find it!')
       END
     ELSE
       BEGIN
         Space := ' ' ;                     { ' ' is an actual Space.  }
         Tab := (Chr(9)) ;                  { Tab is decimal 9.        }
         Count := 0 ;                       { Set the counter to zero. }
```

```
          WordFound := False ;                { Initialize WordFound.    }
          Beep := (Chr(7)) ;                   { Beep is decimal 7.       }


        { Set up a DO loop to continue until   }
        { the End Of Filename (EOF) is Read.   }
      WHILE ( NOT EOF(F)) DO
        BEGIN
          WHILE ( NOT EOLN(F)) DO
            BEGIN
                 { Read the file, character by character }
                 { and test for TRUE/FALSE, Spaces, and  }
                 { Tabs with the "IF...THEN" statements.  }
              Read(F,Ch) ;
              IF (Ch <> Space) AND (Ch <> Tab) THEN
                WordFound := True ;
              IF (WordFound = True) AND ((Ch = Space) OR (Ch = Tab)) THEN
                BEGIN
                  WordFound := False ;
                  Count := Count + 1
                END
            END ;
          IF (WordFound = True) THEN
            BEGIN
              WordFound := False ;
              Count := Count + 1
            END ;
          ReadLn(F)
        END ;
                 { Now that the text file has been }
                 { Read and the DO loops have been }
                 { completed, skip a line at the   }
                 { screen and display the results  }
                 { of the Count.  Insert the name  }
                 { of the text file in the final   }
                 { display.                        }
        LowVideo ;
        GotoXY(22,12) ;
        Write('THE TOTAL NUMBER OF WORDS IN: ') ;
        HighVideo ;
        Write(FileName) ;     { Display the name of the file. }
        LowVideo ;
        Write(' = ') ;
        HighVideo ;
        WriteLn(Count) ;      { Display the total word count in Filename. }
        Write(Beep)           { Sound a beep at the end of the program.   }
      END ;                   { Can you match this END with its BEGIN?    }
    Close(F)                  { Close the text file we had been counting. }
END.
{ End the PROGRAM CntWords }
```

CODE LISITNG FOR CNTWRD

```
(* CNTWRD counts a sequence of characters, except
   spaces and tabs, as a word.  It adds the words
   and prints them as a total count of the number
   of words in the text.
*)

PROGRAM CntWrd ;

  VAR
    Ch,Space : Char ;
    Count,Length : Integer ;
    F : Text ;
    Filename : STRING [14] ;
    IOerr,WordFound : Boolean ;
    Tab : Char ;

  BEGIN
    { CntWrd }
    ClrScr ;
    REPEAT
         (* Start a Repeat-Until loop. *)
      WriteLn ;
         (* Disable the automatic "abort on I/O error".     *)
         (* Otherwise we could have a catastrophic ending. *)
      {$I-}
      REPEAT
        ;
         (* Start another Repeat-Until loop within the first loop. *)
      WriteLn ;
      WriteLn ;
      LowVideo ;
         (* Ask for the name if the file in question. *)
      Write('Name the file whose words are to be counted: ') ;
      HighVideo ;
      ReadLn(Filename) ;
      Assign(F,Filename) ;
      Reset(F) ;
      IOerr := (IOresult <> 0) ;
      IF IOerr THEN
         (* Trap incorrect entries. *)
         (* Display a message if there's trouble with the Filename. *)
         BEGIN
           WriteLn ;
           LowVideo ;
              (* Display the next line in half intensity.    *)
           Write('Sorry, but ') ;
           HighVideo ;
              (* The name of the file is in high intensity. *)
```

14

```
          Write(Filename) ;
          LowVideo ;
              (* Continue the sentence in low intensity.     *)
          WriteLn(' cannot be found!') ;
          WriteLn ;
          Write('Press <Q> to Quit. (Any other key to continue): ') ;
              (* Accept the pressed key's character, but do not echo it. *)
          Read(Kbd,Ch) ;
          IF Ch IN ['Q','q'] THEN
            HALT
      END ;
UNTIL NOT IOerr ;
    (* Restore the automatic IOerror abort. *)
{$I+}
Space := ' ' ;                    (* We use ' ', an actual space.   *)
Tab := (Chr(9)) ;                 (* 9 is the decimal code for Tab. *)
Count := 0 ;
WordFound := False ;
WHILE ( NOT eof(F)) DO            (* Watch for the end-of-file marker. *)
  BEGIN
    WHILE ( NOT eoln(F)) DO   (* Watch for the end-of-line marker. *)
      BEGIN
        Read(F,Ch) ;
        IF (Ch <> Space) AND (Ch <> Tab) THEN
            (* A word has been found. *)
          WordFound := True ;
        IF (WordFound = True) AND (Ch = Space) OR (Ch = Tab) THEN
          BEGIN
            WordFound := False ;
              (* We increment the word counter. *)
            Count := Count + 1
          END
      END ;
    IF (WordFound = True) THEN
      BEGIN
        WordFound := False ;
        Count := Count + 1
      END ;
        (* Continue reading the contents of the file. *)
    ReadLn(F)
  END ;
WriteLn ;
LowVideo ;
    (* Establish the number of repetitions *)
    (* for the line of dashes.              *)
FOR Length := 1 TO 55 DO            (* Start the loop's action. *)
  BEGIN
    Write('-')                         (* Display the dashes.  *)
  END ;                                (* End the FOR-DO loop. *)
    WriteLn ;
        (* Display the start of the sentence in low intensity. *)
```

```
      Write('Total Word Count for ') ;
      HighVideo ;
           (* Then go to high intensity for the Filename. *)
      Write(Filename) ;
      LowVideo ;
           (* Back to low intensity for the word 'is'.     *)
      Write(' is: ') ;
      HighVideo ;
           (* Display the total count in high intensity. *)
      WriteLn(Count) ;
           (* Do same action as the previous FOR-DO loop. *)
      FOR Length := 1 TO 55 DO
        BEGIN
        LowVideo ;
        Write('-')
        END ;
      WriteLn ;
      WriteLn ;
           (* Here's an option coming next. *)
      Write('Press <Q> to Quit. (Any other key to continue): ') ;
           (* "Read the keyboard, but do not echo the character. *)
      Read(Kbd,Ch) ;
      (* If the character-key pressed is an upper or lowercase Q, the *)
      (* program's over. Otherwise, go back to the first "REPEAT".    *)
   UNTIL Ch IN ['Q','q']
END.
{ CntWrd }
```

Chapter 4

Histogram Maker for Graphics Presentations

Histograms, data represented as bars of relative length, are among the most common of all graphics used in the sciences and in business environments. This HISTO program will take numeric data points that are keyed in and convert them to strings of symbolic characters. When these characters are printed end to end, according to the size of the numeric entry, they appear to be a bar. The larger the data entry, the longer the bar.

The restraint of an 80-column video screen and printers sets a pragmatic limit on the number of characters that can be displayed or printed end to end. Normally, the limit would be 80-character bars; however, 80 is an inconvenient number to work with. Therefore I've put an algorithm in the code that enables you to display histogram bars representing data values as large as 100 on a single screen by the simple expedient of dividing the values of data entries by 2. Therefore, 1 character is printed for every two units of value. In other words, if you enter a data value of 100, 50 characters will be displayed and printed; a data value of 50 generates 25 end-to-end characters; and so on.

The bars are printed and displayed horizontally. The value you enter for a bar is displayed and printed at the base of that bar with two decimal places to the right of the integer for each bar; however, since the video monitor and the printer cannot display or print fractions of characters, the data value is rounded off before processing.

Histograms display data in a step-function order. This is especially valuable when you want to gain an overall, visual comparison of relative values. Bar charts accomplish this by placing bars of varying length or height side-by-side against a reference scale.

The length of each bar, if presented horizontally, or the height of each bar, if presented vertically, represents a numeric value. Histograms are widely used in statistical quality control. In a manufacturing or research process, for example, they suggest the outline of the frequency curve that represents the underlying probability law that governs the variation pattern.

This chapter presents a Turbo Pascal version of a program that accepts information entered at the keyboard and converts it into a string or series of asterisks that represents the bar. The choice of the character that simulates a bar is entirely a matter of individual preference. Although the asterisk is very popular for such applications, you may prefer to use a capital X, a capital O, or even a capital H. You can experiment with various characters and use the one that, in your view, is most acceptable.

As the program is listed in this chapter, each histogram value entered at the keyboard is computed by the program in such a way as to produce a string of asterisks equal to half the value that is entered. The series or strings of asterisks are displayed simultaneously on the screen, and if it is turned on, at the printer. The program has a built-in error trap to restrict to 100 the maximum length of any individual entry of data that will be converted to asterisks. This is necessary because of the limitations of the computer screen. The majority of screens used with microcomputers cannot display more than a total of 80 characters on a single horizontal line. Below each display of asterisks on the screen, a scale is shown with markers at every tenth place. For example.

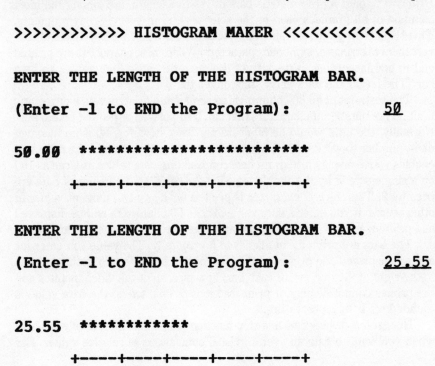

>>>>>>>>>>>> HISTOGRAM MAKER <<<<<<<<<<<<

ENTER THE LENGTH OF THE HISTOGRAM BAR.

(Enter −1 to END the Program):   50

50.00   ************************

        +----+----+----+----+----+

ENTER THE LENGTH OF THE HISTOGRAM BAR.

(Enter −1 to END the Program):   25.55

25.55   ************

        +----+----+----+----+----+

```
  2.00 : X
  4.00 : XX
 20.00 : XXXXXXXXX
 33.00 : XXXXXXXXXXXXXXXX
 13.00 : XXXXXX
 66.00 : XXXXXXXXXXXXXXXXXXXXXXXXXXXXXXXX
 10.00 : XXXX
 90.00 : XXXXXXXXXXXXXXXXXXXXXXXXXXXXXXXXXXXXXXXXXXXX
100.00 : XXXXXXXXXXXXXXXXXXXXXXXXXXXXXXXXXXXXXXXXXXXXXXXXXX
 45.00 : XXXXXXXXXXXXXXXXXXXXXX
  3.00 : XX
 23.00 : XXXXXXXXXXX
 11.00 : XXXXX
 33.33 : XXXXXXXXXXXXXXXX
 22.22 : XXXXXXXXXX
 11.11 : XXXXX
  0.00 :
```

Fig. 4-1. A sample printout from the Histrogram program.

```
  2.22 : X
  4.44 : XX
  8.88 : XXXX
 16.00 : XXXXXXX
 24.24 : XXXXXXXXXXX
 35.00 : XXXXXXXXXXXXXXXXX
 70.00 : XXXXXXXXXXXXXXXXXXXXXXXXXXXXXXXXXXX
 80.00 : XXXXXXXXXXXXXXXXXXXXXXXXXXXXXXXXXXXXXXXX
 85.00 : XXXXXXXXXXXXXXXXXXXXXXXXXXXXXXXXXXXXXXXXXX
 90.00 : XXXXXXXXXXXXXXXXXXXXXXXXXXXXXXXXXXXXXXXXXXXX
 95.00 : XXXXXXXXXXXXXXXXXXXXXXXXXXXXXXXXXXXXXXXXXXXXXX
100.00 : XXXXXXXXXXXXXXXXXXXXXXXXXXXXXXXXXXXXXXXXXXXXXXXX
100.00 : XXXXXXXXXXXXXXXXXXXXXXXXXXXXXXXXXXXXXXXXXXXXXXXX
 95.00 : XXXXXXXXXXXXXXXXXXXXXXXXXXXXXXXXXXXXXXXXXXXXXX
 90.00 : XXXXXXXXXXXXXXXXXXXXXXXXXXXXXXXXXXXXXXXXXXXX
 85.00 : XXXXXXXXXXXXXXXXXXXXXXXXXXXXXXXXXXXXXXXXXX
 80.00 : XXXXXXXXXXXXXXXXXXXXXXXXXXXXXXXXXXXXXXXX
 70.00 : XXXXXXXXXXXXXXXXXXXXXXXXXXXXXXXXXXX
 35.00 : XXXXXXXXXXXXXXXXX
 24.24 : XXXXXXXXXXX
 16.00 : XXXXXXX
  8.88 : XXXX
  4.44 : XX
  2.22 : X
```

Fig. 4-2. A sample printout from the Histogram program.

As each bar is displayed at the screen, the value entered and the line of asterisks are duplicated at the printer (if it is turned on) just as they appear at the screen. On the printer, however, the reference scale is printed only when a − 1 is entered at the keyboard to end the program. The printout shows the bars alongside each other, with the scale printed last. This makes the printout suitable for inclusion in a document. The scale of the bar is deliberately limited to 100 maximum, which causes a total of 50 asterisks to be printed. This ensures that the string of asterisks, the simulated bar, will not run off the right edge of the page.

SAMPLE HISTOGRAM PRINTOUTS

Figures 4-1 and 4-2, showing sample Histogram printouts are included. Figure 4-1 represents a display of individual quantities. Figure 4-2 is an example of a distribution of data that forms a bell curve, as might be found in a statistical analysis.

The program is surprisingly short. It is commented to help you understand the code and to guide you in revising it to meet your special requirements.

CODE LISTING FOR HISTO

```
{ Generates and prints histograms based on data entries. }

PROGRAM Histo ;

  VAR
    Ch : Char ;
    J,Y : Integer ;
    Number : Real ;

  BEGIN
    { Histo }
    ClrScr ;
    HighVideo ;
    GotoXY(20,5) ;
    Write('!!!  TURN ON THE PRINTER, PLEASE  !!!') ;  { Good advice! }
    GotoXY(20,10) ;
    Write('Press any key when ready to continue.') ;  { Any key will do. }
    Read(Kbd,Ch) ;                       { Do not echo the key's character. }
    ClrScr ;
    GoToXY(10,5) ;                        { Start at column 10, row 5.       }
    LowVideo ;                           { Low intensity video.             }
    Write('*******************>> ') ;     { Start the banner display.        }
    HighVideo ;                          { High intensity video.            }
    Write('HISTOGRAM') ;
    LowVideo ;
    Write(' <<*********************!') ;
    WriteLn ;
    REPEAT              { Continue until the UNTIL argument is satisfied. }
```

```
      WriteLn ;
      LowVideo ;
      WriteLn('Enter the Length of the bar.') ;   { Maximum value is 100. }
      Write('(Type -1 to END the program):   ') ;
      HighVideo ;
      Read(Number) ;                              { Get the bar's length.  }
      IF (Number >= 0) AND (Number <= 100.0) THEN
        BEGIN                                     { Or go to the next IF...THEN. }
          WriteLn ;
          Write(Number:6:2,' : ') ;               { Format 6 digits; 2 decimals. }
          Write(LST,Number:6:2,' : ') ;
          Y := Round(Number / 2) ;     { Divide Number by 2 to fit space. }
          FOR J := 1 TO Y DO
            BEGIN                                 { Show the bars: "X" }
              Write('X') ;                        { on the screen and  }
              Write(LST,'X') ;                    { on the printout.   }
            END ;
          WriteLn ;
          WriteLn(LST) ;                          { Skip a line at the printer. }
          Close(LST) ;                            { Dump the printer's buffer.  }
        END ;
      IF (Number > 100.0) THEN                    { A simple error trap. }
        WriteLn('     *** Maximum Length Is 100 ***') ;
    UNTIL (Number < 0)    { Actually, any negative value terminates Histo. }
  END.
  { Histo }
```

Chapter 5

Determining the Contribution To Profit

There are many ways to measure the value of a product or a service to the company marketing them. In taking such measurements, arithmetic and judgment must be combined to give the manager of a business operation a reasonable appraisal of the contribution a particular product or service makes to the company's financial or market position. The appraisal is then used in making dynamic decisions concerning actions to be taken that can dramatically affect the life of a specific product or service, and of course, the welfare of the company.

The judgement factors are human considerations and are not left to the computer. On the other hand, the arithmetic can be more rapidly and possibly even more accurately dealt with by a computer operating with appropriate software.

Surprisingly few companies know the specific contributions that any one product makes to overall profitability. If a product is not meeting the targets for profit, the conclusion appears to be obvious. Get rid of it! Remove it from the catalog! Profit targets, however, are often set arbitrarily, on the basis of intuition and gut feel rather than as the result of a comprehensive study and analysis of the market and the competition. The decision to continue or remove a product offering must take into account the real contributions it makes to the company's overall operation. One important method for determining this is called contribution analysis.

Contribution is the selling price of the item less the variable costs associated with its production and marketing. *Variable costs* are those directly affected by the production and sales volumes of the item. They include materials, labor, shipping, royalties paid, commissions paid, and other miscellaneous costs of manufacturing and marketing that can be attributed to or that vary with quantity or volume.

Why is contribution analysis important? Given the limits of resources and fixed costs, all businesses have a finite capacity to produce. For example, a dealer may be able to sell a variety and a varying quantity of video products with no significant change in fixed overhead costs, assuming he does not have to rent additional storage space and thereby increase his fixed costs. A consultant may be able to do several different kinds of studies and reports for his clients without affecting his overhead costs for rent, utilities, and administrative labor. In fact, if he has no work at all, his fixed costs may continue at the same level, unrelated to the amount of work at hand. A product manufacturer is in the same situation with respect to fixed costs, because overhead remains essentially the same for a specific facility, regardless of the level or production.

In these cases, is contribution to profit the major measure of merit? Isn't contribution to paying for overhead also important in measuring the merits of a product? The answer is obvious. Contribution to paying for overhead makes good sense. It is, however, too often overlooked. Managers often try to maximize sales for a specific product or service purely on the basis of measured profit dollars.

With two nearly identical items on the shelf, one priced at $40 and one at $50, a manager might be tempted to push the $50 item, deemphasizing the $40 one. This could be an error, if contribution analysis is overlooked. Assume that the $50 item cost $30 to move off the shelf after all variable costs have been paid. The contribution is $20 each. Assume that the $40 item's variable costs are $15, resulting in a contribution of $25. On this basis it would be better to concentrate on moving the $40 item, even to the extent of placing a relatively larger sales commission on it than on the higher-priced item. On the basis of these assumptions, it would be more prudent to concentrate on contribution than to focus on sales dollars.

For various reasons, it is not always possible to discontinue certain items if they are needed to round out the line. It is not always practical to ignore the remainder of the line and concentrate on only those with maximum contribution. Total contribution over a time period must be considered. If the manager can move more of the $50 items than of the $40 ones during a special sales promotion, or if the higher-priced item can sell (turnover) faster than the $40 item for whatever reason, it is possible the $50 item will make a greater total contribution than the lower cost item. The point is that maximization of sales dollars should not be used as the only measure of merit for a product's performance in the marketplace or for deciding whether or not to continue a product. By making comparisons for contribution among various products, it becomes relatively easy to resolve questions concerning the life of a product and where to place sale emphasis. The same examination for contribution should be made when considering adding new products or services to the catalog.

Perhaps it's a fundamental mistake to measure the performance of sales and merchandising managers purely on the basis of gross sales. It would seem to make good sense to measure their performance on the basis of contribution to profit.

The CONTRIB program provides a means for doing a rapid analysis of the contribution to fixed costs and overhead for a single product or service. By running the program several times, once for each item in the line, a comparison table that helps to resolve the problem can be developed. Also, by changing the input data for a single product, the right mix of variable cost elements can be developed and analyzed to attain an appropriate contribution level.

RUNNING THE CONTRIB PROGRAM

Here is a sample run of CONTRIB, with the screen's questions shown at the left and your responses underscored at the right:

WHAT IS THE NAME OR MODEL OF THE UNIT?   WIDGET-1A

WHAT IS THE SELLING PRICE PER WIDGET-1A?   59.95

  VARIABLE COST DETAIL:

   WHAT IS THE COST FOR MATERIALS PER UNIT?   11.23

   WHAT IS THE DIRECT LABOR COST PER UNIT?   4.87

   WHAT IS THE SHIPPING COST PER UNIT?   .92

   WHAT COMMISSION DOLLARS ARE PAID PER UNIT?   5.99

   WHAT ROYALTIES ARE PAID PER UNIT?   1.79

   ENTER ANY MISCELLANEOUS DIRECT COSTS: 0

After making the last entry and pressing RETURN, the screen clears and instantly displays a summary of the data you entered plus the calculations that have been programmed:

```
=========================================================
            WIDGET-1A -- CONTRIBUTION ANALYSIS
=========================================================
```

SELLING PRICE PER UNIT:		$59.95
LESS THE VARIABLE COSTS:		
MATERIALS:	$11.23	
DIRECT LABOR:	$4.87	
SHIPPING:	$0.92	
COMMISSIONS:	$5.99	
ROYALTIES:	$1.79	
MISC. COSTS:	$0.00	
TOTAL VARIABLE COSTS:		$24.80
UNIT CONTRIBUTION TO PROFIT:		$35.15

DO ANOTHER CALCULATION?   (Y/N) :

Thus, quickly, the story is unfolded for WIDGET-1A. One product or service can be compared with another as a means for quantifying the contribution-to-profit each makes.

If you do not press the <N> or <Y> key in response to the last line's query, you can make a hard copy of the screen's display by pressing one of the two shift keys on the keyboard simultaneously with the <Prt Sc> or grey asterisk <*> print-screen key. Be sure the printer is turned on. The screen and the program will remain in place, ready for another calculation if you press the <Y> key or an exit if you press the <N> or the Enter key.

The code provided with this chapter is intended to fulfill the arithmetic requirements. The code and the algorithms are quite straight forward and can, at the very least, serve as models upon which more complex, more powerful programs can be built for determining the dollars-and-cents contribution to profit being generated by a product or a service.

CODE LISTING FOR CONTRIB

```
{ CONTRIB helps determine the contribution to profit  }
{ made by a product or a service.  Costs are totalled }
{ and then subtracted from the selling price.         }
PROGRAM Contrib ;
```

```
TYPE
  StringType = STRING[80] ;

VAR
  Ch : Char ;
  Commission : Real ;
  DirLabor : Real ;
  L : Integer ;
  Materials : Real ;
  Misc : Real ;
  Name : StringType ;
  Royalties : Real ;
  SellPrice : Real ;
  ShipCost : Real ;

PROCEDURE Draw_A_Line(VAR OutFile:Text) ;

  BEGIN
    { Draw_A_Line }
    LowVideo ;
    FOR L := 1 TO 60 DO     { Draw a character 60 times in a row. }
      BEGIN
              { Here's the character to draw.  You can change it. }
        Write(OutFile,'-') ;
      END
  END ;
{ Draw_A_Line }

PROCEDURE SignOn ;              { Display the startup message. }

  BEGIN
    { SignOn }
    ClrScr ;
    GotoXY(12,12) ;
    LowVideo ;
    Draw_A_Line(CON) ;      { CON is the console, the video display. }
    GotoXY(24,14) ;
    HighVideo ;
    WriteLn('CONTRIB -- CONTRIBUTION ANALYSIS') ;
    GotoXY(12,16) ;
    LowVideo ;
    Draw_A_Line(CON) ;      { Again, call the PROCEDURE Draw_A_Line.  }
    Delay(1500)             { Display the above name for 1.5 seconds. }
  END ;
{ SignOn }

PROCEDURE StartingConditions ;              { Get the input data. }

  BEGIN
    { StartingConditions }
    ClrScr ;
```

```
      LowVideo ;
      Write('What is the name or model of the unit?      ') ;
      HighVideo ;
      ReadLn(Name) ;
      WriteLn ;
      LowVideo ;
      Write('What is the selling price per ',Name,'?      ') ;
      HighVideo ;
      ReadLn(SellPrice) ;
      WriteLn ;
      LowVideo ;
      Write('What is the cost of materials per unit?      ') ;
      HighVideo ;
      ReadLn(Materials) ;
      WriteLn ;
      LowVideo ;
      Write('What is the direct labor cost per unit?      ') ;
      HighVideo ;
      ReadLn(DirLabor) ;
      WriteLn ;
      LowVideo ;
      Write('What is the shipping cost per unit?          ') ;
      HighVideo ;
      ReadLn(ShipCost) ;
      WriteLn ;
      LowVideo ;
      Write('What commission-dollars are paid per unit? ') ;
      HighVideo ;
      ReadLn(Commission) ;
      WriteLn ;
      LowVideo ;
      Write('What royalty-dollars are paid per unit?      ') ;
      HighVideo ;
      ReadLn(Royalties) ;
      WriteLn ;
      LowVideo ;
      Write('Enter any miscellaneous direct costs:        ') ;
      HighVideo ;
      ReadLn(Misc) ;
      ClrScr
    END ;
{ StartingConditions }


PROCEDURE MakeReport ;                       { Display the final report. }

  VAR
    Sum : Real ;

  BEGIN
    { MakeReport }
```

```
        LowVideo ;
        Draw_A_Line(CON) ;
        WriteLn ;
        HighVideo ;
        WriteLn('            ',Name,' -- CONTRIBUTION ANALYSIS') ;
        LowVideo ;
        Draw_A_Line(CON) ;
        WriteLn ;
        WriteLn ;
        NormVideo ;
            { Reserve a format of 10 spaces, including }
            { integers, decimal point and two digits.  }
        WriteLn('Selling Price/Unit:            ',SellPrice:10:2) ;
        WriteLn ;
        HighVideo ;
        WriteLn('Less the Variable Costs:') ;
        LowVideo ;
            { List the cost-categories and format to  }
            { to two decimal places, as above.        }
        WriteLn('   Materials:        ',Materials:10:2) ;
        WriteLn('   Direct labor:     ',DirLabor:10:2) ;
        WriteLn('   Shipping:         ',ShipCost:10:2) ;
        WriteLn('   Commission:       ',Commission:10:2) ;
        WriteLn('   Royalties:        ',Royalties:10:2) ;
        WriteLn('   Misc. Costs:      ',Misc:10:2) ;
            { Now sum the above six categories. }
        Sum := Materials + DirLabor + ShipCost +
               Commission + Royalties + Misc ;
        HighVideo ;
            { Display the calculated sum of Variable Costs. }
        WriteLn('Total Variable Costs:          ',Sum:10:2) ;
        WriteLn ;
            { Contribution to profit is the Selling Price  }
            { minus the Variable Costs.                    }
        WriteLn('Unit contribution to profit:  ',SellPrice - Sum:10:2) ;
        WriteLn
    END ;
{ MakeReport }


BEGIN
  { Contrib }
  SignOn ;                  { Call the SignOn PROCEDURE.                }
  REPEAT

    StartingConditions ;    { Call the StartingConditions PROCEDURE. }
    MakeReport ;
    Draw_A_Line(CON) ;      { ...and the Draw_A_Line PROCEDURE.        }
    WriteLn ;
    WriteLn ;
    Write('Do another calculation?  (Y/N): ') ;
```

```
   Read(Kbd,Ch) ;
  UNTIL (Ch = 'N') OR (Ch = 'n')  { Repeat until an "N" is entered. }
END.
{ Contrib }
```

Chapter 6

Measuring Cash in Float with DAYSCRED

It's the nature of our economy to do business on credit. And the tendency toward credit purchases, whether through credit cards or open or self-funded revolving-credit accounts, is on the rise. It may be an oversimplification, but it is realistic to say that because of rising credit-sales more and more business operations are waiting for their money, which means some of their money is tied up and not readily available to the business for its own use. The period of waiting for the money is the collection period. It is important to know how long, on the average, the collection period is.

When interest charges are at high rates (especially high for small business operations who usually must pay a premium above the prime rates on bank loans), the days that people take to "live" on their credit can become a significant cost factor for doing business.

By periodically measuring the days-of-credit, the manager can keep track of the cash movement and the cost of doing business on credit (the credit extended by the business to its customer accounts, not the credit suppliers extend to the business).

This chapter's program, DAYSCRED, is important to the business operation's health and important to the credit manager who must make yes/no decisions on continuing a line of credit to a customer. (It also provides a valuable and easily comprehended exercise in writing code for the Turbo Pascal compiler.)

The DAYSCRED program queries the user for the number of days to be considered in doing the calculations. Ninety days, a fiscal quarter, is the usual number. Then the user is asked to enter the dollar value of sales made during the period. Naturally, because you are dealing with accounts receivable, you consider only sales made on credit. Cash sales are not "accounts receivable." They are closed when paid, which is immediately upon delivery of the goods or services to the buyer. The last two questions concern the dollar value of accounts receivable at the start and at the end of the period.

A business normally selling on terms of net-30 would expect to have the previous 30-days' sales-dollars outstanding. But if sales that occurred 40 or 50 days earlier are still displayed on the balance sheet, the indication is that some of the customers are experiencing some difficulty in meeting their commitments or may be abusing their credit privileges. At any rate, an effective job of collection is not being done. This affects cash flow.

CLASSIFYING LATE PAYERS

A measure of the effectiveness of a business's credit terms and collections can be made by *aging* the accounts, that is, by classifying individual accounts into tabular columns such as 30 days, 45 days, 60 days, and 90 days, each column indicating the number of days past the due date. The rows contain the names of the accounts. Accounts past due, depending on the net terms you allowed, are totaled in dollars under the appropriate column headings. The table of data then pinpoints the accounts that need attention.

ACCOUNTS RECEIVABLE AND LIQUIDITY

If your enterprise sells on credit terms, accounts and notes receivable are a significant part of working capital. In assessing the quality of your working capital, it is important to gain some knowledge of the quality and liquidity of the receivables. Quality and liquidity of accounts receivable are affected by the rate of turnover. The longer receivables remain outstanding, the lower is the probability that they will be collected in full. Turnover is a reflection of the age of the receivables when compared with an expected turnover rate determined by the credit terms that have been granted.

USING THE TURNOVER RATIO

The receivable turnover rate is a ratio computed by dividing the net credit sales by the average accounts receivable for a specific period. To make the formula manageable, and because it is today's practice to buy and sell primarily on credit, all sales are usually included in the numerator, which is net credit sales.

If you can separate cash sales from credit sales, so much the better for accuracy. Cash sales do not create accounts receivable. Average accounts receivable is derived by adding the outstanding receivables at the start of a period to the receivables outstanding at the end of the period and dividing by two. Using monthly or quarterly sales figures is proper. The use of longer periods may introduce distortion unless the average is more carefully calculated for the extended period. Notes receivable generated by normal sales activities also should be included in the accounts receivable total in computing the turn-over ratio.

MAKING COMPARISONS TO DETERMINE TRENDS

As with most financial data, and certainly with ratios, it is important to watch for trends and analyze the causes and effects. The average receivables turnover rate indicates how many times, on the average, the receivables revolve, that is, how often they are generated and collected during the year. For example, if net credit sales for a period are $60,000, accounts receivable at the start of the same period are $7,500, and accounts receivable at the end of the same period are $12,500, then the receivable turnover ratio is:

$$\frac{60000}{(7500 + 12500)/2} = \frac{60000}{1000} = 6 \text{ times}$$

The "6 times" figure can be used to compare the selected period with previous periods for trend analysis. There is, however, greater value in using the turnover ratio to calculate the collection period, which reflects the number of day's sales in accounts receivable.

THE COLLECTION PERIOD

How many days, on average, does it take to collect accounts and notes receivable? The number of days is computed by dividing the number of days in the accounting period under review by the receivable turnover ratio. It has been a popular practice among accountants to use the number 360 when doing calculations for a full year. The number 360 was easier to deal with, manually, than 365 or 366 (leap year). With a computer, however, it is just as easy to use the actual term of the calendar year. Using the data developed in the preceding example and a hypothetical calendar year, the following formula can abe developed.

$$\frac{\text{Number of Days' Sales}}{\text{Average Acconts Receivable Turnover}} = \text{Collection Period}$$

$$\frac{365}{6} = 60.8 \text{ days}$$

It's permissible to use any other value for the number of day's sales as long as you are consistent in your treatment. Otherwise, valid comparisons cannot be made. Collection periods can be compared to industry averages or to credit terms granted by competitors and their receivables (if such valuable information can be obtained).

RUNNING THE DAYSCRED PROGRAM

DAYSCRED enables you to determine rapidly the data for any specific period of time, for any account, or for all accounts. To run the program, you need to know and enter only the net credit sales for the period and the starting and ending receivables. For example:

===

COLLECTION PERIOD FOR ACCOUNTS RECEIVABLE

===

(CREDIT SALES ONLY)

HOW MANY DAYS ARE IN THE SALES YOU WILL COMPUTE?	<u>91</u>
WHAT ARE THE NET SALES ($) ON CREDIT FOR THE PERIOD?	<u>60000</u>
AT THE START OF THE PERIOD, WHAT WERE ACCOUNTS RECEIVABLE?	<u>20000</u>
AT THE END OF THE PERIOD, WHAT WERE ACCOUNTS RECEIVABLE?	<u>40000</u>

Press the Enter key after last entry and the computer takes over, clears the screen, and displays these lines of calculated data:

AVERAGE ACCOUNTS RECEIVABLE TURNOVER RATIO: **2.0**

AVERAGE DAILY SALES FOR THE PERIOD: **$659.34**

DAYS SALES IN ACCOUNTS RECEIVABLE (COLLECTION PERIOD): 45.5

Try the same calculation again, but this time enter 180 instead of 91 for the number in the first line. The turnover ratio doesn't change, of course, because it doesn't consider "days' sales" at this point in the calculation. The average daily sales for the period decreases to $333.33, approximately half that of the 91-day period because you have not adjusted the net-sales dollars entry; sales were effectively half as high, and the collection period increased to 90.0 days. Try 360 days and 365 days for the year's computation period; use whichever one makes you feel most comfortable or agrees with past calculations. Adjust the net sales figure and the accounts receivables to represent a full year of operations.

When making comparisons, always use the same relative period; for instance, the same 91-day period of the previous year should be compared with the current 91-day period.

The program directs all output to the default device, CON, the video monitor. It is a useful exercise to practice revising the code to make the program direct its output to the printer (LST) or adding code to send the program's output to both CON and LST simultaneously.

CODE LISTING FOR DAYSCRED

```
{ Analyzing accounts-receivable; for video display only. }

PROGRAM DaysCred ;

  TYPE
    StringType = STRING[80] ;

  VAR
    Ch : Char ;
    Line_Length : Integer ;
    End_Receivables : Real ;          (* Real enables the use of decimal values. *)
    Fiscal_Period : Real ;
    Start_Receivables : Real ;
    Sales_Dollars : Real ;
    Turnover_Ratio : Real ;

  PROCEDURE Deco_Line ;                    (* Decorative line used as a border. *)

    BEGIN
      { Deco_Line }
      LowVideo ;
      FOR Line_Length := 1 TO 80 DO
        BEGIN
          Write(Chr(15))                (* Sunburst-character for video display. *)
        END ;
      HighVideo
    END ;
  { Deco_Line }

  PROCEDURE Sign_On ;                          (* Display the startup message. *)

    BEGIN
      { Sign_On }
      ClrScr ;
      GotoXY(15,10) ;
      LowVideo ;
      FOR Line_Length := 1 TO 50 DO
        BEGIN
          Write(Chr(15)) ;          (* Write the character 50 times on one line. *)
        END ;
      GotoXY(20,12) ;
      HighVideo ;
```

```
          Write('DAYSCRED -- AVERAGE AGE OF RECEIVABLES') ;   (* The title. *)
          GotoXY(15,14) ;
          LowVideo ;
          FOR Line_Length := 1 TO 50 DO
            BEGIN
              Write(Chr(15))
            END ;
        Delay(1500) ;        (* Hold the display for 1.5 seconds, 1500 millisecs. *)
        ClrScr
      END ;
{ Sign_On }


PROCEDURE Get_Data ;                          (* Get the data from the keyboard. *)

    BEGIN
      { Get_Data }
      Deco_Line ;            (* Call the Deco_Line PROCEDURE; then return here. *)
      GotoXY(20,2) ;
      WriteLn('COLLECTION PERIOD FOR ACCOUNTS RECEIVABLE') ;
      Deco_Line ;
      WriteLn ;
      GotoXY(28,4) ;
      WriteLn('(Credit Sales_Dollars Only)') ;
      WriteLn ;
      LowVideo ;
      Write('Enter the number of days in the period to be computed:     ') ;
      HighVideo ;
      ReadLn(Fiscal_Period) ;
      WriteLn ;
      LowVideo ;
      Write('Now, enter the net sales ($) on credit for the period:     ') ;
      HighVideo ;
      ReadLn(Sales_Dollars) ;
      WriteLn ;
      LowVideo ;
      Write('And accounts receivable ($) at the start of the period:    ') ;
      HighVideo ;
      ReadLn(Start_Receivables) ;
      WriteLn ;
      LowVideo ;
      Write('Then the accounts receivable ($) at the end of the period: ') ;
      HighVideo ;
      ReadLn(End_Receivables) ;
      WriteLn ;
      WriteLn               (* Data collection is complete. END this PROCDURE. *)
    END ;
{ Get_Data }


PROCEDURE Make_Report ;   (* Generate the report with two-place arithmetic. *)

    BEGIN
```

```
     { Make_Report }
     WriteLn('Average accounts-receivable turnover ratio: ',
             Turnover_Ratio:8:2) ;
     WriteLn ;
     WriteLn('Average daily sales for the period:         $',
             Sales_Dollars / Fiscal_Period:8:2) ;
     WriteLn ;
     WriteLn('Days sales in accounts receivable:          ',
             Fiscal_Period / Turnover_Ratio:8:2) ;
     WriteLn ;
     Deco_Line                (* Display the border at the bottom of the report. *)
   END ;
{ Make_Report }

BEGIN
  { DaysCred }
   (* Note that this main part of the program calls *)
   (* the PROCEDURES in their natural sequence.      *)
  Sign_On ;                  (* PROCEDURE-call to display the program's name. *)
  REPEAT                     (* REPEAT the program UNTIL... (see below)        *)
    ClrScr ;
    Get_Data ;
        (* Initialize or assign a value to Turnover_Ratio. *)
    Turnover_Ratio := Sales_Dollars / ((Start_Receivables +
                      End_Receivables) / 2) ;
    Make_Report ;
    WriteLn ;
    WriteLn ;
    LowVideo ;
    Delay(1000) ;              (* Call a 1-second delay; just for the effect. *)
    WriteLn('Do another?  (''N'' key for NO. Any other key for YES): ') ;
    Read(Kbd,Ch) ;
  UNTIL Ch IN ['N','n']    (* 'N' ends the program. Any other key continues. *)
END.
{ DaysCred }
```

Chapter 7

A Checkbook Program: Excellent Code Practice

You may be able to maintain your checking account records more easily by hand than with a computer, especially if you have very few checkbook transactions to record. There is, however, always something for the would-be programmer to learn when code is written to perform tasks, especially if the tasks are familiar ones. So, I offer the source code in Turbo Pascal for this CHKBOOK program without suggesting you actually use it for your own checking account. The program, however, does work well. I have heard that several business people are using it to maintain and update records of their own, small companies' checking accounts. Even if you don't put it to work as they do, you'll certainly find the code interesting.

Although every business operation has a checking account, not all business managers with decision-making responsibility and accountability have easy access to the status of the company's checking account. There are many questions whose answers should be but are not always within ready reach. Is the balance being maintained at a healthy level for the specific type of operation? When was the last deposit made? How much was it? What are the ledger and journal references (or locations) for the detail to support the sources of funds that were deposited? How many checks have been written during the same period of time? What was the total amount of all the checks written? What are the check numbers? What was the beginning balance? Was the account overdrawn at any time? What is the ending balance? What is our direction with respect to managing the checking account? Should we change our self-designed standards for the minimum balance or for the number of checks we write during a given period? Do we have a problem at all? If a problem seems to be developing, how can we spot it in time to "cut it off at the pass?"

These questions, if not answered promptly and accurately, can present problems for the manager to solve in a crisis mode. And many decisions made during a crisis are bad or faulty. Such a situation, with its high risk factors, can be prevented by keeping an up-to-date checking-transaction report close at hand. The computer, with appropriate software, is one of the ideal tools for providing the manager with data on a real-time basis.

A FINANCIAL SNAPSHOT

This program generates a snapshot view of the status of the company's checking account; it can show deposits and checks written for any point in time or for any fiscal period. It is designed to identify potential problems before they get out of control and to help guide the direction for constructive management decision making.

When the deposit slip is prepared for checks that have been received and are ready for entry into the company's account, the bookkeeper, secretary, or you can enter the information into the computer using this program. In no time at all, the computer produces a single page report that is a summary of the status of the checking account. Also, the report provides room to enter references to more detailed records in the company's journals and ledgers. Thus, if the manager or the company's accountant wants to audit the books, the locations of the supporting details are in the report and point an auditor in the right direction.

When checks are written, it is common practice to enter the supporting details in a check register. As the manager, you may not need or want all the detail. Very often, however, you will want a snapshot of the number of checks written and a clear statement of what impact they had on the account's bottom-line balance on a specific date.

MONITORING AND WATCHING FOR TRENDS

You can use this program to determine whether you have problems or appear to be developing problems by regularly running the program and saving the hard-copy reports in a binder or a folder. Read the important data they generate. Watch for trends or sudden changes in balances and in checks written; then take whatever action may be indicated to correct or preclude a crisis situation. Continue to generate and read the reports as a means of monitoring checking account activity.

This same program, CHKBOOK, is well suited for use with your personal checking account. You can ignore the query that the computer makes for "journal or ledger references" in connection with deposits. Or you can insert coded responses of your own invention. You can insert abbreviations or full names as an aid to identifying the sources of funds. You could even enter individual dollar amounts. You can type in several lines of information, letters, numbers, and punctuation marks before the printer shouts "enough, already!"

Comments have been placed within the code to explain statements that might not be self-evident. It is also good practice to include comments in the source code you may write or in any modifications you may introduce to CHKBOOK so that, should you set the program aside for a while, you will have a minimum of difficulty in recalling the meanings or the purposes of some of the statements you wrote. It is easy to forget how or why a specific line or a series of lines were written. The comments eliminate this problem.

Each of us handles or treats comments differently. Note the way I did it in this program. Then, as an exercise after you have worked with the program for a bit, try to improve on the quantity and quality of the comments to suit your preferences or needs.

RUNNING THE CHKBOOK PROGRAM

This sample run demonstrates how to use the program and what the printout looks like. Enter, compile, and run CHKBOOK.

First the SignOn procedure is called. It clears the screen and displays the *banner*. In the banner the name of the program appears at the center of the screen in two levels of brilliance. The borders are in low intensity (LowVideo). The line of text in between the two borders is in high intensity (HighVideo).

==

CHKBOOK -- CHECKBOOK-TRANSACTION REPORT

==

The following advisory is displayed below the banner:

*** THE PRINTER MUST BE TURNED ON ***

And, directly below it is the message:

`Press any key when ready to continue`

The printer, if you have indeed turned it on, automatically starts printing the heading for the printout. (If you have not turned the printer on, the program will run with information appearing only on the screen.) After a 1.5 seconds delay, the screen is cleared automatically, and the GetTheFacts procedure is called immediately.

In the example given below, the bold type represents the program's requests for information that appear on the screen. The underlined information represents the responses that you enter through the keyboard. Of course, you must press the Enter key after completing the answer to each question. Do not use commas or dollar signs when entering financial information.

Enter the date of the first transaction.

(Use the Format MM/DD/YY):   10/01/85

Enter the date of the last transaction.

(Use the Format MM/DD/YY):   10/31/85

Type the Beginning ($) Balance: ?   21435.29

The information you enter is sent to the printer, and the next three lines displayed on the screen offer a selection of two categories in which to enter data and the opportunity to quit the program.

To enter the total of a new Deposit......Type 'D'.

To enter total of all Checks Written.....Type 'C'.

To Quit this program and return to DOS...Type 'Q'.

Then the screen instructs you to make a selection:

Enter one letter (D, C or Q):   D

The selection is made through a CASE statement. If any key other than D, C or Q is pressed, an error-message appears on the screen:

Wrong letter selected! Please retype the letter.

Then the previous four lines reappear. The process will continue endlessly until one of the three choices D, C, or Q is made. I choose D, the MakeDeposit procedure is called, and the program continues:

Enter the DATE of the Deposit: 10/01/85

And the ($) Amount of the Deposit: 32796.55

Give the Journal references:

(Space between entries, please): <u>ABC12 ABC13 CBA24</u>

As soon as you press the Enter key, the printer goes to work again and the screen simultaneously displays the new balance. The four lines reappear to ask you to select D, C or Q. This time select the letter <C> to enter the information concerning checks written. The program calls the WriteChecks procedure and continues:

What is the ($) amount of checks written? <u>39842.45</u>

How many checks were written? <u>4</u>

What are the check numbers?

(Put a space between each number): <u>1004 1005 1006 1007</u>

The printer goes to work again, and adds the above information to the hardcopy that is being generated:

Total amount of Checks written: **$39842.45**

The number of Checks written: **4**

The numbers of the Checks are: **1004 1005 1006 1007**

Press the Enter key, and the familiar four selection lines reappear. This time press the <Q> and the Enter keys to quit the program. The WrapUp procedure is called. The printer responds, and the screen displays a message:

===> ENDING BALANCE IS $ 14389.39 <===

If you had entered data that caused the account to be overdrawn or had created a negative balance, the ENDING BALANCE message would have displayed a negative number representing the amount of the overdraft with a warning notice:

===> THE ACCOUNT IS OVERDRAWN! <===

SAMPLE PRINTOUTS FROM THE CHKBOOK PROGRAM

Figures 7-1 and 7-2 shows sample reproductions of the hard-copy print-out of the information entered above. Note that there are differences in the presentation and layout because of the fact that the printout combines the questions and answers that were asked at the screen and responded to at the keyboard.

In the first sample, I entered the RECORD OF DEPOSITS ahead of the RECORD OF CHECKS WRITTEN. Thus, the BALANCE was substantial, more than adequate to cover the amounts written for the checks. In the sec-

```
===================================================================

      CHKBOOK -- CHECKBOOK-TRANSACTION REPORT

===================================================================


This report is from: 10/01/85 to: 10/31/85

---> Beginning Balance is: $   21435.29 <---

RECORD OF DEPOSITS
---------------------------
  The 10/01/85 deposit was: $   32796.55
  Journal or Ledger references are: ABC12 ABC13 CBA24


Balance now is: $   54231.84


RECORD OF CHECKS WRITTEN
---------------------------
  Total amount of Checks written: $   39842.45
  The number of Checks written:       4
  The numbers of the Checks Are:      1004 1005 1006 1007


Balance now is: $   14389.39


---> ENDING BALANCE IS: $   14389.39 <---


===================================================================
```

Fig. 7-1. A sample printout from the Checkbook program.

```
==================================================

    CHKBOOK -- CHECKBOOK-TRANSACTION REPORT

==================================================

This report is from: 10/01/85 to: 10/31/85

---> Beginning Balance is: $   21435.29 <---

RECORD OF CHECKS WRITTEN
-------------------------------------
  Total amount of Checks written: $   39842.45
  The number of Checks written:     4
  The numbers of the Checks Are:    1004 1005 1006 1007


Balance now is: $ -18407.16


===> THE ACCOUNT IS OVERDRAWN! <===


RECORD OF DEPOSITS
---------------------------
  The 10/01/85 deposit was: $   32796.55
  Journal or Ledger references are: ABC12 ABC13 CBA24


Balance now is: $   14389.39


---> ENDING BALANCE IS: $   14389.39 <---

==================================================
```

Fig. 7-2. A sample printout from the Checkbook program.

ond sample, I entered the checks before the deposits. The effect was to overdraw the account, at least until the deposits were entered into the record. This overdrawn condition is called out as a warning when the balance is negative.

CODE LISTING FOR CHKBOOK

```
{ Checking account record-generator. }

PROGRAM ChkBook ;
```

```
VAR
   Balance : Real ;                       { The account balance.         }
   Ch : Char ;                            { The user's menu choice.      }
   EndPeriod : STRING[80] ;               { The ending date.             }
   L : Integer ;                          { Utility for line lengths.    }

   { This program demonstrates FORWARD declarations. }

   { In planning or designing a Pascal program, care }
   { and attention must be given to the sequence in  }
   { which PROCEDUREs appear in the source code.      }

   { One PROCEDURE may call another PROCEDURE.  If   }
   { the PROCEDURE being called has not yet appeared }
   { or been declared in the source code before the  }
   { calling PROCEDURE's appearance, the code will    }
   { not compile or be executable.  If, for reasons  }
   { of code complexity or whatever, the occurences   }
   { of the PROCEDURES cannot be or are not placed    }
   { in a tidy and orderly sequence, the compiler's   }
   { requirements can be satisfied through the use    }
   { FORWARD declarations.                            }

   { The FORWARD declarations are placed in the      }
   { source code immediately after the VARiables     }
   { have been defined, and just ahead of the        }
   { occurrence of the first PROCEDURE.               }

   { The two FORWARD declarations used in this code  }
   { are listed in alphabetical order only for con-  }
   { venience; a desirable technique when a large     }
   { number of FORWARD declarations are made.         }

FUNCTION MakeDeposit : Real ;
   FORWARD ;

FUNCTION WriteChecks : Real ;
   FORWARD ;

   { The FORWARD declarations have been made. }
   { The program can now proceed normally.    }


PROCEDURE SignOn ;            { Generate the startup message. }

   BEGIN
   { SignOn }
   ClrScr ;
   GotoXY(10,8) ;              { Locate the next command at column 10, row 8. }
   LowVideo ;                  { Low intensity video display. }
   FOR L := 1 TO 60 DO        { Do the next action 60 times. }
```

```
          BEGIN
            Write(CHR(178))      { The border is composed of graphics char #178. }
          END ;
        GotoXY(22,10) ;          { Start the next display at column 22, row 8.   }
        HighVideo ;
        Write('CHKBOOK -- CHECKBOOK-TRANSACTION REPORT') ;  { Title. }
        GotoXY(10,12) ;          { Column 10, row 12. }
        LowVideo ;
        FOR L := 1 TO 60 DO      { Same as above. }
          BEGIN
            Write(CHR(178)) ;
          END ;
        GotoXY(20,16) ;          { Column 20, row 16. }
        HighVideo ;
        Write('*** THE PRINTER MUST BE TURNED ON ***') ;
        GotoXY(20,20) ;          { Column 20, row 20. }
        Write('Press any key when ready to continue') ;
        Read(Kbd,Ch) ;          { Get the keyboard character; do not display it. }
        FOR L := 1 TO 50 DO      { Now, send to the printer. }
          BEGIN
            Write(LST,'=') ;    { Print a border of equal signs. }
          END ;
        WriteLn(LST) ;          { Send a carriage return to the printer. }
        WriteLn(LST) ;          { Again. }
        WriteLn(LST,'      CHKBOOK -- CHECKBOOK-TRANSACTION REPORT') ;
        WriteLn(LST) ;          { Again. }
        FOR L := 1 TO 50 DO      { Print a border, as above. }
          BEGIN
            Write(LST,'=') ;
          END ;
        WriteLn(LST) ;
        Delay(1500) ;           { Delay 1.5 seconds. }
        ClrScr ;                { Clear the screen.  }
        HighVideo               { High intensity video display. }
      END ;
{ SignOn }

PROCEDURE GetTheFacts ;
    { Get the first and last transaction }
    { dates and the beginning balance.   }

  VAR
    StartPeriod : STRING [80] ;
    StopPeriod : STRING [80] ;

  BEGIN
    { GetTheFacts }
    GotoXY(1,5) ;
    LowVideo ;
    WriteLn('Enter the date of the first transaction.') ;
    Write('               (Use the Format MM/DD/YY):  ') ;
```

```
      HighVideo ;
      Read(StartPeriod) ;    { Get the response from the keyboard. }
      WriteLn ;              { Skip a line on the video display.  }
      WriteLn ;              { Again. }
      LowVideo ;
      WriteLn('Enter the date of the last transaction.') ;
      Write('          (Use the Format MM/DD/YY):  ') ;
      HighVideo ;
      Read(StopPeriod) ;     { Get the response from the keyboard. }
      WriteLn ;
      WriteLn ;
      LowVideo ;
      Write('         Type the Beginning ($) Balance:  ') ;
      HighVideo ;
      Read(Balance) ;        { Get the response from the keyboard. }
      WriteLn(LST) ;
      WriteLn(LST,'This report is from: ',StartPeriod,' to: ',StopPeriod) ;
      WriteLn(LST) ;
      WriteLn(LST,'---> Beginning Balance is: $',Balance:10:2,' <---') ;
   END ;
{ GetTheFacts }


FUNCTION MakeDeposit ;    { Make a deposit and update the balance. }

   VAR
      DepAmt : Real ;
      DepDate : STRING [80] ;
      JournalRef : STRING [80] ;

   BEGIN
      { MakeDeposit }
      ClrScr ;
      GotoXY(5,5) ;
      LowVideo ;
      Write('Enter the DATE of the Deposit:       ') ;
      HighVideo ;
      Read(DepDate) ;
      GotoXY(5,7) ;
      LowVideo ;
      Write('And the ($) Amount of the Deposit: ') ;
      HighVideo ;
      Read(DepAmt) ;
      GotoXY(5,9) ;
      LowVideo ;
      WriteLn('Give the Journal references.') ;
      Write('    (Space between entries, please): ') ;
      HighVideo ;
      Read(JournalRef) ;
      WriteLn(LST) ;                { Update the listing }
      WriteLn(LST,'RECORD OF DEPOSITS') ;
      WriteLn(LST,'--------------------') ;
```

```pascal
      WriteLn(LST,' The ',DepDate,' deposit was: $',DepAmt:10:2) ;
      WriteLn(LST,' Journal or Ledger references are: ',JournalRef) ;
      WriteLn(LST) ;
      MakeDeposit := DepAmt     { MakeDeposit now has the value of DepAmt. }
   END ;
{ MakeDeposit }


FUNCTION WriteChecks ;          { Enter the checks and report the balance. }

   VAR
      CheckNumbers : STRING [80] ;
      CheckAmt : Real ;
      NumChecks : STRING [80] ;

   BEGIN
      ClrScr ;
      GotoXY(1,5) ;
      LowVideo ;
      Write('What is the ($) amount of checks written? ') ;
      HighVideo ;
      Read(CheckAmt) ;
      WriteLn ;
      WriteLn ;
      LowVideo ;
      Write('How many checks were written?            ') ;
      HighVideo ;
      Read(NumChecks) ;
      WriteLn ;
      WriteLn ;
      LowVideo ;
      WriteLn('What are the check numbers?') ;
      Write('(Put a space after each number): ') ;
      HighVideo ;
      Read(CheckNumbers) ;
      WriteLn(LST) ;
      WriteLn(LST,'RECORD OF CHECKS WRITTEN') ;
      WriteLn(LST,'----------------------------') ;
      WriteLn(LST,' Total amount of Checks written: $',CheckAmt:10:2) ;
      WriteLn(LST,' The number of Checks written:    ',NumChecks) ;
      WriteLn(LST,' The numbers of the Checks Are:   ',CheckNumbers) ;
      WriteLn(LST) ;
      WriteChecks := CheckAmt     { WriteChecks now has the value of CheckAmt. }
   END ;
{ WriteChecks }


PROCEDURE WrapUp ;
   { This procedure sends a closing message }
   { to both the screen and to the printer. }

   BEGIN
      WriteLn ;
```

```
      WriteLn ;
      WriteLn('---> ENDING BALANCE IS: $',Balance:10:2,' <---') ;
      WriteLn(LST) ;
      WriteLn(LST,'---> ENDING BALANCE IS: $',Balance:10:2,' <---') ;
      WriteLn(LST) ;
      FOR L := 1 TO 50 DO
        BEGIN
          Write(LST,'=') ;
        END ;
      WriteLn(LST)
    END ;
{ WrapUp }


BEGIN
  { ChkBook }
  SignOn ;               { Execute the SignOn PROCEDURE. }
  GetTheFacts ;
   { Get the command.  Note that we double the   }
   { apostrophes to indicate a real apostrophe. }
  WriteLn ;
  WriteLn ;

  WriteLn('To enter the total of a new Deposit......Type `D''.') ;
  WriteLn('To enter total of all Checks written.....Type `C''.') ;
  WriteLn('To Quit this program and return to DOS...Type `Q''.') ;
  REPEAT
    WriteLn ;
    Write('          Enter one letter (D, C or Q): ') ;
    Read(Kbd,Ch) ;    { Get the user's response. }

        { Calculation of the balance is done here to make }
        { it relatively easy to make modifications.       }
        { MakeDeposit and WriteCheck get the information   }
        { from the user about transactions.  Then they    }
        { return the number so the balance can be updated }
        { here.  If appropriate, an OVERDRAWN warning      }
        { is displayed and printed.                       }
        { Note these multiple selections can be }
        { processed with the CASE statement.    }
        { Options are paired in the table.      }
    CASE (Ch) OF
      'D','d' : Balance := Balance + MakeDeposit ;
      'C','c' : Balance := Balance - WriteChecks ;
      'Q','q' :
      ;    { This is a NULL - we don't want to do anything. }

          { If a wrong key is pressed, an error message is }
          { displayed.  The code is still inside the       }
          { REPEAT...UNTIL loop, so the program returns to }
          { the beginning of the loop and continues on.    }
```

```
        ELSE
          WriteLn ;
          WriteLn ;
          WriteLn('Wrong letter selected! Please retype the letter!')
      END ;
      { of the CASE statement. }

      IF (Ch <> 'Q') AND (Ch <> 'q') THEN
            { Continue the program if the letter is not a Q or q. }
        BEGIN
          WriteLn ;
          WriteLn ;
          WriteLn('Balance now is: $',Balance:10:2) ;
          WriteLn ;
          WriteLn(LST) ;
          WriteLn(LST,'Balance now is: $',Balance:10:2) ;
          WriteLn(LST)
        END ;

      IF (Balance < 0.00) THEN
            { Display a warning, if account is overdrawn. }
        BEGIN
          WriteLn ;
          WriteLn ;                    { Display it on the screen.    }
          WriteLn('===> THE ACCOUNT IS OVERDRAWN! <===') ;
          WriteLn(LST) ;          { Print it in the report, too. }
          WriteLn(LST,'===> THE ACCOUNT IS OVERDRAWN! <===') ;
          WriteLn(LST)
        END ;
   UNTIL (Ch = 'Q') OR (Ch = 'q') ;
                              { Stop if the user enters a Q or a q }
                              { and go on to the next statement.   }
   WrapUp ;                   { Execute the WrapUp PROCEDURE. }
   WriteLn(LST,Chr(12))  { Eject the paper to the top of the form. }
END.
{ CHKBOOK }
```

Chapter 8

Depreciating
Capital Assets

There's a variety of IRS-approved methods for calculating depreciation for tax-reporting purposes. As with all processes and procedures, however, they aren't all applicable to specific situations. Tax regulations are dynamic. (Need I tell you?) They are constantly changing or being changed. It takes a specialist in taxation to keep up with the IRS regulations. Further, it takes a specialist to comprehend them and know which depreciation method is best suited to a company's situation and need, within the guidelines of the IRS.

In my use of the term "assets" I refer to tangible items used in the operation of a business but not held or intended for sale in the regular course of the business. These are classified on the balance sheet as plant or fixed assets; they may also be identified as property, plant, and equipment. More specifically, such assets include furniture, tools, machinery, buildings, and land.

There are no standard criteria for the minimum length of life necessary for classification as a *plant asset*. The asset must be capable of repeated use and ordinarily is expected to last or have a useful life of more than a year. The IRS has a serious interest in the application and calculation of the depreciation of assets. The IRS publishes a system of Class Life Asset Depreciation that serves as a guideline for what the IRS views as the normal useful life of various classes of assets, which is the minimum number of years allowed for full depreciation of a capital asset.

In effect, depreciation is an annual expense allowed by the IRS for the exhaustion, wear and tear, and obsolescence of property used in your income-producing activity. You may not charge the entire cost of acquiring an asset to operating expenses in the year of acquisition, but you must take into account the number of years the asset will continue to be useful.

The acquisition cost can be computed as a separate line item in the balance sheet and should be included in the profit and loss (P & L) statement as a depreciation expense. The IRS is concerned with the annual effect on taxes and the depreciation method used in the computations.

The formula used to compute annual depreciation is not complex. First, you determine the asset's total cost (cost basis), including all costs directly related to purchasing, shipping, and installing the asset in your plant. Repairs and maintenance after the installation is completed are not included in the cost basis. Next, you determine the salvage value of the asset at the end of its useful life. The salvage value may be nothing more than the scrap-metal content and therefore is often referred to as scrap value. Subtract the scrap value from the total acquisition cost, and then deduct the remainder through annual charges over the useful life of the asset as defined by the IRS guidelines.

The annual depreciation charges may be equal or they may be prorated geometrically, depending on the allowable and desirable impact on taxes. For balance sheet data, the annual charges can be displayed as a cumulative or accrued depreciation figure.

The useful life of the asset may not be the same as its physical life or its life if it were owned by some other company. You may make your own estimate of useful life considering the frequency with which you intend to use the asset, its age and condition when you acquired it, the environment in which it will be used, and obsolescence that may be brought about through technical developments.

SCRAP VALUE

The IRS permits you to use scrap value or net salvage (less cost of removal) in determining depreciation. But you must be consistent in your treatment of the subject. Generally, an asset may not be depreciated below salvage or scrap value. In some cases, end-of-useful-life value can be disregarded, thus increasing the annual depreciation. If the value is disregarded, however, the basis of the asset will be reduced at the end of its useful life. This can cause an increase in gain or a decrease in loss when the property is disposed of or is traded in on the acquisition cost of a new or replacement asset.

REAL ESTATE AND DEPRECIATIOIN

Generally, land or the site on which the plant is located is not depreciated according to useful life. Exceptions are land that has been acquired specifically for its mineral, oil, timber or other natural resources that diminish in value with time and use. In such cases, the allowance rules are similar to but not the same as depreciation; they are known as *depletion allowances.*

The IRS allows you to use any reasonable method to compute depreciation, provided it is consistently applied. Among the many methods are the following: straight line, annuity, appraisal, appropriation, combined depreciation and upkeep, composite life, age life, declining balance or diminishing provision, policy, replacement, retirement, sinking fund, unit summation, working hours, service capacity, and sum-of-years-digits.

The methods above are essentially variations of several common methods of depreciation with diverse degrees of refinement and sophistication. Therefore, my program DEPREC computes only three commonly used methods. The straight line method calculates a linear progression, allowing the same amount to be deducted for the class-life of the asset until the declared scrap value is reached. The sum-of-years-digits and the Declining Balance methods compute a larger amount of depreciation in the early years of asset life, with the amount that is depreciated diminishing each year until the scrap value is reached. In no case, as the display and printout of the declining balance table will remind you, can the depreciation be taken below the stated scrap value.

If you acquire or dispose of an asset during the year, regular depreciation is allowed only for that part of the year you own the property. To simplify the accounting, these accounting conventions are generally used: acquisitions and disposals are effective on the first day of the following month; on the first day of the month, if they occur in the first half of the month; or as of the last day of the month, if they occur in the last half of the month.

You should take the allowable depreciation deduction in each tax year. You may not deduct unclaimed depreciation for prior years in the current year or in a later tax year. The IRS does permit you to file an amended return to claim depreciation that may have been overlooked. Any failure to take the allowable depreciation in the appropriate year or by an amended return reduces the asset's adjusted basis and increases your gain when you dispose of the property.

DEPREC is purely for computing the numbers in helping you decide which method of depreciation seems best suited to your needs. Because the rules are dynamic and frequently changing, your tax adviser, tax attorney, or certified public accountant should be consulted prior to filing your return with the IRS.

RUNNING THE DEPREC PROGRAM

The program displays the information on the screen and prints a hard copy of the results of its calculations at the same time. The series of queries shown below in boldface print is displayed on the screen. The responses at the keyboard are underlined.

Name the item to be depreciated: NEC Printer

Describe the NEC Printer: Model 7710 Letter Quality Printer

Give the acquisition cost of NEC Printer: 2000

Enter the useful life in years: 5

```
================================================================
                    DEPRECIATION SCHEDULES
================================================================

Name of the item to be depreciated: NEC Printer
NEC Printer are described as: Model 7710 Letter Quality Printer
Acquisition cost: 2000.00
Useful life is  5 years.
Scrap value at end of  5 years: 100.00


===========>> STRAIGHT-LINE METHOD

       Current Year     Cumulative              Book
Year   Depreciation     Depreciation            Value
----------------------------------------------------------------
  0          0.00              0.00            2000.00
  1        380.00            380.00            1620.00
  2        380.00            760.00            1240.00
  3        380.00           1140.00             860.00
  4        380.00           1520.00             480.00
  5        380.00           1900.00             100.00

===========>> SUM-OF-YEARS-DIGITS

       Current Year     Cumulative              Book
Year   Depreciation     Depreciation            Value
----------------------------------------------------------------
  0          0.00              0.00            2000.00
  1        633.33            633.33            1366.67
  2        506.67           1140.00             860.00
  3        380.00           1520.00             480.00
  4        253.33           1773.33             226.67
  5        126.67           1900.00             100.00

==========>> DECLINING BALANCE with 150.00 PERCENT FACTOR

       Current Year     Cumulative              Book
Year   Depreciation     Depreciation            Value
----------------------------------------------------------------
  0          0.00              0.00            2000.00
  1        600.00            600.00            1400.00
  2        420.00           1020.00             980.00
  3        294.00           1314.00             686.00
  4        205.80           1519.80             480.20
  5        144.06           1663.86             336.14
```

Fig. 8-1. A sample printout from the Depreciation program.

```
==================================================================
                    DEPRECIATION SCHEDULES
==================================================================


Name of the item to be depreciated: ZEKIAH Printer & Software
ZEKIAH Printer & Software are described as: LaserJet w/2 Meg RAM
Acquisition cost: 7955.45
Useful life is  8 years.
Scrap value at end of  8 years: 250.00


==========>> STRAIGHT-LINE METHOD
```

Year	Current Year Depreciation	Cumulative Depreciation	Book Value
0	0.00	0.00	7955.45
1	963.18	963.18	6992.27
2	963.18	1926.36	6029.09
3	963.18	2889.54	5065.91
4	963.18	3852.72	4102.72
5	963.18	4815.91	3139.54
6	963.18	5779.09	2176.36
7	963.18	6742.27	1213.18
8	963.18	7705.45	250.00

```
==========>> SUM-OF-YEARS-DIGITS
```

Year	Current Year Depreciation	Cumulative Depreciation	Book Value
0	0.00	0.00	7955.45
1	1712.32	1712.32	6243.13
2	1498.28	3210.60	4744.85
3	1284.24	4494.85	3460.60
4	1070.20	5565.05	2390.40
5	856.16	6421.21	1534.24
6	642.12	7063.33	892.12
7	428.08	7491.41	464.04
8	214.04	7705.45	250.00

```
=========>> DECLINING BALANCE with 150.00 PERCENT FACTOR
```

Year	Current Year Depreciation	Cumulative Depreciation	Book Value
0	0.00	0.00	7955.45
1	1491.65	1491.65	6463.80
2	1211.96	2703.61	5251.84
3	984.72	3688.33	4267.12
4	800.09	4488.41	3467.04
5	650.07	5138.48	2816.97
6	528.18	5666.67	2288.78
7	429.15	6095.81	1859.64
8	348.68	6444.49	1510.96

Fig. 8-2. A sample printout from the Depreciation program.

Type the scrap value at the end of 5 years: <u>100</u>

Factor (%) for Declining Balance Calculations is: <u>150</u>

Immediately after you respond to the last query and press the Enter key, the calculations are performed. The results begin to appear in table form at the screen. At the same time, the printer is producing a complete form, including the tables, the queries, and your responses. Three tables are produced: (1) the straight-line method, (2) the sum-of-years-digits method, and (3) the declining balance method with the Factor based on straight-line calculations.

SAMPLE DEPREC PRINTOUTS

Figure 8-1 was produced during the above sample run. Figure 8-2 shows the printout for an asset with a longer useful life period. Note the precision with which the program calculates the depreciation to the declared scrap value.

You'll certainly find the algorithms and the code interesting to learn form and work with. Introduce your own variations in the screen's presentations. I must repeat the suggestion that for the actual tax report to the IRS, it is prudent to seek the counsel of a specialist in taxation or a C.P.A. who keeps abreast of IRS regulations and can advise you about the many methods of depreciation available and suggest the one that best suited to your specific situation.

CODE LISTING FOR DEPREC

```
(* This program generates three types of
   depreciation tables for capital assets:

      (1) Straight Line (SL)
      (2) Sum-Of-Years-Digits (SOYD)
      (3) Declining Balance with Factor (DB)
*)

PROGRAM Deprec ;

  TYPE
    DeprecType = (SL,SOYD,DB) ;
    StringType = STRING[80] ;

  VAR
    AcquisCost : Real ;
    AllDone : Boolean ;
    BookValue : Real ;
    Ch : Char ;
    CumDeprec : Real ;
    CurrentYr : Real ;
    DBFactor : Real ;
    I : Integer ;
```

```
   ItemDescr : StringType ;
   ItemName : StringType ;
   L : Integer ;
   ListOut : Text ;                            { ListOut is assigned later as LST, printer. }
   ScrapValue : Real ;
   StraightLn : Real ;
   UsefulLife : Real ;
   YrsLeft : Real ;

PROCEDURE SignOn ;                             { Display the startup message. }

   BEGIN
     { SignOn }
     ClrScr ;
     GotoXY(15,10) ;                           { Send cursor to column 15, row 10. }
     LowVideo ;
     Write('-------------------------------------------------------') ;
     GotoXY(22,12) ;                           { Now, cursor to column 22, row 12. }
     HighVideo ;
     Write('THREE-METHOD DEPRECIATION CALCULATOR') ;
     GotoXY(15,14) ;                           { And, cursor to column 15, row 14. }
     LowVideo ;
     Write('-------------------------------------------------------') ;
     Delay(1000) ;                             { Delay the next Write for 1 sec.     }
     GotoXY(10,18) ;                           { Send cursor to column 10, row 18    }
     HighVideo ;                               { top display the printer message.     }
     Write('*** Printout is automatic.  Please turn on the printer ***') ;
     Delay(2500) ;                             { Delay 2.5 seconds more.             }
     HighVideo ;                               { Restore high video intensity.       }
     ClrScr ;                                  { And, clear the screen.              }
   END ;
 { SignOn }

PROCEDURE GetData ;                            { Get the user's data via the keyboard. }

   BEGIN
     { GetData }
     GotoXY(0,5) ;
     LowVideo ;
     Write('Name the item to be depreciated: ') ;
     HighVideo ;
     ReadLn(ItemName) ;
     WriteLn ;
     LowVideo ;
     Write('Describe the ',ItemName,': ') ;
     HighVideo ;
     ReadLn(ItemDescr) ;
     WriteLn ;
     LowVideo ;
     Write('Give the acquisition cost of ',ItemName,': ') ;
```

```
      HighVideo ;
      ReadLn(AcquisCost) ;
      WriteLn ;
      LowVideo ;
      Write('Enter the useful life in years: ') ;
      HighVideo ;
      ReadLn(UsefulLife) ;
      WriteLn ;
      LowVideo ;
      Write('Type the scrap value at the end of ',UsefulLife:2:0,' years: ') ;
      HighVideo ;
      ReadLn(ScrapValue) ;
      WriteLn ;
      LowVideo ;
      Write('Factor (%) for Declining Balance calculations is: ') ;
      HighVideo ;
      ReadLn(DBFactor) ;
      ClrScr
    END ;
{ GetData }

PROCEDURE Method_Headers(VAR ListOut:Text ; WhatKind:DeprecType) ;

  BEGIN
    { Method_Headers }
    WriteLn(ListOut) ;
    CASE (WhatKind) OF                    (* Headers for the three methods. *)
      SL : WriteLn(ListOut,'=========>> STRAIGHT-LINE METHOD') ;
      SOYD : WriteLn(ListOut,'=========>> SUM-OF-YEARS-DIGITS') ;
      DB : WriteLn(ListOut,'========>> DECLINING BALANCE with ',DBFactor:5:2
                  ,' PERCENT FACTOR') ;
    END ;                                 { CASE }
    WriteLn(ListOut) ;
    WriteLn(ListOut,'        Current Year       Cumulative               Book'
            ) ;
    WriteLn(ListOut,
            'Year      Depreciation     Depreciation             Value') ;
    WriteLn(ListOut,
            '-----------------------------------------------------------------')
  END ;
{ Method_Headers }

PROCEDURE Draw_A_Line(VAR ListOut:Text) ;

  BEGIN
    { Draw_A_Line }
    LowVideo ;
    FOR L := 1 TO 65 DO
      BEGIN
        Write(ListOut,'=')
      END ;
```

```
      HighVideo
    END ;
{ Draw_A_Line }

PROCEDURE Print_Main_Headings ;

  BEGIN
    { Print_Main_Headings }
    Draw_A_Line(ListOut) ;
    WriteLn(ListOut) ;
    Write(ListOut,'                        ') ;
    WriteLn(ListOut,'DEPRECIATION SCHEDULES') ;
    Draw_A_Line(ListOut) ;
    WriteLn(ListOut) ;
    WriteLn(ListOut) ;
    WriteLn(ListOut,'Name of the item to be depreciated: ',ItemName) ;
    WriteLn(ListOut,ItemName,' are described as: ',ItemDescr) ;
    WriteLn(ListOut,'Acquisition cost: ',AcquisCost:6:2) ;
    WriteLn(ListOut,'Useful life is ',UsefulLife:2:0,' years.') ;
    WriteLn(ListOut,'Scrap value at end of ',UsefulLife:2:0,' years: ',
            ScrapValue:6:2) ;
    WriteLn(ListOut) ;
    Draw_A_Line(CON) ;        (* Use CON as the output parameter for display. *)
    WriteLn(CON) ;
    Write(CON,'                        ') ;
    WriteLn(CON,'DEPRECIATION SCHEDULES') ;
    Draw_A_Line(CON) ;
    WriteLn(CON) ;
    WriteLn(CON) ;
    WriteLn(CON,'Name of the item to be depreciated: ',ItemName) ;
    WriteLn(CON,ItemName,' are described as: ',ItemDescr) ;
    WriteLn(CON,'Acquisition cost: ',AcquisCost:6:2) ;
    WriteLn(CON,'Useful life is ',UsefulLife:2:0,' years.') ;
    WriteLn(CON,'Scrap value at end of ',UsefulLife:2:0,' years: ',ScrapValue
            :6:2) ;
    WriteLn(CON)
  END ;
{ Print_Main_Headings }

PROCEDURE WriteValue(VAR ListOut:Text ;
                     YearNum:Real ;
                     CurYr:Real ;
                     Cumul:Real ;
                     Book:Real) ;

  BEGIN
    { WriteValue }
    WriteLn(ListOut,YearNum:2:0,'            ',CurYr:10:2,'          ',Cumul:10:2,
            '          ',Book:10:2)
  END ;
```

```
{ WriteValue }

BEGIN
  { Deprec }
  Assign(ListOut,'LST:') ;
  Rewrite(ListOut) ;
  SignOn ;
  GetData ;
  Print_Main_Headings ;
  Method_Headers(CON,SL) ;
  Method_Headers(ListOut,SL) ;
  CumDeprec := 0 ;
  WriteValue(CON,0,0,0,AcquisCost) ;
  WriteValue(ListOut,0,0,0,AcquisCost) ;
  FOR I := 1 TO TRUNC(UsefulLife) DO
    BEGIN
      CurrentYr := (AcquisCost - ScrapValue) / UsefulLife ;
      CumDeprec := CumDeprec + CurrentYr ;
      BookValue := AcquisCost - CumDeprec ;
      StraightLn := (UsefulLife * UsefulLife + UsefulLife) / 2.0 ;
    WriteValue(CON,I,CurrentYr,CumDeprec,BookValue) ;
    WriteValue(ListOut,I,CurrentYr,CumDeprec,BookValue)
  END ;
Method_Headers(CON,SOYD) ;
Method_Headers(ListOut,SOYD) ;
CumDeprec := 0 ;
WriteValue(CON,0,0,0,AcquisCost) ;
WriteValue(ListOut,0,0,0,AcquisCost) ;
FOR I := 1 TO TRUNC(UsefulLife) DO
  BEGIN
    YrsLeft := UsefulLife - I + 1 ;
    CurrentYr := YrsLeft / StraightLn * (AcquisCost - ScrapValue) ;
    CumDeprec := CumDeprec + CurrentYr ;
    BookValue := AcquisCost - CumDeprec ;
    WriteValue(CON,I,CurrentYr,CumDeprec,BookValue) ;
    WriteValue(ListOut,I,CurrentYr,CumDeprec,BookValue)
  END ;
Method_Headers(CON,DB) ;
Method_Headers(ListOut,DB) ;
CumDeprec := 0 ;
WriteValue(CON,0,0,0,AcquisCost) ;
WriteValue(ListOut,0,0,0,AcquisCost) ;
DBFactor := (DBFactor / 100.0) / UsefulLife ;
CurrentYr := AcquisCost * DBFactor ;
I := 1 ;
AllDone := False ;
REPEAT
  YrsLeft := UsefulLife - I + 1 ;
  CumDeprec := CumDeprec + CurrentYr ;
  BookValue := AcquisCost - CumDeprec ;
```

```
WriteValue(CON,I,CurrentYr,CumDeprec,BookValue) ;
WriteValue(ListOut,I,CurrentYr,CumDeprec,BookValue) ;
CurrentYr := BookValue * DBFactor ;
I := I + 1 ;
IF (BookValue < ScrapValue) THEN
    (* Display and print a special note re the SOYD method. *)
  BEGIN
    AllDone := True ;
    WriteLn ;
    WriteLn(ListOut) ;
    WriteLn('Cannot take depreciation below book value of ',ScrapValue:6:
         2) ;
    WriteLn(ListOut,'Cannot take depreciation below book value of ',
         ScrapValue:6:2)
  END ;
 IF (I > TRUNC(UsefulLife)) THEN
    AllDone := True
UNTIL (AllDone) ;
WriteLn(ListOut,Chr(12)) ;          (* Eject the paper to top of the form. *)
WriteLn(CON) ;
WriteLn(CON) ;
  HighVideo ;
  (* Display an all-done message and sound the beep. *)
  WriteLn(CON,'                    *** ALL DONE ***',Chr(7))
END.
{ Deprec }
```

Chapter 9

Evaluating Investments

You made an investment a while back. What's its effective value today? The program INVSTVAL asks for the dollar value of an investment. It goes on to ask how long ago the investment was made, and what it is worth today. The program computes the amount of change in terms of dollars gained or lost, and displays the equivalent or effective change as a percentage of the investment. The secondary objective of the program (the primary objective is to provide a Turbo Pascal listing) is to give the user a rapid way of comparing investments.

For instance, if the program calculates that my investment has increased 100% in the five years I've owned or held it, how does it compare with other investment opportunities that were available to me or that may still be available to me for the future? INVSTVAL can help me make a decision for the future that, on the basis of historic fact, is possibly the best one.

Whether you are an active investor, trader, speculator, or a "paper player" who enjoys the risk free challenge of watching the dynamics of the market, you have many decisions to make. Should you hold? Buy? Sell? There are so many good looking buys that it can be difficult to decide which way to go. How about the 200 shares of common stock you bought 10 years ago at $19 a share? You held it when it dropped to $16. You held it when it split and climbed rapidly to $154. You now hold 498 shares. But the bottom has fallen out of the market and the stock's peak of $76,692 has dropped to $45,318. What should you do?

One thing you can do is set a bottom dollar for the stock, at which point you will trade, selling all or some of the shares. To determine the bottom you might pick a reference point, say the interest rate currently being paid on savings accounts, about 5.5 percent a year. As long as your stock is doing better than this, you decide, you will hold onto the stock. You will periodically check the market price and equate your holdings in this particular stock to the interest-earned value of your original investment, which was for 200 shares multiplied by $19 per share plus fees and taxes; roughly $3,850 is what you put into it 10 years ago. Not bad, but, on the other hand, you don't want to just sit on it and lose out if the danger signals become very strong.

INVSTVAL was designed specifically to solve this type of problem. While it can't make the decisions for you, it can give you a rapid statistical analysis that will help you decide.

A SAMPLE RUN OF THE INVSTVAL PROGRAM

Compile INVSTVAL.PAS and call up the INVSTVAL.COM file. Try it out on a hypothetical 10-year-old $3,850 investment. Let's see what its growth has been, when or how it might compare with other investment opportunities when effective interest is the measure of growth. The program displays all queries and your responses on the screen. A printout is not essential and therefore has not been incorporated into the code. Here is the dialog you have with the screen, as ordered by the Get_The_Facts procedure. In this illustration, the screen's queries are shown in bold face. The responses are shown with underlines:

Enter the ORIGINAL amount of the investment: 3850

Enter the MARKET value of the investment now: 45318

Enter the NUMBER OF YEARS it has been held: 10

When you complete the third entry and press the Enter key, the screen clears briefly while the calculations are being performed. The Show_Results procedure is called and executed and, shows the results:

==

The investment's original value has INCREASED!

During the 10 years it has been held

it has increased at the annual rate of: 27.96 percent

The original investment: $3850.00

The current market value: $45318.00

The total change in value: $41468.00

==

62

And then, below the above information, the screen displays:

Do you want to do another set of data? (Y/N):

Out of curiosity, let's do the same type of run using the stock's market value at its peak, which occurred after you had held it for nine and a half years:

Enter the original amount of the investment: 3850

Enter the market value of the investment now: 76692

Enter the number of years it has been held: 9.5

==

The investment's original value has INCREASED!

During the 9.5 years it has been held

it has increased at the annual rate of: 37.01 percent

The original investment: $3850.00

The current market value: $76692.00

The total change in value: $72842.00

==

As an interest earner it's a big winner; you knew that, but now you know exactly how big it is.

As an additional demonstration of the program's action, let's reverse the situation. It was purchased at $45,318 and the value is now $3,850. It's a financial disaster, all right! Let's see how the program handles it:

Enter the original amount of the investment: 45318

Enter the market value of the investment now: 3850

Enter the number of years it has been held: 9.5

==

The investment's original value has DECREASED!

During the 9.5 years it has been held

it has decreased at the annual rate of: −21.85 percent

The original investment: $45318.00

The current market value: $3850.00

The total change in value: −$41468.00

==

CODE LISTING FOR INVSTVAL:

```pascal
PROGRAM InvstVal ;

  TYPE
    StringType = STRING[80] ;

  VAR
    Ch : Char ;
    ChangeValue,Interest : Real ;
    L : Integer ;
    NumYears,OriginalValue,ValueNow : Real ;

  PROCEDURE SignOn ;        { Display the startup message on the screen. }

    BEGIN
      { SignOn }
      ClrScr ;
      GotoXY(15,8) ;        { Start the display at column 15, row 8. }
      LowVideo ;
      Write('$$$$$$$$$$$$$$$$$$$$$$$$$$$$$$$$$$$$$$$$$$$$$$$$$$$$$') ;
      GotoXY(25,10) ;
      HighVideo ;
      Write('INVSTVAL -- INVESTMENT ANALYZER') ;
      GotoXY(15,12) ;
      LowVideo ;
      Write('$$$$$$$$$$$$$$$$$$$$$$$$$$$$$$$$$$$$$$$$$$$$$$$$$$$$$') ;
      HighVideo ;
      Delay(1500) ;         { After 1.5 seconds, clear the screen. }
      ClrScr
    END ;
  { SignOn }

  PROCEDURE Get_The_Facts ;    { Ask for the data. }

    BEGIN
      { Get_The_Facts }
```

64

```pascal
      LowVideo ;
      Write('Enter the ORIGINAL amount of the investment:  $') ;
      HighVideo ;
      ReadLn(OriginalValue) ;
      WriteLn ;
      LowVideo ;
      Write('Enter the MARKET value of the investment now: $') ;
      HighVideo ;
      ReadLn(ValueNow) ;
      WriteLn ;
      LowVideo ;
      Write('Enter the NUMBER OF YEARS it has been held:    ') ;
      HighVideo ;
      ReadLn(NumYears) ;
      WriteLn
   END ;
{ Get_The_Facts }


PROCEDURE MakeBorder ;        { Generate a graphic border. }

  BEGIN
    { MakeBorder }
    Write('  ') ;
    FOR L := 1 TO 60 DO     { Write it 60 times in a row on the screen. }
      BEGIN
        Write(CHR(205))     { This is an extended graphics character.   }
      END ;
  END ;
{ MakeBorder }

PROCEDURE Show_Results ;    { Display the results. }

  BEGIN
    { Show_Results }
    MakeBorder ;
    WriteLn ;
    WriteLn ;
    IF (ChangeValue >= 0) THEN
      BEGIN
        WriteLn('      The investment''s original value has INCREASED!') ;
        WriteLn ;
        WriteLn('      During the ',NumYears:4:2,' years it has been held') ;
        Write('      it has increased at the annual rate of: ') ;
        WriteLn(Interest:5:2,' percent')
      END
    ELSE
      BEGIN
        WriteLn('      The investment''s original value has DECREASED!') ;
        WriteLn ;
        WriteLn('      During the ',NumYears:4:2,' years it has been held') ;
```

```
              Write('      it has decreased at the annual rate of: ') ;
              WriteLn(Interest:5:2,' percent')
           END ;
        WriteLn ;
        WriteLn('      The original investment:    $',OriginalValue:10:2) ;
        WriteLn('      The current market value:   $',ValueNow:10:2) ;
        WriteLn('      The total change in value: $',ChangeValue:10:2) ;
        WriteLn ;
        MakeBorder ;
        WriteLn ;
        WriteLn ;
        WriteLn
     END ;
  { Show_Results }
  BEGIN
     { InvstVal }
     SignOn ;               { Execute the SingOn PROCEDURE. }
     REPEAT
        ClrScr ;
        Get_The_Facts ;     { Execute the Get_The_Facts PROCEDURE. }
        ClrScr ;
           { The calculations are next. }
        ChangeValue := ValueNow - OriginalValue ;
        Interest := Exp(Ln(ValueNow / OriginalValue) * (1.0 / NumYears)) - 1 ;
        Interest := Interest * 100.0 ;
        Show_Results ;       { Execute the Show_Results PROCEDURE. }
        LowVideo ;
        Write('     Do you want to do another set of data? (Y/N): ') ;
        Read(Kbd,Ch) ;
           { Get the keyboard character; do not echo it.       }
           { End when any character but 'Y' or 'y' is typed. }
     UNTIL (Ch <> 'Y') AND (Ch <> 'y') ;

     HighVideo ;
     GotoXY(15,24) ;         { Go to column 15, row 24.         }
                             { Change the signoff message on    }
                             { the next line to suit yourself. }
     Write('Thank you.  We hope the news was good!') ;
  END.
  { InvstVal }
```

Chapter 10

A Mortgage and Loan Table Generator

Here's a comprehensive mathematical-table generator that takes a few snatches of input data and produces a large amount of output data. Forward declarations of some of the procedures are used in the design of MORTLOAN, this chapter's program. They provide an opportunity to learn about and practice with the flowpaths of Pascal procedures. The use of forward declarations can eliminate the need to carefully plan the relative positions of Procedures in the program's structure. Forward declarations are deliberately used in several of the programs in this book. Try to rewrite the code and eliminate the forward declarations in this program and in others in this book by reordering the relative positions of the procedures.

The program has genuine applications in business, professional, and private affairs. There does come a time when additional cash infusions must be obtained. This holds true for the smallest and the largest organizations, whether they are start ups or veterans, sole proprietorships, partnerships, or publicly or closely held corporations.

In business and financial operations, as an aid to solving cash-flow problems, money can be borrowed for short terms, typically with due-dates of 30, 90, 180, or 360 days for repayment of the loan with interest earned by the lender.

As a borrower or as a lender, your questions that need answers are usually, "How much will the money cost (or earn) for the term of the loan?" "What is the amount of the periodic repayments?" "How much of each payment goes toward reducing the principal amount of the loan? How much of the amount is interest?" And, "What is the total interest I will pay (or earn) by the time the loan is fully paid off?"

The MORTLOAN program is designed to answer all these questions rapidly and precisely based on the answers given to the program's questions.

The compiled program begins with a call to the SignOn procedure, which displays the program's banner heading and a message to turn on the printer.

The GetInfo procedure is called and asks for:

Enter the principal amount of the mortgage/loan: <u>5000</u>

And the interest rate in percent: <u>13.5</u>

What is the term of the mortgage/loan in months: <u>6</u>

The remainder of the procedures do the calculations and cause the table of data to be printed. Figures 10-1 and 10-2 show sample runs based on the brief amount of data entered in the above example. Figure 10-1 is for six months, and Fig. 10-2 is for 12 months.

```
=================================================================
                    MORTGAGE/LOAN SCHEDULE
=================================================================

Month        Monthly      Interest      Principal     Principal
             Payment          Paid        Reduced       Balance
-----------------------------------------------------------------
  0             0.00          0.00           0.00       5000.00
  1           866.45         56.25         810.20       4189.80
  2           866.45         47.14         819.32       3370.48
  3           866.45         37.92         828.53       2541.95
  4           866.45         28.60         837.85       1704.09
  5           866.45         19.17         847.28        856.81
  6           866.45          9.64         856.81          0.00
                           ---------
      Total Interest:        198.71
   Interest Rate (%):         13.50


=================================================================
```

Fig. 10-1. A sample printout from the Mortgage and Loan program.

```
===================================================================
                    MORTGAGE/LOAN SCHEDULE
===================================================================

Month          Monthly      Interest     Principal    Principal
               Payment      Paid         Reduced      Balance
-------------------------------------------------------------------
  0              0.00         0.00          0.00       5000.00
  1            447.76        56.25        391.51       4608.49
  2            447.76        51.85        395.91       4212.58
  3            447.76        47.39        400.37       3812.21
  4            447.76        42.89        404.87       3407.33
  5            447.76        38.33        409.43       2997.91
  6            447.76        33.73        414.03       2583.87
  7            447.76        29.07        418.69       2165.18
  8            447.76        24.36        423.40       1741.78
  9            447.76        19.60        428.17       1313.61
 10            447.76        14.78        432.98        880.63
 11            447.76         9.91        437.85        442.78
 12            447.76         4.98        442.78          0.00
                          ----------
     Total Interest:        373.12
  Interest Rate (%):         13.50

===================================================================
```

Fig. 10-2. A sample printout from the Mortgage and Loan program.

CODE LISTING FOR MORTLOAN

```
{ Mortgage and loan payment calculator. }

PROGRAM MortLoan ;

  TYPE
    StringType = STRING[80] ;

  VAR
    Ch : Char ;
    I : Integer ;
    Interest,IntrstPaid : Real ;
    MonthlyPay,Principal,PrincPaid : Real ;
    Temp,Term,Total : Real ;

  { The FORWARD declarations are listed in alphabetical order. }
```

69

```
PROCEDURE Border_Graphics(VAR OutFile:Text) ;
   FORWARD ;

PROCEDURE DoHeading(VAR OutFile:Text ; IsStraightLine:Boolean) ;
   FORWARD ;

PROCEDURE Format_Values(VAR OutFile:Text ;
                        MonthNum,MonthPay,IntrPaid:Real ;
                        PrinReduced,PrinBal:Real) ;
   FORWARD ;

PROCEDURE WrapUp(VAR OutFile:Text) ;
   FORWARD ;

PROCEDURE SignOn ;                     { Display the banner with the program's name. }

   BEGIN
     { SignOn }
     ClrScr ;
     GotoXY(20,10) ;              { Go to column 20, row 10 to start the display. }
     LowVideo ;
     Write('$$$$$$$$$$$$$$$$$$$$$$$$$$$$$$$$$$$$$$$$$$$$$$$$$$$') ;
     GotoXY(23,12) ;                         { Now to column 23, row 12. }
     HighVideo ;
     Write('MORTGAGES & LOANS -- SHORT-TERM COST OF MONEY') ;
     GotoXY(20,14) ;                         { Column 20, row 14. }
     LowVideo ;
     Write('$$$$$$$$$$$$$$$$$$$$$$$$$$$$$$$$$$$$$$$$$$$$$$$$$$$') ;
     GotoXY(26,18) ;   { Column 26, row 18 reminds the user about the printer. }
     HighVideo ;
     Write('**** TURN ON THE PRINTER, PLEASE ****') ;
     GotoXY(26,22) ;                { And, if everything's set, press a key. }
     Write('Press any key when ready to continue') ;
     Read(Kbd,Ch) ;   { Read the character, but do not echo it. }
     HighVideo ;
     ClrScr ;
   END ;
 { SignOn }

PROCEDURE Get_Info ;                       { Get the data. }

   BEGIN
     { Get_Info }
     LowVideo ;
     Write('Enter the principal amount of the mortgage/loan:  ') ;
     HighVideo ;
     ReadLn(Principal) ; { Read the keyboard entry and display it. }
     WriteLn ;
     LowVideo ;
     Write('And the interest rate in percent:                 ') ;
     HighVideo ;
```

70

```
      ReadLn(Interest) ;
      Interest := Interest / 100 ;
      WriteLn ;
      LowVideo ;
      Write('What is the term of the mortgage/loan in months:  ') ;
      HighVideo ;
      ReadLn(Term) ;
  END ;
{ Get_Info }


PROCEDURE WrapUp ;              { Create the table of data. }

  BEGIN
    { WrapUp }
    WriteLn(OutFile,'                        -----------') ;
    WriteLn(OutFile,'    Total Interest:     ',Total:10:2) ;
    WriteLn(OutFile,'Interest Rate (%):      ',Interest * 100.0:10:2) ;
    WriteLn(OutFile) ;
    Border_Graphics(OutFile) { Execute the Border_Graphics PROCEDURE. }
  END ;
{ WrapUp }


PROCEDURE DoHeading ;          { Display the headings. }

  BEGIN
    { DoHeading }
    Border_Graphics(OutFile) ;
    WriteLn(OutFile,'                 ','MORTGAGE/LOAN SCHEDULE') ;
    Border_Graphics(OutFile) ;
    WriteLn(OutFile) ;
    WriteLn(OutFile,
          'Month        Monthly      Interest    Principal      Principal') ;
    WriteLn(OutFile,
          '             Payment         Paid       Reduced        Balance') ;
    LowVideo ;
    FOR I := 1 TO 60 DO
      BEGIN
        Write(OutFile,'-')   { A line of 60 hyphens. }
      END ;
    WriteLn(OutFile) ;
    HighVideo
  END ;
{ DoHeading }


PROCEDURE Border_Graphics ; { Send a border-line (equals sign) to OutFile. }

  BEGIN
    { Border_Graphics }
    LowVideo ;
    FOR I := 1 TO 60 DO
```

```pascal
          BEGIN
            Write(OutFile,'=')       { A line of 60 equals signs. }
          END ;
        WriteLn(OutFile) ;
        HighVideo
      END ;
  { Border_Graphics }

  PROCEDURE Format_Values ;          { Format and write values. }

      BEGIN
        { Format_Values }
        WriteLn(OutFile,MonthNum:2:0,'          ',MonthPay:10:2,'     ',IntrPaid:10:2,
                '     ',PrinReduced:10:2,'      ',PrinBal:10:2)
      END ;
  { Format_Values }

  BEGIN
    { MortLoan }
    SignOn ;        { Execute the SignOn PROCEDURE. }
    Get_Info ;      { Same for Get_Info.           }
    ClrScr ;
    ;
    DoHeading(CON,True) ; { Ditto ... CON is the video display. }
    DoHeading(LST,True) ; { Ditto ... LST is the printer.       }
    Temp := Exp(Term * Ln(1.0 + (Interest / 12.0))) ;
    MonthlyPay := Principal * (Interest / 12.0) / (1.0 - (1.0 / Temp)) ;
    Total := 0 ;                              { Set the counter to zero. }
    Format_Values(CON,0,0,0,0,Principal) ;
    Format_Values(LST,0,0,0,0,Principal) ;
    FOR I := 1 TO Trunc(Term) DO
      BEGIN
        IntrstPaid := Principal * Interest / 12.0 ;
        PrincPaid := MonthlyPay - IntrstPaid ;
        Principal := Principal - PrincPaid ;
        Total := Total + IntrstPaid ;
        Format_Values(CON,I,MonthlyPay,IntrstPaid,PrincPaid,Principal) ;
        Format_Values(LST,I,MonthlyPay,IntrstPaid,PrincPaid,Principal)
      END ;
    WrapUp(CON) ;    { Execute WrapUp ... on the video monitor. }
    WrapUp(LST) ;    { Execute WrapUp ... at the printer.       }
    { Send a carriage return to the printer as a means of }
    { making certain the printer's buffer is emptied.     }
    WriteLn(LST)
  END.
  { MortLoan }
```

Chapter 11

Calculating Your Net Worth

Searching for a loan from a bank? If you are operating an enterprise as a sole proprietorship, a partnership, or a closely held corporation still in its start up stages, the bank will most likely ask you to prepare a personal financial statement. If the loan is approved, it will probably be on the basis of your personal net worth rather than on the assets of the enterprise.

If you want to finance any major purchase that requires the use of credit, you usually have to prepare a detailed personal financial statement. If you should engage an estate planner, a tax attorney, or a CPA to help you define, manage, and improve your financial affairs, you will have to prepare a personal financial statement before anything else can be done.

NETWORTH, the next program in Turbo Pascal, is designed to fit the needs of the majority of prospective lenders, creditors, and financial advisers. Its primary objective is to mathematically determine your net worth as an individual. As you may know, in a company's balance sheet total assets must always be equal to (in exact balance with) total liabilities. In the personal financial statement, which has the general appearance of a balance sheet, we expect there to be a difference between the two totals. The difference is your financial net worth. The difference should be a positive value.

If your total liabilities (which are the debts you have, or the amount of money you owe) exceed your total assets (which are the things you own or which can be quickly converted to cash to pay off your debts), your net worth in dollars is negative. As with a company's balance sheet, a personal financial statement that is periodically prepared clearly reveals trends in your material growth.

In preparing a company's balance sheet, there are two accepted formats: *account* and *report*. In preparing a personal financial statement the report form is the one that is generally used. And this is exactly what I have done in designing the program NETWORTH in Turbo Pascal.

A TEST RUN OF NETWORTH

NETWORTH is highly interactive and is set up to ensure that you correctly follow the procedure for completing the detailed input of data. The output is a neatly printed sheet that contains all the calculations and their results. Compile the code. When you call up the executable program (NET-WORTH.COM), the printer must be turned on and the paper properly adjusted.

After the banner is displayed by the SignOn procedure, the screen advises you:

*** TURN ON THE PRINTER ***

*** Press any key when ready ***

When you press any key, the screen clears and a series of queries is displayed:

Please type your full name: CONFIDENTIAL

Enter the date of this statement (MM/DD/YY):   08/31/85

The heading, with the name and date you entered, is then printed.

The program continues as the Show__How procedure is called to display a set of instructions on the screen. (See the NETWORTH code listing for the actual text.) The next procedure to be called is List__Assets. Individual queries are displayed for the asset items. Each time you enter an amount in response to a query the screen displays another question:

Is the amount correct? (Y/N):

If you respond <Y> and press the Enter key, the line with the amount you confirmed to be correct is sent to the printer. Because of the REPEAT ... UNTIL loop in this procedure, if you respond <N>, the item is repeated and no action occurs at the printer until you respond <Y>, the amount is correct. Thus, you are able to correct any errors in data you have entered immediately. If the amount for any line is zero, just press the Enter key or type the zero digit. In either case you will be prompted for confirmation before the

```
========================================

STATEMENT OF PERSONAL NET WORTH
FOR:   CONFIDENTIAL
AS OF: 08/31/85


========================================

ASSETS
------

         Cash (Money On Hand)      832.45
             Savings Accounts     2356.89
            Checking Accounts     1200.00
                        CD's         0.00
                  Money Mart      2500.00
               Stocks, Bonds     12575.00
             Other Securities     5000.00
             Notes Receivable        0.00
      Life Insurance Cash Val     25000.00
       Rebates/Refunds Owed You     175.84
                     Vehicles     5695.00
                  Real Estate     79500.00
            Annuities/Pensions        0.00
          Furniture/Appliances     7500.00
         Jewelry/Cameras/Tools     2500.00
          Valuable Collections     1000.00
                 Other Assets        0.00
         ----------------------------------
            TOTAL ASSETS:       145835.18
         ----------------------------------


LIABILITIES
-----------

          Contracts Outstanding    2976.88
       Promissory Notes Payable    3000.00
           Taxes Due and Unpaid     395.89
             Loans Outstanding    1000.00
         Mortgages (Princ. Amts)  55000.00
          Court-Ordered Payments      0.00
                   Other Debts    2500.00
         ----------------------------------
            TOTAL LIABILITIES:     64872.77
         ----------------------------------



========================================

             NET WORTH:          80962.41

========================================
```

Fig. 11-1. A sample printout from the Net Worth program.

computer accepts the amount and sends it to the printer.

After completing your responses to the queries concerning your assets, the screen displays and the printer prints the total assets in dollars.

The program continues in the same manner with the List__Liabilities procedure; it displays individual items and waits for your entry before asking the same question each time:

Is the amount correct?   (Y/N):

After completing your responses to the queries about your debts, the screen displays and the printer prints the total of your declared debts and the difference between your TOTAL ASSETS and your TOTAL DEBTS, which is your NET WORTH.

Figure 11-1 is a sample of a complete printout of a run of NETWORTH, and the code listing follows.

CODE LISTING FOR NETWORTH

```
{ Calculate material net worth of an individual }
{ on the basis of assets and liabilities.        }

PROGRAM Net_Worth ;

  TYPE                                { List of labels to be used by the arrays. }
    AssetType = (Cash,Savings,Checking,CD,MoneyMart,Stocks,Securities,Notes,
                 LifeIns,Rebates,Vehicles,RealEstate,Annuities,Furniture,
                 Jewelry,Collections,OtherAsset) ;
    LiabilType = (Contracts,PromisNotes,Taxes,Loans,Mortgages,Payments,Debts) ;
    StringType = STRING[80] ;

  VAR
    Asset : ARRAY [AssetType] OF Real ;
    Asset_Name : ARRAY [AssetType] OF StringType ;
    Ch : Char ;
    Date : StringType ;
    L : Integer ;
    Liability : ARRAY [LiabilType] OF Real ;
    Liab_Name : ARRAY [LiabilType] OF StringType ;
    Name : StringType ;
    Total_Assets : Real ;
    Total_Liabilities : Real ;

  PROCEDURE Initialize ;           { Assign string values to the arrays' labels. }

    BEGIN
      { Initialize }
      LowVideo ;
      Asset_Name[Cash] := ' Cash (Money On Hand)' ;
      Asset_Name[Savings] := ' Savings Accounts' ;
      Asset_Name[Checking] := ' Checking Accounts' ;
```

```
      Asset_Name[CD] := ' CD''s' ;
      Asset_Name[MoneyMart] := ' Money Mart' ;
      Asset_Name[Stocks] := ' Stocks, Bonds' ;
      Asset_Name[Securities] := ' Other Securities' ;
      Asset_Name[Notes] := ' Notes Receivable' ;
      Asset_Name[LifeIns] := ' Life Insurance Cash Val' ;
      Asset_Name[Rebates] := ' Rebates/Refunds Owed You' ;
      Asset_Name[Vehicles] := ' Vehicles' ;
      Asset_Name[RealEstate] := ' Real Estate' ;
      Asset_Name[Annuities] := ' Annuities/Pensions' ;
      Asset_Name[Furniture] := ' Furniture/Appliances' ;
      Asset_Name[Jewelry] := ' Jewelry/Cameras/Tools' ;
      Asset_Name[Collections] := ' Valuable Collections' ;
      Asset_Name[OtherAsset] := ' Other Assets' ;
      Liab_Name[Contracts] := ' Contracts Outstanding' ;
      Liab_Name[PromisNotes] := ' Promissory Notes Payable' ;
      Liab_Name[Taxes] := ' Taxes Due and Unpaid' ;
      Liab_Name[Loans] := ' Loans Outstanding' ;
      Liab_Name[Mortgages] := ' Mortgages (Princ. Amts)' ;
      Liab_Name[Payments] := ' Court-Ordered Payments' ;
      Liab_Name[Debts] := ' Other Debts' ;
      Total_Assets := 0.0 ;                  { Set the counter to zero. }
      Total_Liabilities := 0.0              { Set the counter to zero. }
   END ;
{ Initialize }

PROCEDURE SignOn ;              { Clear the screen. Display the program's name. }

   BEGIN
      { SignOn }
      ClrScr ;
      GotoXY(12,10) ;
      LowVideo ;
      FOR L := 1 TO 30 DO                { Do a task 30 times. }
        BEGIN                            { Start the tasks; a loop. }
          Write(Chr(175)) ;             { Task one: display a character. }
          Write(Chr(174)) ;          { Task two: display another character. }
        END ;                           { End the loop. }
      GotoXY(17,12) ;
      HighVideo ;
      Write('NETWORTH - STATEMENT OF PERSONAL FINANCIAL NET WORTH') ;
      GotoXY(12,14) ;
      LowVideo ;
      FOR L := 1 TO 30 DO               { This is the same as the above loop. }
        BEGIN
          Write(Chr(175)) ;
          Write(Chr(174))
        END ;
      Delay(1500) ;          { Display the sign-on banner for 1500 milliseconds. }
      ClrScr ;                              { Clear the screen. }
      HighVideo ;                  { Set the high intensity video display mode. }
```

```
      END ;
{ SignOn }

PROCEDURE Show_How ;                          { Display instructions for the user. }

   BEGIN
     { Show_How }
     HighVideo ;
     WriteLn('     Please enter `amounts'' when requested.') ;
     WriteLn('     Do not enter commas.  Do enter decimal points.') ;
     WriteLn('     Respond `Y'' or `N'' when asked to confirm.') ;
     WriteLn ;
     WriteLn('     Don''t be concerned about errors.') ;
     WriteLn('     You will be able to correct them with `N''') ;
     WriteLn('     when you are asked to confirm each entry.') ;
     WriteLn
   END ;
{ Show_How }


PROCEDURE Broken_line(VAR OutFile:Text) ;  { Draw a "broken line." }

   BEGIN
     { Broken_line }
     FOR L := 1 TO 38 DO        { Write the character 38 times in sequence. }
       BEGIN
         Write(OutFile,'-') ;
       END ;
     WriteLn(OutFile)
   END ;
{ Broken_line }

PROCEDURE Double_Line(VAR OutFile:Text) ;  { Draw a "double line." }

   BEGIN
     { Double_Line }
     FOR L := 1 TO 38 DO        { Write the character 38 times in sequence. }
       BEGIN
         Write(OutFile,'=') ;
       END ;
     WriteLn(OutFile)
   END ;
{ Double_Line }

PROCEDURE List_Assets ;                       { Collect information about assets. }

   VAR
     AsstCtr : AssetType ;

   PROCEDURE Asset_Total(VAR OutFile:Text) ;
```

```
      BEGIN
        { Asset_Total }
        Broken_line(OutFile) ;                      { Execute the PROCEDURE. }
        WriteLn(OutFile,' TOTAL ASSETS: ':26,' ',Total_Assets:10:2) ;
        Broken_line(OutFile)                  { Execute it again.        }
      END ;
    { Asset_Total }

  BEGIN
    { List_Assets }
    WriteLn(LST,'ASSETS') ;
    WriteLn(LST,'------') ;
    WriteLn ;
    WriteLn('This section is for your assets......') ;
    WriteLn('(Everything you own with cash value).') ;
    WriteLn ;
    { Colect data for each asset. }
    FOR AsstCtr := Cash TO OtherAsset DO
      BEGIN
        REPEAT
          LowVideo ;                         { Low intensity video for the query. }
          WriteLn ;
          Write(Asset_Name[AsstCtr],': ') ;   { Display the asset's name. }
          HighVideo ;                        { High intensity for the response.  }
          ReadLn(Asset[AsstCtr]) ;                        { Enter the value. }
          Write('  Is the amount correct? (Y/N) ') ; { Verify the data. }
          Read(Trm,Ch)              { "Trm" echos the character that is typed. }
        UNTIL (Ch = 'Y') OR (Ch = 'y') ;    { Accept the data, if correct. }
        Total_Assets := Total_Assets + Asset[AsstCtr] ;
        WriteLn(LST,Asset_Name[AsstCtr]:26,' ',Asset[AsstCtr]:10:2)
      END ;
    Asset_Total(CON) ;                        { Display the total for the assets. }
    Asset_Total(LST)                          { Print the same information.       }
  END ;
{ List_Assets }

PROCEDURE List_Liabilities ;         { Collect information about liabilities.}

  VAR
    LiabCtr : LiabilType ;

  PROCEDURE LiabWrapup(VAR OutFile:Text) ;

    BEGIN
      { LiabWrapup }
      Broken_line(OutFile) ;
      HighVideo ;
      WriteLn(OutFile,'TOTAL LIABILITIES: ':26,' ',Total_Liabilities:10:2) ;
      Broken_line(OutFile) ;
      WriteLn(OutFile)
```

```
      END ;
   { LiabWrapup }

   BEGIN
     { List_Liabilities }
     WriteLn ;
     WriteLn ;
     WriteLn('This section is for your debts (liabilities)') ;
     WriteLn ;
     WriteLn(LST) ;
     WriteLn(LST,'LIABILITIES') ;
     WriteLn(LST,'------------') ;
     FOR LiabCtr := Contracts TO Debts DO
       BEGIN
         REPEAT
           LowVideo ;
           WriteLn ;
           Write(Liab_Name[LiabCtr],': ') ;   { Display the item's name.}
           HighVideo ;
           ReadLn(Liability[LiabCtr]) ;     { Give the value of the item.  }
           Write('    Is the amount correct? (Y/N) ') ; { Verify it. }
           Read(Trm,Ch) ;
         UNTIL (Ch = 'Y') OR (Ch = 'y') ;  { Accept the data, if correct. }
         Total_Liabilities := Total_Liabilities + Liability[LiabCtr] ;
         WriteLn(LST,Liab_Name[LiabCtr]:26,'  ',Liability[LiabCtr]:10:2)
       END ;
     LiabWrapup(CON) ;           { Execute the PROCEDURE; display the total. }
     LiabWrapup(LST)             { Execute the PROCEDURE; print the total.   }
   END ;
 { List_Liabilities }

PROCEDURE Finale(VAR OutFile:Text) ;         { Calculate the net worth. }

   BEGIN
     { Finale }
     WriteLn(OutFile) ;
     Double_Line(OutFile) ;
     WriteLn(OutFile) ;
     WriteLn(OutFile,'NET WORTH: ':26,'  ',
                     Total_Assets - Total_Liabilities:10:2) ;
     WriteLn(OutFile) ;
     Double_Line(OutFile) ;
     WriteLn(OutFile)
   END ;
 { Finale }

BEGIN                                      { The main part of the program. }
  { Net_Worth }
  Initialize ;                             { The program actually starts here. }
  SignOn ;                                 { Execute the SignOn PROCEDURE.     }
  ClrScr ;
```

```
        GotoXY(25,8) ;
        Write('*** TURN ON THE PRINTER ***') ;  { Do just what it says. }
        GotoXY(23,14) ;
        Write('*** Press any key when ready ***') ;
        Read(Kbd,Ch) ;             { "Kbd" makes it unneccessary to press Return. }
        ClrScr ;
        LowVideo ;
        Write('Please type your full name: ') ;
        HighVideo ;
        ReadLn(Name) ;
        WriteLn ;
        LowVideo ;
        Write('Enter the date of this statement (MM/DD/YY): ') ;
        HighVideo ;
        ReadLn(Date) ;
        Double_Line(LST) ;
        WriteLn(LST) ;
        WriteLn(LST,'STATEMENT OF PERSONAL NET WORTH') ;
        WriteLn(LST,'FOR:   ',Name) ;
        WriteLn(LST,'AS OF: ',Date) ;
        WriteLn(LST) ;
        Double_Line(LST) ;
        WriteLn(LST) ;
        WriteLn ;
        Show_How ;
        List_Assets ;
        List_Liabilities ;
        Finale(CON) ;                           { Display the final number. }
        Finale(LST) ;                           { Print it, too.           }
        Write(LST,Chr(12))        { Eject the paper to the next top of form. }
    END.
    { Net_Worth }
```

Chapter 12

Generate Detailed Reports and Summaries of Trip Expenses

The methodical problem solver has an insatiable appetite for data on which to base decisions that have high probabilities for success. Although the experienced business person knows that it takes time and costs money up front merely to get to and from the customer's location, he recognizes this as a necessary evil, one that must be controlled to ensure that the pay back is a reasonable return on the time and money invested.

One of the best ways to exercise control over this investment is to itemize and record all reasonable details. Then the data that has been accumulated can be analyzed, the investment can be tallied in a form of direct-cost accounting, and when the business deal or the purpose of the trip has ben realized, the *return on investment* (ROI) can be quantified. Also, if an analysis indicates a budgeting problem, appropriate adjustments and alternative future paths can be defined. This can preclude problems or minimize the nonproductive use of time and money expended on business trips. The result is a probable increase in the ROI in business travel.

TRIPRPT is designed to provide a record and an analysis of travel costs. It has a built-in extra value. If you used an automobile during your business trip, the program will group the automobile related costs and will print out a detailed report on a series of factors useful in determining the costs of operating an automobile for business travel.

The program examines the data and calculates such items as average miles per gallon or litre for the trip, average speed, cost of fuel per mile, and total cost of operation per mile. By periodically recording and analyzing this information, you can track changing trends in the costs of operation.

TRIPRPT deals directly with the many problems of controlling the all-inclusive cost of a trip beyond those of the operation of an automobile. The program prints a summary of nonautomobile expenses as separate group, which includes car rentals, taxis, trains, airplanes, lodgings, meals, tips, and other familiar travel costs. Figures 12-1 and 12-2 are printouts of the results generated by the compiled code, Fig. 12-1 shows a trip in which an automobile was used, and Fig. 12-2 shows a trip for which an automobile was not used.

It's well worth the time to compare the source code for this program with the source code in the previous chapter. There are certain similarities in the performance requirements of the two programs. This one, however, doesn't use arrays. The items are treated individually be name. Forward declarations are used in this program to provide you with an opportunity to learn to order the sequence of the procedures.

Forward declarations are a valid programming technique; however, they do add several lines of code to the listing. Normally, there are no differences in performance. As a learning experience, try your hand at revising the sequence of the procedures to preclude the need for the forward declarations.

```
            AUTORPT -- AUTOMOBILE TRAVEL EXPENSE REPORT


REPORT FOR PERIOD: 11/11/85 THROUGH 11/15/85

Objective of the 5 day trip: Sales calls
Cities visited: Dallas  Houston  San Antonio

The trip required:   1250 miles of driving.
The automobile used: 119.00 gallons or litres of fuel.
The automobile got:  10.50 miles per gallon or litre.
Average speed was:    54.35 miles per hour.
Cost of fuel/mile:  $  0.14

        Total fuel cost:     $170.17
        Tolls paid for car:  $ 12.50
        Parking fees:        $ 39.85
        Oil added to car:    $  2.34
        Repairs to car:      $  0.00
        Miscellaneous:       $ 12.00

Cost of operation per mile: $  0.19


TOTAL COST FOR 1250 MILES OF AUTOMOBILE OPERATION: $236.86
```

Fig. 12-1. A sample printout from the Auto Trip Report program.

```
        TRIPRPT -- TRAVEL EXPENSE RECORD
```

```
TRIP REPORT: 12/01/85 THROUGH 12/06/85

Objective of the 6 day trip: Market studies
Cities visited: New Orleans  Tampa  Miami   Sarasota


        Airplane fares:  $904.00
        Train fares:     $  9.95
        Taxicab fares:   $ 35.85
        Car rentals:     $123.45
        Meals for self:  $189.95
        Lodgings:        $324.77
        Telephone calls: $ 33.33
        Tips paid:       $ 53.50
        Entertainment:   $195.35
        Valet services:  $ 15.50
        Miscellaneous:   $ 10.00


TOTAL COSTS REPORTED FOR THE TRIP: $1895.65
```

Fig. 12-2. A sample printout from the Travel Expense Report program.

CODE LISTING FOR AUTORPT

```
{ An automobile expense report. }

PROGRAM AutoRpt ;

  TYPE
    StringType = STRING[80] ;

  VAR
    AutoCosts : Real ;         { Total auto expenses    }
    CarMaintain : Real ;       { Car maintenance        }
    CarRent : Real ;           { Car rental             }
    Ch : Char ;                { Keyboard character     }
    Cities : StringType ;      { Cities visited         }
    Days : Integer ;           { Number of days         }
    DateEnd : StringType ;     { When the trip ended    }
    DateStart : StringType ;   { When the trip started  }
    DrivTime : Real ;          { Driving time           }
    Fuel : Real ;              { Amt of fuel used       }
    FuelPrice : Real ;         { Price paid for fuel    }
```

```pascal
    I : Integer ;                        { Counter used in loops }
    Miles : Real ;                       { Miles driven          }
    Misc : Real ;                        { Miscellaneous expense }
    Oil : Real ;                         { Oil for car           }
    Parking : Real ;                     { Parking fees          }
    Tolls : Real ;                       { Tolls paid            }
    TripPurpose : StringType ;           { Purpose of trip       }
    { The FORWARD declarations and PROCEDURES }
    { are listed in alphabetical order only   }
    { for convenience in finding them by eye.  }

PROCEDURE Auto_Out(VAR F:Text) ;
  FORWARD ;

PROCEDURE Basic_Facts ;
  FORWARD ;

PROCEDURE Basic_Report(VAR F:Text) ;
  FORWARD ;

PROCEDURE Car_Facts ;
  FORWARD ;

PROCEDURE Instruct ;
  FORWARD ;

PROCEDURE SignOn(VAR F:Text) ;
  FORWARD ;

PROCEDURE Auto_Out ;                     { Calculate time, speed, operating costs. }

  BEGIN
    { Auto_Out }
    AutoCosts := 0 ;                         { Start with the costs at zero. }
    WriteLn(F,'The trip required:   ',Miles:4:0,' miles of driving.') ;
    WriteLn(F,'The automobile used: ',Fuel:4:2,
            ' gallons or litres of fuel.') ;
    WriteLn(F,'The automobile got:  ',Miles / Fuel:4:2,
            ' miles per gallon or litre.') ;
    WriteLn(F,'Average speed was:   ',Miles / DrivTime:6:2,
            ' miles per hour.') ;
    WriteLn(F,'Cost of fuel/mile:  $',FuelPrice / (Miles / Fuel):6:2) ;
    WriteLn(F) ;
    WriteLn(F,'       Total fuel cost:    $',FuelPrice * Fuel:6:2) ;
    WriteLn(F,'       Tolls paid for car: $',Tolls:6:2) ;
    WriteLn(F,'       Parking fees:       $',Parking:6:2) ;
    WriteLn(F,'       Oil added to car:   $',Oil:6:2) ;
    WriteLn(F,'       Repairs to car:     $',CarMaintain:6:2) ;
    WriteLn(F,'       Miscellaneous:      $',Misc:6:2) ;
    AutoCosts := (FuelPrice * Fuel) + Tolls + Parking +
                 Oil + CarMaintain + Misc ;
```

```pascal
      WriteLn(F) ;
      WriteLn(F,'Cost of operation per mile: $',AutoCosts / Miles:6:2) ;
      WriteLn(F) ;
      WriteLn(CON,'TOTAL OF ABOVE COSTS: ',AutoCosts:6:2) ;   { To the screen }
      WriteLn(CON) ;
    END ;
{ Auto_Out }

PROCEDURE Basic_Facts ;                          { Get information from the keyboard. }

  BEGIN
    { Basic_Facts }
    GotoXY(1,5) ;
    LowVideo ;
    { Write statements, the queries, are }
    { displayed in low intensity video.  }
    Write('Briefly, state the trip''s purpose?  ') ;
    HighVideo ;
    { ReadLn responses are displayed }
    { in high intensity.             }
    ReadLn(TripPurpose) ;
    WriteLn ;
    LowVideo ;
    Write('How many days did the trip take?    ') ;
    HighVideo ;
    ReadLn(Days) ;
    LowVideo ;
    Write('What was the starting date?         ') ;
    HighVideo ;
    ReadLn(DateStart) ;
    LowVideo ;
    Write('What was the ending date?           ') ;
    HighVideo ;
    ReadLn(DateEnd) ;
    WriteLn ;
    LowVideo ;
    Write('Name the cities visited: ') ;
    { This could have been 'customers' as well as cities. }
    { You can modify the words to suit your preference.    }
    HighVideo ;
    ReadLn(Cities) ;
    WriteLn ;
  END ;
{ Basic_Facts }

PROCEDURE Basic_Report ;                  { Print the information from Basic_Facts. }

  BEGIN
    { Basic_Report }
    ClrScr ;
    WriteLn(F) ;
```

```
      WriteLn(F) ;
      WriteLn(F,'REPORT FOR PERIOD: ',DateStart,' THROUGH ',DateEnd) ;
      WriteLn(F) ;
      WriteLn(F,'Objective of the ',Days,' day trip: ',TripPurpose) ;
      WriteLn(F,'Cities visited: ',Cities) ;  { Or customers.  Or ? }
      WriteLn(F) ;
    END ;
{ Basic_Report }


PROCEDURE Car_Facts ;                    { Collect facts about the use of the car. }

    BEGIN
      { Car_Facts }
      WriteLn ;
      LowVideo ;
      Write('How many miles did you drive on this trip?      ') ;
      HighVideo ;
      ReadLn(Miles) ;
      LowVideo ;
      Write('How many gallons or litres of fuel did you use? ') ;
      HighVideo ;
      ReadLn(Fuel) ;
      LowVideo ;
      Write('What price did you pay per gallon or litre?     ') ;
      HighVideo ;
      ReadLn(FuelPrice) ;
      LowVideo ;
      Write('What was the actual driving time in hours?      ') ;
      HighVideo ;
      ReadLn(DrivTime) ;
      WriteLn ;
      WriteLn('Enter the ($) Amounts Spent For: ') ;
      WriteLn ;
      LowVideo ;
      Write('Tolls:    ') ;
      HighVideo ;
      ReadLn(Tolls) ;
      LowVideo ;
      Write('Parking: ') ;
      HighVideo ;
      ReadLn(Parking) ;
      LowVideo ;
      Write('Oil:      ') ;
      HighVideo ;
      ReadLn(Oil) ;
      LowVideo ;
      Write('Repairs or maintenance: ') ;
      HighVideo ;
      ReadLn(CarMaintain) ;
      LowVideo ;
```

```
      Write('Miscellaneous expenses: ') ;
      HighVideo ;
      ReadLn(Misc) ;
      WriteLn
   END ;
{ Car_Facts }

PROCEDURE Instruct ;                          { Display instructions for the user. }

   BEGIN
     { Instruct }
     GotoXY(20,5) ;                  { Start instructions at column 20, row 5. }
     Write('This program provides information') ;
     GotoXY(20,6) ;
     Write('concerned with travel expenses,') ;
     GotoXY(20,7) ;
     Write('specifically the costs of using an') ;
     GotoXY(20,8) ;
     Write('automobile...company or personal.') ;
     GotoXY(20,10) ;
     Write('Answer the questions and allow the') ;
     GotoXY(20,11) ;
     Write('computer to do all calculations.') ;
     GotoXY(20,13) ;
     Write('If no expenses were incurred for an') ;
     GotoXY(20,14) ;
     Write('item, enter a zero and press Return.') ;
     GotoXY(20,16) ;
     Write('A hard-copy report will be provided.') ;
     GotoXY(20,19) ;
     Write('*** BE SURE THE PRINTER IS READY ***') ;
     GotoXY(20,22) ;
     Write(' ... Press any key to continue ...') ;
     Read(Kbd,Ch) ;          { Wait for any key to be pressed. Then continue. }
     ClrScr
   END ;
{ Instruct }

PROCEDURE SignOn ;                            { Create the startup display. }

   BEGIN
     { SignOn }
     ClrScr ;
     GotoXY(10,10) ;
     LowVideo ;
     FOR I := 1 TO 65 DO
       BEGIN
         Write(F,CHR(205))
       END ;
     WriteLn(F) ;
     GotoXY(12,12) ;
```

```
      HighVideo ;
      Write(F,'                AUTORPT -- AUTOMOBILE TRAVEL EXPENSE REPORT') ;
      WriteLn(F) ;
      GotoXY(10,14) ;
      LowVideo ;
      FOR I := 1 TO 65 DO
        BEGIN
          Write(F,CHR(205))
        END ;
      Write(F) ;
      Delay(1500) ;
      HighVideo ;
      ClrScr ;
    END ;
{ SignOn }


BEGIN                           (* The main part of the program begins here. *)
  { AutoRpt }
  SignOn(CON) ;
  Instruct ;
  Basic_Facts ;                                { Get the basic information. }
  Car_Facts ;
  Basic_Report(CON) ;
  WriteLn ;
  Auto_Out(CON) ;
  Write('*** Press any key to continue ***') ;
  Read(Kbd,Ch) ;
  ClrScr ;
  GotoXY(10,8) ;                    { Now get ready to do the printed report. }
  Write('*** Turn on the printer --') ;   { Remind the user.  }
  WriteLn(' check and adjust the paper ***') ;  { Ready, get set... }
  GotoXY(18,12) ;
  Write('*** Press any key when ready to print *** ') ;
  Read(Kbd,Ch) ;                             { ...and print it!  }
  ClrScr ;
  GotoXY(20,10) ;
  { Display a notice. }
  WriteLn('*** A hard-copy will now be printed ***') ;
  { Hold the notice on the screen for 2 seconds. }
  Delay(2000) ;
  { Start printing. }
  SignOn(LST) ;
  Basic_Report(LST) ;
  Auto_Out(LST) ;
  FOR I := 1 TO 65 DO
    BEGIN
      Write(LST,Chr(205))
    END ;
  WriteLn(LST) ;
  WriteLn(LST,'TOTAL COST FOR ',Miles:4:0,' MILES OF AUTOMOBILE OPERATION: $'
```

```
                ,AutoCosts:6:2) ;
      FOR I := 1 TO 65 DO
        BEGIN
          Write(LST,Chr(205))
        END ;
      ClrScr ;
      GotoXY(25,10) ;
      WriteLn('*** End of the Auto Expense Report ***') ;
      WriteLn(LST) ;                          { Empty the printer's buffer.        }
      Write(LST,Chr(12))                      { Send a form feed to the printer. }
    END.
    { AutoRpt }
```

CODE LISTING FOR TRIPRPT

```
{ A detailed trip-expense report. }

PROGRAM TripRpt ;

  TYPE
    StringType = STRING[80] ;

  VAR
    Airplane : Real ;                  { Airplane fares paid   }
    CarRent : Real ;                   { Car rental            }
    Ch : Char ;                        { Keyboard character    }
    Cities : StringType ;              { Cities visited        }
    Days : Integer ;                   { Number of days        }
    DateEnd : StringType ;             { When the trip ended   }
    DateStart : StringType ;           { When the trip started }
    Entertain : Real ;                 { Business entertain    }
    I : Integer ;                      { Counter used in loops }
    ItemCosts : Real ;                 { Itemized expenses     }
    Laundry : Real ;                   { Laundry/tailor/valet  }
    Lodging : Real ;                   { Lodgings on trip      }
    Meals : Real ;                     { Meals on the road     }
    Misc : Real ;                      { Miscellaneous expense }
    Phone : Real ;                     { Phone charges         }
    Taxis : Real ;                     { Taxicab fares paid    }
    Tips : Real ;                      { Tips                  }
    Trains : Real ;                    { Train fares paid      }
    TripPurpose : StringType ;         { Purpose of trip       }
    { The FORWARD declarations and PROCEDURES }
    { are listed in alphabetical order only   }
    { for convenience in finding them by eye. }

  PROCEDURE Basic_Facts ;
    FORWARD ;

  PROCEDURE Basic_Report(VAR F:Text) ;
    FORWARD ;
```

```
PROCEDURE Instruct ;
   FORWARD ;

PROCEDURE Items(VAR F:Text) ;
   FORWARD ;

PROCEDURE SignOn(VAR F:Text) ;
   FORWARD ;

PROCEDURE Trip_Facts ;
   FORWARD ;

PROCEDURE Basic_Facts ;                          { Get information from the keyboard. }

   BEGIN
     { Basic_Facts }
     GotoXY(1,5) ;
     LowVideo ;
     { Write statements, the queries, are }
     { displayed in low intensity video.  }
     Write('Briefly, state the trip''s purpose?  ') ;
     HighVideo ;
     { ReadLn responses are displayed }
     { in high intensity.             }
     ReadLn(TripPurpose) ;
     WriteLn ;
     LowVideo ;
     Write('How many days did the trip take?    ') ;
     HighVideo ;
     ReadLn(Days) ;
     LowVideo ;
     Write('What was the starting date?          ') ;
     HighVideo ;
     ReadLn(DateStart) ;
     LowVideo ;
     Write('What was the ending date?            ') ;
     HighVideo ;
     ReadLn(DateEnd) ;
     WriteLn ;
     LowVideo ;
     Write('Name the cities visited: ') ;
     { This could have been 'customers' as well as cities. }
     { You can modify the words to suit your preference.    }
     HighVideo ;
     ReadLn(Cities) ;
     WriteLn ;
   END ;
{ Basic_Facts }

PROCEDURE Basic_Report ;              { Print the information from Basic_Facts. }
```

```
   BEGIN
     { Basic_Report }
     ClrScr ;
     WriteLn(F) ;
     WriteLn(F) ;
     WriteLn(F,'TRIP REPORT: ',DateStart,' THROUGH ',DateEnd) ;
     WriteLn(F) ;
     WriteLn(F,'Objective of the ',Days,' day trip: ',TripPurpose) ;
     WriteLn(F,'Cities visited: ',Cities) ;   { Or customers. }
     WriteLn(F) ;
   END ;
{ Basic_Report }

PROCEDURE Instruct ;                          { Display instructions for the user. }

   BEGIN
     { Instruct }
     GotoXY(20,5) ;                      { Start instructions at column 20, row 5. }
     Write('This program provides information') ;
     GotoXY(20,6) ;
     Write('concerned with travel expenses,') ;
     GotoXY(20,7) ;
     Write('excluding the costs of using an') ;
     GotoXY(20,8) ;
     Write('automobile...company or personal.') ;
     GotoXY(20,10) ;
     Write('Answer the questions and allow the') ;
     GotoXY(20,11) ;
     Write('computer to do all calculations.') ;
     GotoXY(20,13) ;
     Write('If no expenses were incurred for an') ;
     GotoXY(20,14) ;
     Write('item, enter a zero and press Return.') ;
     GotoXY(20,16) ;
     Write('A hard-copy report will be provided.') ;
     GotoXY(20,19) ;
     Write('*** BE SURE THE PRINTER IS READY ***') ;
     GotoXY(20,22) ;
     Write(' ... Press any key to continue ...') ;
     Read(Kbd,Ch) ;                  { Wait for a key to be pressed, then continue. }
     ClrScr
   END ;
{ Instruct }

PROCEDURE Items ;

   BEGIN
     { Items }
     ItemCosts := 0 ;                          { Set the item costs to zero. }
     WriteLn(F) ;
     WriteLn(F,'      Airplane fares:  $',Airplane:6:2) ;
```

```
        WriteLn(F,'     Train fares:      $',Trains:6:2) ;
        WriteLn(F,'     Taxicab fares:    $',Taxis:6:2) ;
        WriteLn(F,'     Car rentals:      $',CarRent:6:2) ;
        WriteLn(F,'     Meals for self:   $',Meals:6:2) ;
        WriteLn(F,'     Lodgings:         $',Lodging:6:2) ;
        WriteLn(F,'     Telephone calls:  $',Phone:6:2) ;
        WriteLn(F,'     Tips paid:        $',Tips:6:2) ;
        WriteLn(F,'     Entertainment:    $',Entertain:6:2) ;
        WriteLn(F,'     Valet services:   $',Laundry:6:2) ;
        WriteLn(F,'     Miscellaneous:    $',Misc:6:2) ;
        ItemCosts := Meals + Misc + Airplane + Trains + Taxis + Phone + Tips +
            Lodging + Entertain + CarRent + Laundry ;
        WriteLn(F) ;
    END ;
{ Items }

PROCEDURE Trip_Facts ;                  { Collect facts about the trip's costs. }

    BEGIN
        { Trip_Facts }
        WriteLn ;
        HighVideo ;
        WriteLn('Enter the Amount for Each Item of Expense:') ;
        WriteLn ;
        LowVideo ;
        Write('Airplanes:  ') ;
        HighVideo ;
        ReadLn(Airplane) ;
        LowVideo ;
        Write('Trains:     ') ;
        HighVideo ;
        ReadLn(Trains) ;
        LowVideo ;
        Write('Taxicabs:   ') ;
        HighVideo ;
        ReadLn(Taxis) ;
        LowVideo ;
        Write('Car rental: ') ;
        HighVideo ;
        ReadLn(CarRent) ;
        LowVideo ;
        Write('Meals:      ') ;
        HighVideo ;
        ReadLn(Meals) ;
        LowVideo ;
        Write('Lodging:    ') ;
        HighVideo ;
        ReadLn(Lodging) ;
        LowVideo ;
        Write('Telephone:  ') ;
        HighVideo ;
```

```
      ReadLn(Phone) ;
      LowVideo ;
      Write('Tips:        ') ;
      HighVideo ;
      ReadLn(Tips) ;
      LowVideo ;
      Write('Entertainment:   ') ;
      HighVideo ;
      ReadLn(Entertain) ;
      LowVideo ;
      Write('Valet services: ') ;
      HighVideo ;
      ReadLn(Laundry) ;
      LowVideo ;
      Write('Miscellaneous:   ') ;
      HighVideo ;
      ReadLn(Misc) ;
      WriteLn ;
      LowVideo
    END ;
  { Trip_Facts }

PROCEDURE SignOn ;                             { Create the startup display. }

    BEGIN
      { SignOn }
      ClrScr ;
      GotoXY(10,10) ;
      LowVideo ;
      FOR I := 1 TO 65 DO
        BEGIN
          Write(F,CHR(205))
        END ;
      WriteLn(F) ;
      GotoXY(12,12) ;
      HighVideo ;
      Write(F,'            TRIPRPT -- TRAVEL EXPENSE RECORD') ;
      WriteLn(F) ;
      GotoXY(10,14) ;
      LowVideo ;
      FOR I := 1 TO 65 DO
        BEGIN
          Write(F,CHR(205))
        END ;
      Write(F) ;
      Delay(1500) ;
      HighVideo ;
      ClrScr ;
    END ;
  { SignOn }
```

94

```
BEGIN                         (* The main part of the program begins here. *)
  { TripRpt }
  SignOn(CON) ;
  Instruct ;
  Basic_Facts ;                              { Get the basic information. }
  Trip_Facts ;
  Basic_Report(CON) ;
  WriteLn ;
  WriteLn ;
  Items(CON) ;
  Write('      *** Press any key to continue *** ') ;
  Read(Kbd,Ch) ;
  ClrScr ;
  GotoXY(10,8) ;                       { Now get ready to do the printed report. }
  Write('*** Turn on the printer --') ;    { Remind the user.  }
  WriteLn(' check and adjust the paper ***') ;  { Ready, get set... }
  GotoXY(18,12) ;
  Write('*** Press any key when ready to print *** ') ;
  Read(Kbd,Ch) ;                             { ...and print it!  }
  ClrScr ;
  GotoXY(20,10) ;
  { Display a notice. }
  WriteLn('*** A hard-copy will now be printed ***') ;
  { Hold the notice on the screen for 2 seconds. }
  Delay(2000) ;
  { Start printing now. }
  SignOn(LST) ;
  Basic_Report(LST) ;
  Items(LST) ;
  FOR I := 1 TO 65 DO
    BEGIN
      Write(LST,Chr(205))
    END ;
  WriteLn(LST) ;
  Write(LST,'TOTAL COSTS REPORTED FOR THE TRIP: $',ItemCosts:6:2) ;
  WriteLn(LST) ;
  FOR I := 1 TO 65 DO
    BEGIN
      Write(LST,Chr(205))
    END ;
  ClrScr ;
  GotoXY(25,10) ;
  WriteLn('*** End of the Trip Report ***') ;
  WriteLn(LST) ;                             { Empty the printer's buffer.      }
  Write(LST,Chr(12))                         { Send a form feed to the printer. }
END.
{ TripRpt }
```

Chapter 13

Send Control
Codes to a Printer

Most popular printers will accept external commands entered at the computer keyboard. Under software control these printers can be instructed to change fonts, faces, spacing, and other printing characteristics within the printers' capabilities. The command sequences are usually found in the documentation supplied with the printers. This chapter's program, SETPRNTR, provides the structure and basic code that can be adapted to virtually any printer that will accept commands issued from a remote source such as the computer to which it is connected.

SETPRNTR clears the screen and displays a menu of a dozen commands. The program uses the Case construction for the response to selected commands, which are letters of the alphabet. The Case structure recognizes both upper-case or lowercase letters. If a key is pressed that is not on the menu (not in the Case construction), an error message is displayed and the menu waits for a valid selection.

The commands given in the code listing for SETPRNTR are intended for the IBM dot-matrix printer, and, of course, those compatible printers that use the same commands. The control codes given in the Case construction can be changed to conform to your specific printer or to perform other printer functions. The menu can be expanded to include the complete alphabet, numbers, or other characters that can then become part of the CASE statement. In SETPRNTR, the letter X is used for printing a four-line sample of the mode that has been selected from the menu. Y resets the printer to its default status. Z ends the program and returns the system to the DOS command line.

CODE LISTING FOR SETPRNTR

```
{ Program to set control characters for IBM   }
{ and command-compatible printers from a menu. }
{ A large number of Procedures are used to     }
{ simplify making changes for other printers.  }

PROGRAM SetPrntr ;

  CONST
    Width = 27 ;

  VAR
    I  : Integer ;
    Ch : Char ;

  PROCEDURE SetCase ;       { Here's the CASE construction. }

    VAR
      OK : Boolean ;

    BEGIN
      OK := True ;
      CASE Ch OF
        'A','a' : BEGIN                      (* EXPANDED *)
                  { Chr(27) is the escape code.     }
                  Write(LST,(Chr(27)),(Chr(87)),(Chr(1))) ;
                  Write(LST,(Chr(7)))     { Chr(7) is the console's beep. }
                  END ;
        'B','b' : BEGIN                      (* COMPRESSED *)
                  Write(LST,(Chr(15))) ;
                  Write(LST,(Chr(7)))
                  END ;
        'C','c' : BEGIN                      (* ELITE *)
                  Write(LST,(Chr(27)),(Chr(77))) ;
                  Write(LST,(Chr(7)))
                  END ;
        'D','d' : BEGIN                      (* PROPORTIONAL *)
                  Write(LST,(Chr(27)),(Chr(112)),(Chr(1))) ;
                  Write(LST,(Chr(7)))
                  END ;
        'E','e' : BEGIN                      (* ITALICS *)
                  Write(LST,(Chr(27)),(Chr(52))) ;
                  Write(LST,(Chr(7)))
                  END ;
        'F','f' : BEGIN                      (* DOUBLE STRIKE *)
                  Write(LST,(Chr(27)),(Chr(71))) ;
                  Write(LST,(Chr(7)))
                  END ;
        'G','g' : BEGIN                      (* EMPHASIZED *)
```

```pascal
                Write(LST,(Chr(27)),(Chr(69))) ;
                Write(LST,(Chr(7)))
             END ;
      'H','h' : BEGIN                          (* SUPERSCRIPT *)
                Write(LST,(Chr(27)),(Chr(83)),(Chr(0))) ;
                Write(LST,(Chr(7)))
             END ;
      'I','i' : BEGIN                          (* SUBSCRIPT *)
                Write(LST,(Chr(27)),(Chr(83)),(Chr(1))) ;
                Write(LST,(Chr(7)))
             END ;
      'J','j' : BEGIN                          (* UNDERLINE *)
                Write(LST,(Chr(27)),(Chr(45)),(Chr(1))) ;
                Write(LST,(Chr(7)))
             END ;
      'K','k' : BEGIN                          (* DOUBLE SPACE *)
                Write(LST,(Chr(27)),(Chr(51)),(Chr(60))) ;
                Write(LST,(Chr(7)))
             END ;
      'L','l' : BEGIN                          (* SINGLE SPACE *)
                Write(LST,(Chr(27)),(Chr(2))) ;
                Write(LST,(Chr(7)))
             END ;
      'M','m' : BEGIN                          (* LINE FEED *)
                Write(LST,(Chr(10))) ;
                Write(LST,(Chr(7)))
             END ;
      'N','n' : BEGIN                          (* FORM FEED *)
                Write(LST,(Chr(12))) ;
                Write(LST,(Chr(7)))
             END ;
      'X','x' : BEGIN                          (* TEST PRINT *)
                WriteLn(LST,('ABCDEFGHIJKLMNOPQRSTUVWXYZ')) ;
                WriteLn(LST,('abcdefghijklmnopqrstuvwxyz')) ;
                WriteLn(LST,('1234567890')) ;
                WriteLn(LST,('!@#$%^&*()_+=-{}[]":;,<>?/|\~'')) ;
                Write(LST,(Chr(10))) ;  { Do a line feed after the test. }
                Write(LST,(Chr(7)))
             END ;
      'Y','y' : BEGIN                          (* RESET *)
                Write(LST,(Chr(27)),(Chr(64))) ;
                Write(LST,(Chr(7)))
             END ;
      'Z','z' : ;   (* ";" is the NULL character that ends the program. *)

   ELSE
   OK := False
END ;
IF ( NOT OK) THEN
  BEGIN
    WriteLn ;
```

```
              WriteLn ;
              HighVideo ;
              Write('              +++ INVALID SELECTION +++ ') ;
              Delay(1000)  (* Hold the INVALID message for 1 second. *)
           END ;
      END ;

   PROCEDURE Header ;     (* This is the heading for the menu. *)

      VAR
        I : integer ;

      BEGIN
        { Header }
        WriteLn ;
        WriteLn ;
        WriteLn ;
        LowVideo ;
        FOR I := 1 TO Width DO
          Write('\') ;
        FOR I := 1 TO Width DO
          Write('/') ;
        WriteLn ;
        Write(' >>>>>>>>   ') ;
        HighVideo ;
        Write('   IBM PRINTER CONFIGURATOR   ') ;
        LowVideo ;
        WriteLn('   <<<<<<<<') ;
        FOR I := 1 TO Width DO
          Write('/') ;
        FOR I := 1 TO Width DO
          Write('\') ;
        WriteLn
      END ;
   { Header }

   PROCEDURE Menu_Part1 ;  (* The menu is divided into two parts. *)

      BEGIN
        { Menu_Part1 }
        WriteLn ;
        HighVideo ;
        WriteLn('-----------------CHARACTER STYLES--------------------') ;
        WriteLn ;
        LowVideo ;
        WriteLn('    A) Expanded               F) Double Strike') ;
        WriteLn('    B) Compressed             G) Emphasized') ;
        WriteLn('    C) Elite                  H) Superscript') ;
        WriteLn('    D) Proportional           I) Subscript') ;
        WriteLn('    E) Italics                J) Underline')
      END ;
```

```
{ Menu_Part1 }

PROCEDURE Menu_Part2 ;

  BEGIN
    { Menu_Part2 }
    WriteLn ;
    HighVideo ;
    WriteLn('----------------------PAPER MOVEMENT----------------------') ;
    WriteLn ;
    LowVideo ;
    WriteLn('    K) Double Space              M) Line Feed') ;
    WriteLn('    L) Single Space              N) Form Feed') ;
    WriteLn ;
    HighVideo ;
    WriteLn('----------------------------------------------------------') ;
    LowVideo ;
    WriteLn('    X) TEST PRINT    Y) RESET    Z) RETURN TO DOS') ;
    HighVideo ;
    WriteLn('----------------------------------------------------------') ;
    WriteLn ;
    WriteLn
  END ;
{ Menu_Part2 }

BEGIN
  { SetPrntr }
  REPEAT
    ClrScr ;
    Header ;            (# Execute the Header PROCEDURE. #)
    Menu_Part1 ;        (# Execute the Menu PROCEDUREs.  #)
    Menu_Part2 ;
    Write(Chr(7)) ;     (# Sound the bell or beep.       #)
    HighVideo ;
    Write(':----------< Select One Option at a Time >------------: ') ;
    Read(Kbd,Ch) ;
    SetCase ;           (# Execute the PROCEDURE.        #)
  UNTIL (Ch = 'Z') OR (Ch = 'z')
  { An alternate line of code is: }
  {     UNTIL Ch IN ['Z','z']     }
  { Both lines do the same thing. }
END.
{ SetPrntr }
```

Chapter 14

Use Time-trend Analysis to Smooth the Rough Spots

When you examine the day-to-day or month-to-month histories of a company's performance, you often discover that a graph of the data resembles the profile of an amusement park's roller coaster. Therefore, preparing a forecast or a budget on the basis of historic data can seriously test the expertise and know-how of the forecaster. But you must build on historic data, and you can, after it has been made meaningful or translated into a usable form.

Trends may lie hidden in the data, however, and there are many techniques for discovering and quantifying those trends. One of the methods is known as *time-trend analysis*. It is also known as *calculating the moving average*. This chapter's program, TIMETRND, takes raw data for a series of quantitative events and continuously averages the data. The effect is to smooth out the peaks and valleys and in this way to make the trend of the data quite clear and unambiguous. If the data were to be plotted, you would see immediately whether the direction was up, down, or static.

TIMETRND queries the user for the raw data and the number of periods for the moving-average calculations. A complete table of data, raw and smoothed, is computed, displayed, and if desired, it can be printed.

Many companies, financial and marketing managers, and statisticians use this approach to data analysis. Moving averages developed for raw data that cover reasonably short periods of time, say 15 months or so, can be quite revealing. The calculation of moving averages, however, is not limited to short-term data analysis. Financial institutions may use 20-year moving averages to determine or test the reasonableness of bad debt provisions for federal income tax purposes.

Although the formulas and the process are not complex, they are time consuming, and at the very least, somewhat of a bore to do manually or even with the aid of a hand-held electronic calculator. The TIMETRND program does all the calculations for you, displays the results on the screen and at your signal, makes as many printouts as you want.

A MARKETING MANAGER'S PROBLEM SOLVER

In forecasting sales of products, systems, components, or services, the most recent historic data are the important bases for improving the accuracy of the forecast. Such data are always related to time—days, months, quarters, years, and so on. In a multiproduct marketing company or in a service operation, sales and financial forecasts (budgets) must be developed for each item in the catalog. A forecast also must be developed for the aggregate of all products and services.

Historic reviews of the movement of products or services with respect to time periods, when tabulated and displayed or graphed as raw or actual data, often resemble the teeth of a defective saw blade or the jagged profile of a cliff more than they resemble a smooth, idealistic, upward-moving line. It can be difficult and sometimes impossible to determine the direction of the trend from the raw data. MOVAVGE accepts the data, regardless of how "sharp its teeth" or how "jagged its edges," and at microcomputer speed, calculates and redisplays it to reveal the unambiguous trend of the data. Moreover, on the basis of the computed trend, the program suggests and displays a forecast for the next time period as an aid to planning and budgeting.

In this chapter I will use moving averages to analyze relatively short-term trends in marketing and manufacturing. The numbers may relate to days, weeks, months, or years; and to pennies, dollars, or units—whichever suits the need. Dollar signs are not used in the program. Therefore the references or the classifications for the type of data are for you to define.

Moving averages can be used to reveal trends in productivity, be it the output produced by a single assembly-line, by a combination of facilities, or by a complete plant. The analysis of trends in sales, which have a significant effect on production, becomes a valuable aid in pinpointing problem areas, in comparing two or more product lines, in budgeting, and in forecasting. For an analysis of production, the data entered can be classified as units of time, head counts, parts used, input, output, dollars, open jobs, and so on.

A SAMPLE RUN

Let's simulate a typical run as might be created by a sales or marketing manager. In this example, numbers that have distinctly sharp peaks and valleys will be used as raw actual data; notice how TIMETRND handles them.

The data will span a 16-month period of sales activity for fictitious company ABC. There is no magic to the number 16. It happens to be the number of time periods for which the hypothetical marketing or sales manager of company ABC has accurate information. More important, it covers what has been a rather volatile period, one in which the sales volume moved up and down alarmingly, making it difficult to ascertain any sort of meaningful trend.

The requests for information that are displayed on the screen are shown in boldface. The responses that are typed in are shown underlined, at the right of each request:

===

TIME TREND ANALYSIS WITH MOVING AVERAGES

===

How many TIME PERIODS are to be entered?:   16

Enter a value for each of the 16 time periods:

1:	11287
2:	15445
3:	23479
4:	14876
5:	15434
6:	27565
7:	22835
8:	9678
9:	11034
10:	10222
11:	14943
12:	17042
13:	38904
14:	16832

15:	<u>5ØØ89</u>
16:	<u>345Ø2</u>

Enter the number of periods to be averaged: <u>3</u>

When you press the Enter key after the last entry, the screen clears and the table of data appears with three headings:

PERIOD　　　　　**RAW DATA**　　　　**SMOOTHED DATA**

The numbers of the 16 individual time periods, in this case equivalent to months, appear in sequence below the PERIOD column. The RAW DATA, the actual, historic data that was entered previously appears appropriately under the center heading. The SMOOTHED DATA that has been generated by the computer appears in the last column. Each smoothed data entry is derived from the average of the immediately previous raw data periods. In this example, three periods are averaged, because 3 was entered in response to the request to "Enter the number of periods to be averaged."

Based on the trend of the data that was smoothed for a moving average of three periods, a forecast is displayed for period 17. As you can see from the hard copy printout, this particular forecast is not terribly exciting. But, it is based on the average of the 14th, 15th, and 16th time periods, which are the most recent historic facts. If the display that has been created is too long to appear in whole on the screen, an option is provided so that the table can be repeatedly brought back to the screen for study:

Repeat the display? (Y/N):

In addition to being able to repeatedly display the table of data, you can change the averaging period as many times as you wish. This is useful for optimizing the smoothed data. The screen asks:

Change the number of periods to be averaged?　(Y/N):

If you type <Y>, the screen asks:

Enter the number of periods to be averaged:

You can change the number as many times as you want until you are satisfied with the SMOOTHED DATA, which changes each time you revise the number of the averaging period.

Then, when you have arrived at an acceptable set of data, you are given the option to make a hard copy. You can make as many printouts as you want by entering the letter <Y> in response to the screen's query. Finally, when you have as many printouts as you want, you can end the program by entering <N> instead of <Y> in response to the prompt:

Do another printout? (Y/N):

```
MOVING AVERAGES - TIME TREND ANALYSIS


   PERIOD          RAW DATA          SMOOTHED DATA
   --------------------------------------------------

      1            11287.0                0.0
      2            15445.0                0.0
      3            23479.0                0.0
      4            14876.0            16737.0
      5            15434.0            17933.3
      6            27565.0            17929.7
      7            22835.0            19291.7
      8             9678.0            21944.7
      9            11034.0            20026.0
     10            10222.0            14515.7
     11            14943.0            10311.3
     12            17042.0            12066.3
     13            38904.0            14069.0
     14            16832.0            23629.7
     15            50089.0            24259.3
     16            34502.0            35275.0


THE TREND FORECASTS PERIOD 17 AS: 33807.7

NUMBER OF PERIODS AVERAGED: 3
```

Fig. 14-1. A sample printout from the Time-Trend Analysis program.

```
          MOVING AVERAGES - TIME TREND ANALYSIS


          PERIOD              RAW DATA              SMOOTHED DATA

            1                 11287.0                   0.0
            2                 15445.0                   0.0
            3                 23479.0                   0.0
            4                 14876.0                   0.0
            5                 15434.0                   0.0
            6                 27565.0                16104.2
            7                 22835.0                19359.8
            8                  9678.0                20837.8
            9                 11034.0                18077.6
           10                 10222.0                17309.2
           11                 14943.0                16266.8
           12                 17042.0                13742.4
           13                 38904.0                12583.8
           14                 16832.0                18429.0
           15                 50089.0                19588.6
           16                 34502.0                27562.0


       THE TREND FORECASTS PERIOD 17 AS: 31473.8

       NUMBER OF PERIODS AVERAGED: 5
```

Fig. 14-2. A sample printout from the Time-Trend Analysis program.

Figures 14-1 and 14-2 are printouts that TIMETREND generated using the raw data from the example. Figure 14-1 demonstrates the smoothing effect when an averaging period of 3 is used. Figure 14-2 takes the same data and smooths it over 5 periods. Note that the forecast for period 17 is changed, as are the calculations for the smoothed data.

CODE LISTING FOR TIMETRND

```
{ TimeTrnd accepts raw, unsmoothed data, and generates a  }
{ smoothed set of data from which it generates a table of }
{ moving averages that reveal trends related to time.     }
```

```
PROGRAM TimeTrnd ;

   CONST
     MaxNumPeriod = 50 ;
     { Change the CONST to modify the  }
     { maximum number of periods the   }
     { program will deal with.         }
     { If this is changed, be sure to  }
     { make similar changes in the     }
     { error-trap message displayed by }
     { PROCEDURE Facts_Only ;          }

   TYPE
     PerNumType = 1..MaxNumPeriod ;
     StringType = STRING[80] ;

   VAR
     Ch : Char ;                           { Keyboard response character.  }
     I,J,K,L : Integer ;                   { Identifiers for the FOR loops. }
     NumAveraged,NumPeriods : Integer ;
     Period_Value : ARRAY [PerNumType] OF Real ;
     Trend_Value : Real ;

   PROCEDURE SignOn ;                      { Display the startup message.  }

     BEGIN                                 { BEGIN the SignOn PROCEDURE.   }
       { SignOn }
       ClrScr ;                            { Clear the screen.             }
       GotoXY(15,8) ;                      { Send the cursor to C15/R8.    }
       LowVideo ;                          { Low-intensity screen chars.   }
       FOR I := 1 TO 50 DO                 { This loop has 50 iterations.  }
         BEGIN                             { Start the FOR...DO loop.      }
           Write(Chr(205))                 { The character to be written.  }
         END ;                             { END of the FOR...DO loop.     }
       GotoXY(20,10) ;                     { Send the cursor to C20/R10.   }
       HighVideo ;                         { High-intensity screen chars.  }
       Write('TIME TREND ANALYIS with MOVING AVERAGES') ;
       GotoXY(15,12) ;                     { Send the cursor to C15/R12.   }
       LowVideo ;                          { Restore low-intensity video.  }
       FOR J := 1 TO 50 DO                 { Same as first FOR...DO loop.  }
         BEGIN                             { Begin the FOR loop.           }
           Write(Chr(205))
         END ;                             { End the FOR loop.             }
       Delay(1500) ;                       { Delay the next screen action. }
       ClrScr                              { Clear the screen.             }
     END ;                                 { End the PROCEDURE.            }
   { SignOn }

   PROCEDURE Averaging_Period ;            { Get the number for averaging. }

     BEGIN
```

```
      WriteLn ;
      LowVideo ;                              { Low intensity for the query.  }
      Write('  Enter the number of periods to be averaged: ') ;
      HighVideo ;                             { High intensity for the answer. }
      ReadLn(NumAveraged) ;
      WriteLn
   END ;
{ Averaging_Period }


PROCEDURE Facts_Only ;                   { Get the facts from the keyboard. }

   VAR
      Period_Counter : PerNumType ;

   BEGIN
      { Facts_Only }
      LowVideo ;            { The "maximum" is the same as the CONST value. }
      Write('How many TIME PERIODS are to be entered? (50 maximum): ') ;
      HighVideo ;
      ReadLn(NumPeriods) ;              { Get the keyboard entry.            }
      IF (NumPeriods > 50) THEN        { The > 50 must be the same as CONST, }
         BEGIN                         { otherwise this error-trap is wrong. }
            WriteLn ;
            Write('That''s more than 50.  Please choose another quantity: ') ;
            ReadLn(NumPeriods)         { Get the keyboard entry, if needed.  }
         END ;
      WriteLn ;
      LowVideo ;
      WriteLn('Enter a value for each of the ',NumPeriods,' periods:') ;
      WriteLn ;
      FOR Period_Counter := 1 TO NumPeriods DO
         BEGIN                         { Loop for counting up to NumPeriods. }
            LowVideo ;
            Write('                    ',Period_Counter:3,':  ') ;
            HighVideo ;
            ReadLn(Period_Value[Period_Counter])
         END ;
      Averaging_Period ;              { Execute the PROCEDURE Averaging_Period. }
      WriteLn ;
      WriteLn ;
      WriteLn
   END ;
{ Facts_Only }


PROCEDURE Pattern_1 (VAR F:Text) ;           { Send a pattern to F. }

   BEGIN
      { Pattern_1 }
      LowVideo ;
      Write(F,' ') ;
```

```
      FOR L := 1 TO 70 DO          { Repeat the `Write' expression 70 times. }
        BEGIN
          Write(F,Chr(205))        { Write the IBM graphics character 205.    }
        END ;
      HighVideo ;
      WriteLn(F)
    END ;
{ Pattern_1 }

PROCEDURE Pattern_2 (VAR F:Text) ;          { Send a pattern to F. }

    BEGIN
      { Pattern_2 }
      LowVideo ;
      Write(F,'              ') ;
      FOR K := 1 TO 50 DO          { Repeat the `Write' expression 50 times. }
        BEGIN
          Write(F,'-') ;           { Write a series of 50 hyphen characters. }
        END ;
      HighVideo ;
      WriteLn(F)
    END ;
{ Pattern_2 }

PROCEDURE Make_The_Table (VAR F:Text) ; { Generate the time trend table. }

    VAR
      Counter : PerNumType ;
      NumSequence : Integer ;

    BEGIN
      { Make_The_Table }
      ClrScr ;
      LowVideo ;
      Pattern_1(F) ;                { Execute the PROCEDURE. }
      WriteLn(F) ;
      HighVideo ;
      WriteLn(F,'            MOVING AVERAGES - TIME TREND ANALYSIS') ;
      WriteLn(F) ;
      LowVideo ;
      Pattern_1(F) ;                { Execute the PROCEDURE. }
      WriteLn(F) ;
      HighVideo ;
      Write(F,'            ') ;
      WriteLn(F,'PERIOD        RAW DATA           SMOOTHED DATA') ;
      Pattern_2(F) ;                { Execute the PROCEDURE. }
      WriteLn(F) ;
      FOR NumSequence := 1 TO NumPeriods + 1 DO
        BEGIN
          Trend_Value := 0 ;        { Set Trend_Value to zero. }
```

```
              IF (NumSequence > NumAveraged) THEN
                BEGIN
                  FOR Counter := 1 TO NumAveraged DO
                        { Set Trend_Value's value. }
                    Trend_Value := Trend_Value +
                                  Period_Value[NumSequence - Counter] ;
                        { Set Trend_Value to a new value. }
                    Trend_Value := Trend_Value / NumAveraged
                END ;
              IF (NumSequence <= NumPeriods) THEN
                BEGIN
                  Write(F,'          ',NumSequence:7) ;
                  Write(F,'            ',Period_Value[NumSequence]:7:1) ;
                  WriteLn(F,'            ',Trend_Value:7:1)
                END
              ELSE
                BEGIN
                  WriteLn(F) ;
                  LowVideo ;
                  Pattern_2(F) ;      { Execute the PROCEDURE. }
                  HighVideo ;
                  Write(F,'          ','THE TREND FORECASTS PERIOD ') ;
                  WriteLn(F,NumSequence,' AS: ',Trend_Value:7:1) ;
                  Pattern_2(F) ;      { Execute the PROCEDURE. }
                  Write(F,'        ') ;
                  WriteLn(F,'NUMBER OF PERIODS AVERAGED: ',NumAveraged)
                END
          END ;
        WriteLn(F) ;
        Pattern_1(F)                  { Execute the PROCEDURE. }
      END ;
{ Make_The_Table }

BEGIN
  { TimeTrnd }
  { This is the main-part of the code. }
  { Each of the PROCEDURES is called   }
  { and executed in turn.              }
  SignOn ;                        { Execute the PROCEDURE. }
  Facts_Only ;                    { Execute the PROCEDURE. }
  ClrScr ;
  REPEAT
    Make_The_Table(CON) ;         { Display the moving averages table. }
    WriteLn ;
    LowVideo ;
    Write(' Repeat the Display?  (Y/N): ') ;   { An option. }
    HighVideo ;
    Read(Kbd,Ch) ;
    IF (Ch = 'Y') OR (Ch = 'y') THEN
      BEGIN
        WriteLn ;
```

```
                LowVideo ;
                Write('  Change the number of periods to be averaged?','  (Y/N): ') ;
                HighVideo ;
                Read(Kbd,Ch) ;
                IF (Ch = 'Y') OR (Ch = 'y') THEN
                    Averaging_Period        { Recalculate for the averaging period. }
                ELSE
                    Make_The_Table(CON)                 { Generate the revised table. }
            END
        UNTIL (Ch = 'N') OR (Ch = 'n') ;
        WriteLn ;
        LowVideo ;
        WriteLn('  For a printout, turn on the printer.') ;
        Write('  When ready, type the letter `Y'', or `N''to QUIT: ') ;
        HighVideo ;
        Read(Kbd,Ch) ;
        WHILE (Ch = 'Y') OR (Ch = 'y') DO
            BEGIN
                Make_The_Table(LST) ;       { Print the moving averages table.  }
                Write(LST,Chr(12)) ;        { Do a form feed after the printout. }
                WriteLn ;
                LowVideo ;
                Write('  Do another printout?  (Y/N): ') ;
                Read(Kbd,Ch)
            END
    END.
    { TimeTrnd }
```

Chapter 15

Plotting Equidistant Data Points

There are many ways to make visual presentations of numeric information. You have already looked at programs in this book that generate tables of data and histograms. Another option is offered with LINEPLOT, a program that presents data as a series of points within the boundaries of an X-axis and a Y-axis. By connecting the data points with a straight edge, one data point to the next data point in succession, you can gain a view of the data that enables rapid trend analysis or other series-related examinations and evaluations.

LINEPLOT contains algorithms that make the code interesting to the Turbo Pascal programmer. As an applications program, it can be exceptionally valuable to the marketer, manufacturer, engineer, and student who deals with data. LINEPLOT queries the user for basic data such as the width of the graph, and the number of data points to be plotted. Then it asks for the data to be entered. When the declared number of data points has been entered, the program prints a graph with the largest data value at the top of the graph and the other data values equidistant from one another in the sequence they were entered.

Each data point is indicated by an asterisk character placed in its appropriate position by the program. The character used to indicate the positions of the data points can be changed to any character within your printer's capability. The completed plot is displayed on the screen. A Yes/No option to print hard copies of the plot is offered.

The plot is printed horizontally. It is properly oriented by rotating the printed plot 90-degrees counter clockwise; the printed width is actually the height of the plot. Connect the data points using a straightedge to complete the plot.

LINEPLOT is easy to use. Instructions are comprehensively displayed on the screen as you move through the program. LINEPLOT provides both screen displays and printouts. Because of the physical limitations of the screen, a print-out is essential for a proper examination of the graph and its data points. Therefore, output to a printer (LST) is a feature incorporated into the code. You can make any number of printouts of the graph.

RUNNING THE PROGRAM

When you compile and execute the program, the SignOn procedure is the first one called. This displays the name of the program for 1.5 seconds. The screen clears and this notice is displayed:

*** TURN ON THE PRINTER BEFORE ENTERING ANY DATA ***

The next instruction and your response (shown with an underline) are:

Give the width of the graph to be printed in inches: 4

If your printer produces 10 characters per inch, the printout of the graph will actually be 4 inches wide. The length of the graph will be related to the number of data points you enter. For 10 data-point entries, a reasonable number, you can generally estimate a length-to-width ratio of about 1.2:1, which is adequate for many purposes. Each data point is equidistant from the preceding and succeeding data points.

It is practical to make the width of the graph proportional to the largest data-value that you will enter. For example, if you are going to make a series of entries with the largest value being 530, respond to the "width of the graph" question with the number 5.3. This will enable you to produce a graph that will be 5.3 inches wide with the value 530 at the top of the Y axis. This ade-quately fits a sheet of printer paper that is 8.5 inches wide. When you are printing at the normal 10 characters-per-inch scale, the maximum graph size is 7.9 inches.

Let's continue to create the sample graph with a width of 4.

How many data points do you want to plot? (50 Max):   10

Do NOT enter negative values.

Now you can start entering values for the data points. The program keeps count until it reaches the number you entered; in the code the number is assigned as the value of <NumPoints>. The letter <I> in the FOR . . . DO loop carries the count, which appears as part of the statement in the BEGIN . . . END expression that follows.

ENTER THE VALUES FOR:

1:	<u>100</u>
2:	<u>150</u>
3:	<u>375</u>
4:	<u>350</u>
5:	<u>400</u>
6:	<u>300</u>
7:	<u>175</u>
8:	<u>250</u>
9:	<u>275</u>
10:	<u>325</u>

The code formats the numbers, which are of the real type, to four places. The printer repeats each value when you press the Enter key. After the value for the 10th data point has been entered, the PrintStatistics procedure is called. The screen and the printer display the summary simultaneously:

Largest data value: 400.

Top of the Graph has a value of: 400.

Width of Graph: 4 inches at 10 cpi.

The printing and displaying of the graph start at this point. The screen and the printer keep pace with one another. After the printout is completed, the screen asks:

Do another printout of the graph? (Y/N):

The REPEAT . . . UNTIL Ch IN ['N', 'n'] routine controls the exit or con-

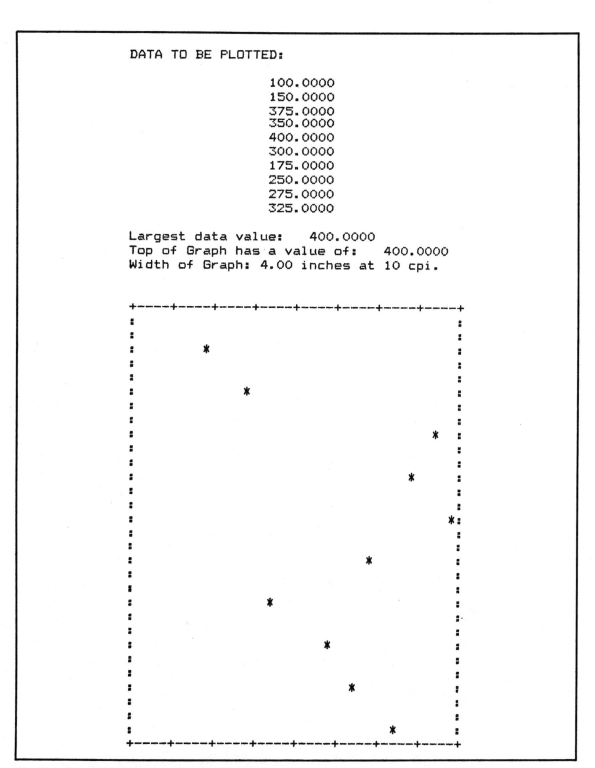

Fig. 15-1. A sample printout from the Line Plot program.

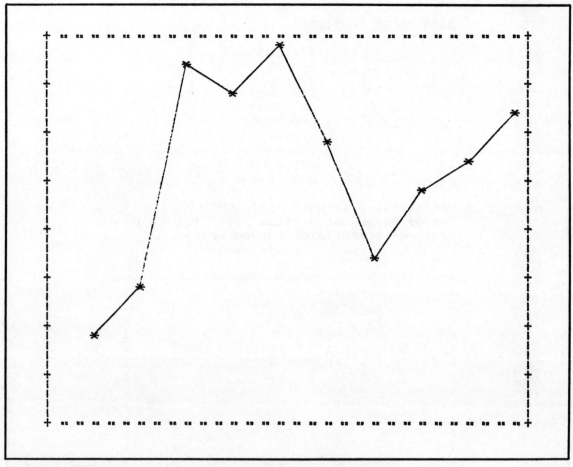

Fig. 15-2. A sample printout from the Line Plot program with points connected.

tinuation of the program. <Y> calls the Write Graph procedure, which sends the output of WriteGraph to the video display (CON) and to the printer (LST). The <N> response ends the program.

A SAMPLE LINEPLOT PRINTOUT

When the plot of the data points is printed within the graph's boundaries, the X and Y-axes appear transposed. The width of the graph, 4 inches in this example, is actually the height. Merely turn the graph sideways when you use it. Draw lines connecting each asterisk to the next. You will have a graphic display of the data that is plotted by this program as a series of points, and you didn't have to buy, rent, or borrow special drawing tools or a plotter-printer.

Figures 15-1 and 15-2 show printouts of the data entered earlier. In Fig. 15-1, the data points are shown in their relative positions on the graph, and in Fig. 15-2, the data points have been linked and the page has ben properly oriented.

116

CODE LISTING FOR LINEPLOT

```
{ Program to plot a set of equidistant data points on a graph. }

PROGRAM LinePlot ;

  CONST
    MaxNumPoints = 50 ;          { 50 is the maximum number of data points. }
                                 { To increase or decrease the "maximum,"   }
                                 { change the number 50 to the desired one. }

  VAR
    Ch : Char ;
    Factor,Largest,TensWidth,Width : Real ;
    I,NumPoints : Integer ;
    Points : ARRAY [1..MaxNumPoints] OF Real ;

  PROCEDURE SignOn ;                              { Display the startup message. }

    BEGIN
      { SignOn }
      ClrScr ;
      LowVideo ;
      GotoXY(18,10) ;                             { Go to column 18, row 10.     }
      FOR I := 1 TO 50 DO
        BEGIN      { DO BEGIN a series of fifty Chr(205)'s for the banner. }
          Write(CHR(205))
        END ;
      GotoXY(21,12) ;
      HighVideo ;
      WriteLn('LINEPLOT - PLOT A GRAPH OF EQUIDISTANT POINTS') ;  { Title. }
      LowVideo ;
      GotoXY(18,14) ;
      FOR I := 1 TO 50 DO
        BEGIN                                  { Same as above, for the banner. }
          Write(CHR(205))
        END ;
      Delay(1500) ;                            { A 1500 milliscond delay. }
      HighVideo ;                              { Restore high intensity video. }
      ClrScr ;                                 { Clear the screen. }
    END ;
  { SignOn }

  PROCEDURE PrintStatistics (VAR OutFile:Text) ;

    BEGIN
      { PrintStatistics }
      WriteLn(OutFile) ;                       { Information for the record. }
      WriteLn(OutFile,'Largest data value: ',Largest:10:4) ;
      WriteLn(OutFile,'Top of Graph has a value of: ',Largest:10:4) ;
```

```pascal
      WriteLn(OutFile,'Width of Graph: ',Width:2:2,' inches at 10 cpi.') ;
      WriteLn(OutFile)
    END ;
{ PrintStatistics }

PROCEDURE WriteGraph (VAR OutFile:Text) ;

  VAR
    I,K : Integer ;
    NumSpaces : Integer ;

  PROCEDURE WriteAxis ;                          { Print and Display the Y axis. }

    VAR
      L : Integer ;

    BEGIN
      { WriteAxis }
      HighVideo ;
      FOR L := 1 TO Trunc(TensWidth / 5.0) DO
        Write(OutFile,'+----') ;
          { The X-axis is composed of sectors of plus and minus signs. }
        WriteLn(OutFile,'+')
    END ;
  { WriteAxis }

  PROCEDURE WriteSpaces (Num:Integer) ;

    VAR
      I : Integer ;

    BEGIN
      { WriteSpaces }
      FOR I := 1 TO Num DO
        Write(OutFile,' ')
    END ;
  { WriteSpaces }

  BEGIN                                  { Print & display the data points }
    { WriteGraph }
    WriteLn(OutFile) ;
    WriteAxis ;
    HighVideo ;
    FOR I := 1 TO NumPoints DO
      BEGIN    { We'll truncate the data points in plotting the graph. }
        FOR K := 1 TO Trunc(0.5 * TensWidth / NumPoints) DO
          BEGIN
            { The colon character outlines the graph. }
            Write(OutFile,':') ;
            WriteSpaces(Trunc(TensWidth - 1)) ;
            WriteLn(OutFile,':')
```

```
           END ;
         NumSpaces := Trunc(Factor * Points[I]) ;
         IF (NumSpaces = 0) THEN              { Point at start. }
            BEGIN
               { The '*' (asterisk character) is the datapoint marker. }
               { It may be changed to any other printable character.   }
               Write(OutFile,'*') ;
               WriteSpaces(Trunc(TensWidth - 1)) ;
                 { The colon character outlines the graph. }
               WriteLn(OutFile,':')
            END
         ELSE IF (NumSpaces = Trunc(TensWidth)) THEN
            BEGIN
               { The colon character outlines the graph. }
               Write(OutFile,':') ;
               WriteSpaces(Trunc(TensWidth - 1)) ;
                 { The '*' (asterisk character) is the datapoint marker. }
                 { It may be changed to any other printable character.   }
               WriteLn(OutFile,'*')
            END
         ELSE
            BEGIN
               { The colon character outlines the graph. }
               Write(OutFile,':') ;
               WriteSpaces(NumSpaces - 1) ;
                 { The '*' (asterisk character) is the datapoint marker. }
                 { It may be changed to any other printable character.   }
               Write(OutFile,'*') ;
               WriteSpaces(Trunc(TensWidth - 1 - NumSpaces)) ;
                 { The colon character outlines the graph. }
               WriteLn(OutFile,':')
            END
      END ;
    WriteAxis
  END ;
{ WriteGraph }

BEGIN
  { LinePlot }
  SignOn ;
  ClrScr ;
  GotoXY(15,3) ;
   { Alert the user.  }
  WriteLn('*** TURN ON THE PRINTER BEFORE ENTERING ANY DATA ***') ;
  GotoXY(5,6) ;
  LowVideo ;
   { Make the request for data to be entered. }
  Write('Give the width of the graph to be printed in inches: ') ;
  HighVideo ;
  ReadLn(Width) ;
  WriteLn ;
```

```
          GotoXY(5,8) ;
          LowVideo ;
           { The "50 Max" statement must match the CONST MaxNumPoints = ? }
          Write('How many data points do you want to plot?  (50 Max): ') ;
          HighVideo ;
          ReadLn(NumPoints) ;     { Enter the number of data points. }
           { If the user enters a number greater than MaxNumPoints, }
           { it will be given the value of CONST MaxNumPoints.      }
          IF (NumPoints > MaxNumPoints) THEN
            NumPoints := MaxNumPoints ;
          GotoXY(5,10) ;
          LowVideo ;
          WriteLn('Do NOT enter negative values.') ;
          GotoXY(10,12) ;
          HighVideo ;
          WriteLn('ENTER THE VALUES FOR:') ;
          WriteLn ;
          WriteLn(LST,'DATA TO BE PLOTTED:') ;
          WriteLn(LST) ;
          FOR I := 1 TO NumPoints DO
            BEGIN
              LowVideo ;
              Write('               Point ',I,': ') ;
              HighVideo ;
              ReadLn(Points[I]) ;
              WriteLn(LST,'               ',Points[I]:10:4)
            END ;
          Largest := 0.0 ;        { Find the greatest data value for scaling. }
          TensWidth := Width * 10.0 ;
          FOR I := 1 TO NumPoints DO
            IF (Largest < Points[I]) THEN
              Largest := Points[I] ;
          Factor := TensWidth / Largest ;
          PrintStatistics(CON) ;
          PrintStatistics(LST) ;
          REPEAT
            WriteGraph(CON) ;                       { Display the graph and do  }
            WriteGraph(LST) ;                       { a printout, too.  Then,   }
            Write(LST,CHR(12)) ;                    { after printing, do a form }
            WriteLn ;                               { feed and offer an option. }
            Write('Do another printout of the graph?  (Y/N): ') ;
            Read(Kbd,Ch) ;
            WriteLn ;
          UNTIL Ch IN ['N','n']                     { If "N" or n"' are not typed, }
                                                    { The program assumes the user }
                                                    { wants another printout.      }
                                                    { "N" or "n" ends the program. }

        END.
        { LinePlot }
```

Chapter 16

Use the CASE Statement in a Program for English/ Metrics Conversions

Here's a fast-running program that helps with the changeover from the English (Standard) system to the metric system of data expression. It takes less than six seconds from the moment you execute the program until you see the main menu of the METRICS program displayed on the screen.

METRICS generates a full-screen menu offering the user 25 options. Options 1 through 12 are for converting quantities from English or Standard to Metric values. Options 13 through 24 are the converse, converting Metric quantities to English or Standard values. Option 25 is for exiting the METRICS program and returning instantly to DOS.

The precision of the calculation is two places to the right of the decimal point. The precision can be extended or reduced by changing the formatting in the CASE statements. Note that the last digit in each statement is :2. The :2 means that the display of the results of calculations should include two digits to the right of the decimal point. This can be changed to :4, for example, providing a format that includes four digits to the right of the decimal point. Note too, the out-of-range error trap coded into the main part of the program.

The first procedure called is SignOn. This displays the name of the program for 1.5 seconds. The Big_Menu procedure is called next; it makes a call from within itself to the very short Artsy_Line procedure that displays an attractive line made up of 38 each of the extended graphics characters 175 and 174. The title is displayed surrounded by the Artsy_Line border.

And, now, the menu itself appears:

1 - Inches to millimeters	13 - Millimeters to inches
2 - Inches to meters	14 - Meters to inches
3 - Feet to meters	15 - Meters to feet
4 - Miles to kilometers	16 - Kilometers to miles
5 - Teaspoons to milliliters	17 - Milliliters to teaspoons
6 - Tablespoons to milliliters	18 - Milliliters to tablespoons
7 - Pints to liters	19 - Liters to pints
8 - Quarts to liters	20 - Liters to quarts
9 - Gallons to liters	21 - Liters to gallons
10 - Ounces to grams	22 - Grams to ounces
11 - Pounds to kilograms	23 - Kilograms to pounds
12 - Fahrenheit to Celsius	24 - Celsius to Fahrenheit
	25 - End the program

When you choose an item from 1 to 24, the menu remains in place and a new instruction appears just below it. Let's choose item 11, converting English pounds to metric kilograms:

Enter the quantity to be converted: <u>3.6789</u>

3.6789 is entered as the number of pounds to be converted to kilograms. Press the Enter key and the computer responds instantly with a new line of information displayed below the previous one:

3.6789 Pounds = 1.67 kilograms

And, below that line appears the instruction:

*** Press any key to continue ***

When you press any key, a series of spaces or blanks is written over the areas that contained the information for the calculation just completed and displayed at column 16 of rows 21, 22, and 25. This ends the Convert__Quantity procedure. The operation REPEATS UNTIL the choice of 25 is made from the menu.

An error trap is incorporated. For example, suppose you inadvertently choose 26, which doesn't exist on the menu. The following line appears below the menu:

*** OUT OF RANGE ***

After a time delay of 1.5 seconds (1500 milliseconds), the out-of-range message clears, and the program is ready for another choice to be made from the menu. Choosing 25 at the menu ends the program.

CODE LISTING FOR METRICS

```
{ Rapid conversions of quantities to-and-from Metrics and English. }

PROGRAM Metrics ;

  VAR
    L,Choice : Integer ;

  PROCEDURE SignOn ;     { Generate and display the program's banner. }

    BEGIN
      { SignOn }
      ClrScr ;                  { Clear the screen and start the }
      GotoXY(15,10) ;           { banner at column 15, row 10.    }
      LowVideo ;
      FOR L := 1 TO 50 DO     { Do the next task 50 times.       }
        BEGIN
          Write('|')     { The task: write the stick character. }
        END ;
      GotoXY(17,12) ;
      HighVideo ;
      Write('METRICS -- METRICS-ENGLISH-METRICS CONVERSIONS') ;
      GotoXY(15,14) ;
      LowVideo ;
      FOR L := 1 TO 50 DO  { Again, do the next task 50 times. }
        BEGIN
          Write('|')             { This, again, is the task.        }
        END ;
      Delay(1500) ;             { 1500 millisecond before }
      ClrScr ;                  { the screen is cleared.  }
      HighVideo ;               { Exit the PROCEDURE with    }
    END ;                       { video set to high intensity. }
  { SignOn }

  PROCEDURE Artsy_Line (VAR OutFile:Text) ;
     { Generate a graphics border. }
    BEGIN                       { Begin the PROCEDURE. }
```

```pascal
      { Artsy_Line }
      LowVideo ;
      FOR L := 1 TO 38 DO          { Loop 38 times.  }
        BEGIN                      { Begin the loop. }
          Write(Chr(175)) ;        { An IBM screen-graphics character. }
          Write(Chr(174))          { A similar graphics character.     }
        END ;                      { End the loop.   }
      HighVideo
    END ;                          { End the PROCEDURE.    }
  { Artsy_Line }

PROCEDURE Big_Menu ;               { Display the menu of options. }

  BEGIN
    { Big_Menu }
    ClrScr ;
    LowVideo ;
    Artsy_Line(CON) ;              { Execute the PROCEDURE. }
    GotoXY(22,2) ;
    HighVideo ;
    WriteLn('METRICS-ENGLISH-METRICS CONVERSIONS') ;
    LowVideo ;
    Artsy_Line(CON) ;              { Execute it again.     }
    HighVideo ;
    WriteLn ;
    WriteLn ;

    (* Display two columns of options. *)
    WriteLn('        1 - Inches to millimeters        ',
           '13 - Millimeters to inches') ;
    WriteLn('        2 - Inches to meters             ',
           '14 - Meters to inches') ;
    WriteLn('        3 - Feet to meters               ',
           '15 - Meters to feet') ;
    WriteLn('        4 - Miles to kilometers          ',
           '16 - Kilometers to miles') ;
    WriteLn('        5 - Teaspoons to milliliters     ',
           '17 - Milliliters to teaspoons') ;
    WriteLn('        6 - Tablespoons to milliliters   ',
           '18 - Milliliters to tablespoons') ;
    WriteLn('        7 - Pints to liters              ',
           '19 - Liters to pints') ;
    WriteLn('        8 - Quarts to liters             ',
           '20 - Liters to quarts') ;
    WriteLn('        9 - Gallons to liters            ',
           '21 - Liters to gallons') ;
    WriteLn('       10 - Ounces to grams              ',
           '22 - Grams to ounces') ;
    WriteLn('       11 - Pounds to kilograms          ',
           '23 - Kilograms to pounds') ;
```

```
    WriteLn('     12 - Fahrenheit to Celsius            ',
            '24 - Celsius to Fahrenheit') ;
    FOR L := 1 TO 41 DO
      BEGIN
        Write(' ')
      END ;
    Write('25 - End the program') ;
    WriteLn
  END ;
{ Big_Menu }

PROCEDURE Convert_Qty (WhichOne:Integer) ;
{ Conversion formulas are contained in this procedure  }
{ which also performs the formatting and calculations. }

  VAR
    Quantity : Real ;
    Ch : Char ;

  BEGIN
    { Convert_Qty }
    WriteLn ;
    GotoXY(16,21) ;
    Write('Enter the quantity to be converted: ') ;
    ReadLn(Quantity) ;
    Write('              ') ;
    CASE (WhichOne) OF    { See the text for the formatting rules. }
      1 : WriteLn('Inches = ',Quantity * 25.4:8:2,' millimeters') ;
      2 : WriteLn('Inches = ',Quantity * 0.0254:8:2,' meters') ;
      3 : WriteLn('Feet = ',Quantity * 0.3048:8:2,' meters') ;
      4 : WriteLn('Miles = ',Quantity * 1.6093:8:2,' kilometers') ;
      5 : WriteLn('Teaspoons = ',Quantity * 5.0:8:2,' milliliters') ;
      6 : WriteLn('Tablespoons = ',Quantity * 15:8:2,' milliliters') ;
      7 : WriteLn('Pints = ',Quantity * 0.4732:8:2,' liters') ;
      8 : WriteLn('Quarts = ',Quantity * 0.9463:8:2,' liters') ;
      9 : WriteLn('Gallons = ',Quantity * 3.7853:8:2,' liters') ;
     10 : WriteLn('Ounces = ',Quantity * 28.3495:8:2,' grams') ;
     11 : WriteLn('Pounds = ',Quantity * 0.453:8:2,' kilograms') ;
     12 : WriteLn('Deg Fahrenheit = ',(Quantity - 32.0) * 5.0 / 9.0:8:2,
                  ' deg Celsius') ;
     13 : WriteLn('Millimeters = ',Quantity * 0.0394:8:2,' inches') ;
     14 : WriteLn('Meters = ',Quantity * 39.37:8:2,' inches') ;
     15 : WriteLn('Meters = ',Quantity * 3.2808:8:2,' feet') ;
     16 : WriteLn('Kilometers = ',Quantity * 0.6214:8:2,' miles') ;
     17 : WriteLn('Milliliters = ',Quantity * 0.2:8:2,' teaspoons') ;
     18 : WriteLn('Milliliters = ',Quantity * 0.0667:8:2,' tablespoons') ;
     19 : WriteLn('Liters = ',Quantity * 2.1134:8:2,' pints') ;
     20 : WriteLn('Liters = ',Quantity * 1.0567:8:2,' quarts') ;
     21 : WriteLn('Liters = ',Quantity * 0.2642:8:2,' gallons') ;
     22 : WriteLn('Grams = ',Quantity * 0.0353:8:2,' ounces') ;
     23 : WriteLn('Kilograms = ',Quantity * 2.2046:8:2,' pounds') ;
```

```pascal
      24 : WriteLn('Deg Celsius = ',(Quantity * 9.0 / 5.0) + 32.0:8:2,
                 ' deg Fahrenheit') ;
      25 :                                      { DUMMY }
    END ;
    { CASE }
    WriteLn ;
    GotoXY(20,25) ;
    Write('*** Press any key to continue *** ') ;
    Read(Kbd,Ch) ;
    { When a key is pressed, write a series of blanks for the }
    { purpose of erasing stuff from lines 21, 22, and 25.     }
    GotoXY(16,21) ;
    Write('                                                   ') ;
    GotoXY(16,22) ;
    Write('                                                   ') ;
    GotoXY(16,25) ;
    Write('                                                   ') ;
  END ;
{ Convert_Qty }

BEGIN                                  { Main part of the program }
  { Metrics }
  SignOn ;                                 { Begin the signon. }
  Big_Menu ;                               { Display the menu. }
  Artsy_Line(CON) ;                        { Display the line. }
  WriteLn ;
  REPEAT
    GotoXY(40,19) ;           { Overwrite line 19, with blanks. }
    Write('            ') ;
    GotoXY(25,19) ;        { Display the make-a-choice message. }
    Write('Choose 1 to 25: ') ;
    ReadLn(Choice) ;        { Get the choice from the keyboard. }
    IF (Choice < 1) OR (Choice > 25) THEN
        { If the number is out of range... }
      BEGIN
        WriteLn ;
        GotoXY(25,21) ;             { Display the error message. }
        Write('*** OUT OF RANGE ***') ;
        Delay(1500) ;  { Hold the message for 1500 millisecs. }
        GotoXY(25,21) ;  { Overwrite the message with blanks. }
        Write('                    ')
      END
    ELSE IF (Choice < 25) THEN
        { If the number chosen is less than 25, }
        { use the quantity-conversion formula.  }
      Convert_Qty(Choice)
        { If the number is 25, end the program. }
  UNTIL (Choice = 25)
END.
{ Metrics }
```

Chapter 17

Alphanumeric Sorting . . . Garbage in, Neatness out

People often need to assemble lists of customer names or account numbers, payroll numbers, addresses, dates, parts numbers, zip codes, routing slips, salespersons' hunt lists, friends' names, association members' card numbers; there are many types of list of alphanumeric information that, when placed in an ordered sequence, become significantly more useful and usable than they were originally. SORTLIST eliminates the time-consuming, patience-testing procedure of manually bringing order to such lists.

This program will sort and order up to 50 separate items, each up to 30 characters long, whether numeric or alphabetic. If some entries start with numbers and there are other items beginning with letters, the items that start with numbers are given priority in the sorting hierarchy.

The ASCII collating sequence prioritizes the digits "0" through "9," the uppercase letters "A" through "Z," and then lowercase "a" through "z." This sequence is universally acceptable in developing a sort of a list of alphanumeric names and data. (De Longine, for example, would appear ahead of de Longine on a list of names sorted according to the ASCII collating sequence.)

The maximum number of lines that can be sorted by SORTLIST is established by the CONST statement "MaxNumInSort = 50 ;". You may change the number 50 to a value you prefer.

Use a text editor that saves the file in ASCII form to create a file with the list of names (or numbers, or both) to be sorted. Give the file a distinctive name when you save it. When the SORTLIST program asks for the name of the file to be sorted, type the name of the file you created, press the Enter key, and the program will take care of the rest. Be sure to turn on the printer. The sorted list will be displayed on the video monitor and printed automatically and simultaneously.

The code for this sorting program is surprisingly simple. The value of such a program, when used as a stand alone, is limited only by the individual's need. For example, if you have a document that must be routed to a large number of people in the organization (I've seen routing lists with more than a hundred names) and you want to avoid the appearance of favoritism (or internal politics), the best way to list the names is in strict alphabetic sequence.

To illustrate what SORTLIST can do, let's simulate actual runs with 12 different items. When you execute the program, the brief how-to-use instruction is displayed, and you are reminded to turn on the printer. The instructions also point out that the program can sort a file or characters you enter at the keyboard.

The screen displays the query and guidance:

Do you want to read from a file? (Y/N).

(Responding 'N' means you want to enter

the information by using the keyboard.):

A <Y> calls the ReadFile procedure, which asks you to:

ENTER THE NAME OF THE FILE TO BE SORTED:

Sorting is performed in the SortBuffer procedure. The Procedure WriteBuffer then displays the sorted file on the screen and prints a hard copy. Then the file that was opened is closed. The printer does a line feed and a carriage return; WriteLn(LST); to ensure that the printer's buffer is emptied, and the program ends.

The sorting process, by some standards, may be slow. However, you should not be disturbed by the fact that SORTLIST takes just a few seconds to sort a 50-entry list; the task is still completed more quickly and probably more accurately than if it had been done by hand. The program's code is heavily commented so that you can follow the sequences and actions of the procedures.

CODE LISTING FOR SORTLIST

```
{ SortList reads unordered information from the }
{ keyboard or from an ASCII file, sorts it and  }
{ prints and displays an ordered, sorted list.  }

PROGRAM SortList ;

  CONST
    MaxNumInSort = 50 ;   { The maximum number of lines to be sorted. }
```

```
TYPE
  SortNum = 1..MaxNumInSort ;
  StringType = STRING[80] ;         { String length is 80 characters. }

VAR
  Ch : Char ;                       { Keyboard response character. }
  L : Integer ;
  Buffer : ARRAY [SortNum] OF StringType ;
  InFile : Text ;                   { Disk file for input.        }
  LineCnt : Integer ;               { Counter for sorted lines.   }

PROCEDURE SignOn ;                              { Display the signon banner. }

  BEGIN
    { SignOn }
    ClrScr ;
    GotoXY(15,8) ;
    LowVideo ;
    FOR L := 1 TO 50 DO
      BEGIN
        Write(Chr(176))
      END ;
    GotoXY(18,10) ;
    HighVideo ;
    Write('SORTLIST -- ALPHANUMERIC SORTING & PRINTING') ;
    GotoXY(15,12) ;
    LowVideo ;
    FOR L := 1 TO 50 DO      { Do the next action 50 times.         }
      BEGIN                  { Begin the FOR-loop action.           }
        Write(Chr(176))      { An extended IBM graphics character.  }
      END ;                  { End the FOR loop-action.             }
    Delay(1500) ;
    ClrScr ;
    GotoXY(20,6) ;  { Display the instructions at column 20, row 6. }
    Write('This program automatically sorts ') ;
    GotoXY(20,7) ;
    Write('up to 50 lines of alphanumerics.') ;
    GotoXY(20,9) ;
    Write('You can also sort a file you''ve') ;
    GotoXY(20,10) ;
    Write('created with an ASCII text editor.') ;
    HighVideo ;
    GotoXY(15,12) ;
    Write('!!! Be sure the printer is turned on !!!') ;
    LowVideo ;
    GotoXY(20,14) ;
    Write('Instructions follow below.')
  END ;
{ SignOn }

PROCEDURE ReadUser ; { ReadUser fills the buffer with keyboard info. }
```

```
VAR
   AllDone : Boolean ;

BEGIN
   { ReadUser }
   ClrScr ;
   AllDone := False ;
   LineCnt := 1 ;         { Initialize the line counter to start at 1. }
   HighVideo ;
   WriteLn('To QUIT entering information and start sorting, ') ;
   WriteLn('press Return at the beginning of any new line.') ;
   LowVideo ;
   WriteLn ;
   WHILE ( NOT AllDone AND (LineCnt <= MaxNumInSort)) DO
     BEGIN
       Write('          Enter info ',LineCnt:2,': ') ;
       HighVideo ;
       ReadLn(Buffer[LineCnt]) ;
       LowVideo ;
       AllDone := (Ord(Buffer[LineCnt][0]) = 0) ;
       LineCnt := LineCnt + 1 ;    { Increment the line counter. }
     END ;
   LineCnt := LineCnt - 2
END ;
{ ReadUser }

PROCEDURE ReadFile ;              { ReadFile reads text from a file. }

   VAR
   Temp : StringType ;

BEGIN
   { ReadFile }
   ClrScr ;
   LowVideo ;
   Write('ENTER THE NAME OF THE FILE TO BE SORTED:  ') ;
   HighVideo ;
   ReadLn(Temp) ;
   Assign(InFile,Temp) ;
   Reset(InFile) ;
   LineCnt := 1 ;
   WHILE ( NOT EOF(InFile) AND (LineCnt <= MaxNumInSort)) DO
       { While we are still inside the File and the  }
       { line count is less than or equal to the     }
       { CONST for MaxNumInSort, DO the next action. }
     BEGIN
       ReadLn(InFile,Buffer[LineCnt]) ;
       LineCnt := LineCnt + 1 ;   { Increment the line count. }
     END ;
   LineCnt := LineCnt - 1
 END ;
```

```
{ ReadFile }

PROCEDURE SortBuffer ;
   { Exchange or swap-sort the buffer's contents. }

  VAR
    HaveExchanged : Boolean ;
    K : SortNum ;
    Temp : StringType ;

  BEGIN
    { SortBuffer }
    REPEAT
      HaveExchanged := False ;
      FOR K := 2 TO LineCnt DO
        IF (Buffer[K - 1] > Buffer[K]) THEN
          BEGIN
            { Do the exchange. }
            HaveExchanged := TRUE ;
            Temp := Buffer[K] ;
            Buffer[K] := Buffer[K - 1] ;
            Buffer[K - 1] := Temp ;
          END
    UNTIL ( NOT HaveExchanged) ;
  END ;
{ SortBuffer }

PROCEDURE WriteBuffer(VAR F:Text) ;

  VAR
    I : SortNum ;
    J : Integer ;

  BEGIN
    { WriteBuffer }
    WriteLn(F,'     Listed in alphanumeric order: ') ;
    WriteLn(F,'     -----------------------------') ;
    WriteLn(F) ;
    FOR I := 1 TO LineCnt DO
      WriteLn(F,'    ',I:3,': ',Buffer[I]) ;
  END ;
{ WriteBuffer }

BEGIN    { This is the main section that calls the PROCEDURES. }
  { SortList }
  SignOn ;
  REPEAT
    WriteLn ;
    HighVideo ;
    GotoXY(15,16) ;
    Write('Do you want to read input from a file?  (Y/N).') ;
```

```
    LowVideo ;
    GotoXY(15,17) ;
    Write('(Responding `N'' means you want to enter ') ;
    GotoXY(15,18) ;
    Write('the information by using the keyboard.):    ') ;
    Read(Kbd,Ch) ;
  UNTIL  Ch  IN  ['Y','y','N','n'] ;
        { Recognize only (Y)es or (N)o. }
  IF Ch IN ['Y','y'] THEN
        { If (Y)es, then read input from a file. }
    ReadFile
  ELSE
        { If (N)o, then read input from the keyboard. }
    ReadUser ;
  SortBuffer ;
  ClrScr ;
  WriteBuffer(CON) ;            { Display the buffer's contents. }
  WriteBuffer(LST) ;            { Print the buffer' contents.    }
  Close(InFile) ;  { Close any files that may have been opened.  }
    WriteLn(LST)    { Make certain the printer's buffer is empty. }
END.
{ SortList }
```

Chapter 18

A Personnel Appraisal Program Provides a Good Session in Writing Code

They say, "When you appraise someone's job performance, you must be wary of the *halo effect*." The halo effect functions when the person appraising or evaluating another's performance is unreasonably influenced by superficial or extraneous aspects of the one being appraised. The aspects are not a requirement for the job and, therefore, have no rightful place in the evaluation. Although the concept of a halo implies a positive effect, it can also cause a negative reaction. In either case, the appraiser may be responding subjectively to factors unrelated to the task at hand.

For example, suppose an evaluator enjoys a specific sense of humor and the person being evaluated demonstrates that kind of humor. It is conceivable the evaluator might, without conscious recognition, tend to overlook areas of performance on the job that are unrelated to the ability to entertain. The evaluator may give an undeservedly high rating to the person being appraised. And, of course, the converse could be true; he could give an undeservedly low rating to the person.

There are many ways to avoid or minimize the misleading halo effect. One of them is to depend entirely on a quantitative appraisal that may, with a properly created reference table, be converted to qualtitative factors. Ideally, the appraiser is not aware of the algorithm that converts the quantitative to the qualitative.

The APPRAISL program written in Turbo Pascal is an attempt to minimize the halo effect by generating a quantitative and a qualitative appraisal. The program queries the appraiser about eleven job-related characteristics.

The appraiser assigns a value from 1 to 5 (1 is lowest, 5 is highest) to each of the characteristics. The program totals the individual scores and assigns a qualitative value to the total score. The total score is valid if it is between 11 and 55; otherwise the appraiser has made an error, an error message is displayed, and the appraisal must be redone.

An option offers a detailed printout of the appraisal. The printed report is automatically dated and has space for the appraiser's initials. The APPRAISL program is not intended to solve all the problem areas inherent in the evaluation and management of human resources. It is intended to provide the Turbo Pascal user with source code that provides instruction, guidance and practice with the language and the compiler.

A SAMPLE RUN OF THE APPRAISL PROGRAM

As usual the program signs on with the ClrScr function. In a short while, the screen clears again and the information identifying the person being appraised is collected from the keyboard by the ID__Stuff procedure. The instructions are displayed as the Show__How procedure is called into action.

The next procedure, Rate__The__Person, is called and the 11 characteristics are assigned values by keying in the appropriate assessment for the level performance:

1 indicates poor performance
2 shows that the employee is just getting by
3 indicates acceptable performance
4 indicates good performance
5 indicates exceptional performance

Error trapping is provided, and warning messages are displayed for total scores that are less than 11 (11 * 1) or greater than 55 (11 * 5). If the total score is within the range of 11 to 55, the score is displayed. The screen continues with:

Print a hard copy for full details? (Y/N):

If the response is <Y>, the printer generates a more comprehensive report with quantitative and qualitative details. An <N> response causes this query to be displayed:

Do you want to do another appraisal? (Y/N):

An <N> response ends the program. Figure 18-1 shows a sample run of the program.

```
++++++++++++++++++++++++++++++++++++++++++++++++++

    Appraisal of: Jonathan Quimbey
    Department:   Shipping
    Appraised on: 12/15/85

++++++++++++++++++++++++++++++++++++++++++++++++++

        Quality:        3
        Knowledge:      4
        Productivity:   4
        Dependability:  3
        Initiative:     3
        Adaptability:   5
        Attitude:       3
        Attendance:     2
        Safety:         3
        Potential:      2
        Personality:    4

The highest possible rating is 55.
The lowest possible rating is 11.
The mid-range rating is 33.
Jonathan Quimbey is rated at:   36

Jonathan Quimbey does an Acceptable Job.

++++++++++++++++++++++++++++++++++++++++++++++++++


Initials of the Appraiser: _____

++++++++++++++++++++++++++++++++++++++++++++++++++
```

Fig. 18-1. A sample printout from the Appraisal program.

CODE LISTING FOR APPRAISL

```
{ Program for appraising, scoring, and qualifying }
{ the capabilities of a manager, supervisor or an }
{ employee on the basis of 11 characterisitcs.    }

PROGRAM Appraisl ;

  TYPE
    StringType = STRING[80] ;
```

```
VAR
   Ch : Char ;
   I,Adaptability,Attendance,Attitude : Integer ;
   Dependability,Initiative,Knowledge : Integer ;
   Personality,Potential,Quality : Integer ;
   Quantity,Safety,Score : Integer ;
   Date,Department,Name : StringType ;

PROCEDURE SignOn ;
   { Display the startup message. }

   BEGIN
     { SignOn }
     ClrScr ;
     GotoXY(15,8) ;              { Send the cursor to column 15, row 8.  }
     LowVideo ;
     FOR I := 1 TO 50 DO                { For 50 times, display the  }
       Write(Chr(205)) ;                { graphics character, #205.  }
     GotoXY(19,10) ;            { Send the cursor to column 19, row 10. }
     HighVideo ;           { Display the next line in high intensity. }
     WriteLn('APPRAISL -- PERFORMANCE MERIT-RATING FORM') ;
     GotoXY(15,12) ;           { Send the cursor to column 15, row 12. }
     LowVideo ;                { Restore the low intensity video mode. }
     FOR I := 1 TO 50 DO                { For 50 times, display the  }
       Write(Chr(205)) ;                { graphics character, #205.  }
     Delay(1500) ;                      { 1500 millisecond delay.    }
     HighVideo ;
     ClrScr
   END ;
{ SignOn }

PROCEDURE Show_How ;
   { Show the instructions for doing an appraisal. }

   BEGIN
     { Show_How }
     WriteLn('You will now appraise ',Name,' for 11 key characteristics.') ;
     Write('Each characteristic is to be assigned') ;
     WriteLn(' a value from ''1 to 5''.') ;
     WriteLn ;
     LowVideo ;
     WriteLn('      `1'' means ',Name,' performs Poorly.') ;
     WriteLn('      `2'' means ',Name,' just Barely Gets By.') ;
     WriteLn('      `3'' means ',Name,' does Acceptable Work.') ;
     WriteLn('      `4'' means ',Name,' delivers Good Performance.') ;
     WriteLn('      `5'' means ',Name,' does Exceptional Work.') ;
     WriteLn ;
     HighVideo ;
     Write('You must rate each of the 11 ') ;
     WriteLn(' characteristics in the range of `1'' to `5''.') ;
```

```
        WriteLn ;
        WriteLn('After you have rated the 11th characteristic,') ;
        WriteLn('all details of the appraisal can be printed.') ;
        WriteLn ;
        WriteLn
      END ;
    { Show_How }

  PROCEDURE ID_Stuff ;
      { Collect initial data from the keyboard. }

    BEGIN
      {ID_Stuff }
      LowVideo ;
      Write('Enter the name of the person to be rated:        ') ;
      HighVideo ;
      ReadLn(Name) ;
      LowVideo ;
      Write('Enter ',Name,'''s department number or name:     ') ;
      HighVideo ;
      ReadLn(Department) ;
      LowVideo ;
      Write('Enter the date of this appraisal (MM/DD/YY):    ') ;
      HighVideo ;
      ReadLn(Date) ;
      WriteLn ;
      WriteLn
    END ;
  {ID_Stuff }

  PROCEDURE Print_A_Border(VAR OutFile:Text) ;

    BEGIN
      { Print_A_Border }
      FOR I := 1 TO 45 DO
        Write(LST,'+') ;       { The border character is a plus sign. }
      WriteLn(LST)             { Send a line feed to the printer.      }
    END ;
  { Print_A_Border }

  PROCEDURE Initial_It ;
      { Print a line for the appraiser's initials. }

    BEGIN
      { Initial_It }
      WriteLn(LST) ;
      Print_A_Border(LST) ;    { Call the PROCEDURE Print_A_Border. }
      WriteLn(LST) ;
      WriteLn(LST) ;
      WriteLn(LST,'Initials of the Appraiser: _____') ;
      WriteLn(LST) ;
```

```
     Print_A_Border(LST) ;                      { Call the procedure. }
     Write(LST,chr(12)) { Eject the paper to the top of the form. }
  END ;
{ Initial_It }

PROCEDURE Print_It ;                             { Print the final report. }

  VAR
    Sum : Real ;

  BEGIN
    { Print_It }
    Print_A_Border(LST) ;           { Call the PROCEDURE   }
                                    { to print the border. }
                                    { Then return here.    }
    WriteLn(LST) ;
    WriteLn(LST,'   Appraisal of: ',Name) ;
    WriteLn(LST,'   Department:   ',Department) ;
    WriteLn(LST,'   Appraised on: ',Date) ;
    WriteLn(LST) ;
    Print_A_Border(LST) ;    { Print the border again.   }
    WriteLn(LST) ;                { Print the characteristics }
                                  { and the scores.           }
    WriteLn(LST,'       Quality:        ',Quality) ;
    WriteLn(LST,'       Knowledge:      ',Knowledge) ;
    WriteLn(LST,'       Productivity:   ',Quantity) ;
    WriteLn(LST,'       Dependability:  ',Dependability) ;
    WriteLn(LST,'       Initiative:     ',Initiative) ;
    WriteLn(LST,'       Adaptability:   ',Adaptability) ;
    WriteLn(LST,'       Attitude:       ',Attitude) ;
    WriteLn(LST,'       Attendance:     ',Attendance) ;
    WriteLn(LST,'       Safety:         ',Safety) ;
    WriteLn(LST,'       Potential:      ',Potential) ;
    WriteLn(LST,'       Personality:    ',Personality) ;
    WriteLn(LST) ;  { Print the ranges. }
    WriteLn(LST,'   The highest possible rating is 55.') ;
    WriteLn(LST,'   The lowest possible rating is 11.') ;
    WriteLn(LST,'   The mid-range rating is 33.') ;
    WriteLn(LST,'   ',Name,' is rated at:  ',Score) ;
    WriteLn(LST) ;
        { Select a statement related to the Score. }
    IF (Score <= 13) THEN
      WriteLn(LST,'   ',Name,' is a ''Poor'' performer.')
    ELSE IF (Score <= 22) THEN
      WriteLn(LST,'   ',Name,' Just Gets By.  Needs Help.')
    ELSE IF (Score <= 43) THEN
      WriteLn(LST,'   ',Name,' does an Acceptable Job.')
    ELSE IF (Score <= 49) THEN
      WriteLn(LST,'   ',Name,' is a Good Performer.')
    ELSE
      WriteLn(LST,'   ',Name,' does Exceptional Work.') ;
```

```
                  { Now, execute the PROCEDURE for the signature line. }
            Initial_It
         END ;
    { Print_It }


    PROCEDURE Rate_The_Person ;
        { Assign a value to each chracteristic. }

      BEGIN
        { Rate_The_Person }
        WriteLn('A - QUALITY') ;
        LowVideo ;
        Write('  Meets quality standards of the job:              ') ;
        HighVideo ;
        ReadLn(Quality) ;
        WriteLn ;
        WriteLn('B - JOB KNOWLEDGE') ;
        LowVideo ;
        Write('  Understanding of all phases of the work:          ') ;
        HighVideo ;
        ReadLn(Knowledge) ;
        WriteLn ;
        WriteLn('C - QUANTITY') ;
        LowVideo ;
        Write('  Level of productivity or output:                ') ;
        HighVideo ;
        ReadLn(Quantity) ;
        WriteLn ;
        WriteLn('D - DEPENDABILITY') ;
        LowVideo ;
        Write('  Works according to instructions:                ') ;
        HighVideo ;
        ReadLn(Dependability) ;
        WriteLn ;
        WriteLn('E - INITIATIVE') ;
        LowVideo ;
        Write('  Originates constructive actions:                ') ;
        HighVideo ;
        ReadLn(Initiative) ;
        WriteLn ;
        WriteLn('F - ADAPTABILITY') ;
        LowVideo ;
        Write('  Ability to learn and adapt to changes:          ') ;
        HighVideo ;
        ReadLn(Adaptability) ;
        WriteLn ;
        WriteLn('G - ATTITUDE') ;
        LowVideo ;
        Write('  Willingness to cooperate and meet demands:       ') ;
        HighVideo ;
```

```
      ReadLn(Attitude) ;
      WriteLn ;
      WriteLn('H - ATTENDANCE') ;
      LowVideo ;
      Write('  Attendance and promptness on the job:          ') ;
      HighVideo ;
      ReadLn(Attendance) ;
      WriteLn ;
      WriteLn('I - SAFETY AND ORDERLINESS') ;
      LowVideo ;
      Write('  Compliance with rules for safety/housekeeping:  ') ;
      HighVideo ;
      ReadLn(Safety) ;
      WriteLn ;
      WriteLn('J - POTENTIAL FOR ADVANCEMENT') ;
      LowVideo ;
      Write('  Rate the person for leadership qualities:       ') ;
      HighVideo ;
      ReadLn(Potential) ;
      WriteLn ;
      WriteLn('K - PERSONALITY') ;
      LowVideo ;
      Write('  Ability to get along with others:              ') ;
      HighVideo ;
      ReadLn(Personality) ;
      WriteLn
    END ;
  { Rate_The_Person }
BEGIN
  { main part of the Appraisl program }
  SignOn ;                  { Execute the PROCEDURE. }
  REPEAT
    ClrScr ;
    ID_Stuff ;              { Execute the PROCEDURE. }
    Show_How ;              { Execute the PROCEDURE. }
    Rate_The_Person ;       { Execute the PROCEDURE. }

      { Assign the total value of the }
      { 11 characteristics to Score.  }
  Score := Quality + Knowledge + Quantity + Dependability +
           Initiative + Adaptability + Attitude + Attendance +
           Safety + Potential + Personality ;

  IF (Score < 11) THEN
    BEGIN                   { This traps an error in scoring and explains it. }
      WriteLn('The score for ',Name,' is below 11.') ;
      LowVideo ;
      WriteLn('An error has been made.') ;
      HighVideo ;
      WriteLn('Please redo the appraisal.') ;
      Delay(3000)    { Hold for 3 seconds. }
```

```
          END
      ELSE IF (Score > 55) THEN
        BEGIN                { A similar trap with an explanation. }
          WriteLn('The score for ',Name,' is above 55.') ;
          LowVideo ;
          WriteLn('An error has been made.') ;
          HighVideo ;
          WriteLn('Please redo the appraisal.') ;
          Delay(3000)    { Hold for 3 seconds. }
        END
      ELSE
        BEGIN       { If the score is in range, display the score. }
          WriteLn ;
          WriteLn ;
          WriteLn(Name,' has a score of ',Score) ;
          WriteLn ;
          Write('Print a hard copy for full details?  (Y/N): ') ;
          Read(Kbd,Ch) ;          { Get the keyboard's character. }
          IF Ch IN ['Y','y'] THEN
              { If keyboard character is a 'Y' or a 'y', then BEGIN. }
            BEGIN
              ClrScr ;
              GotoXY(15,20) ;
               { Display a message. }
              WriteLn('*** Printing now being done ***') ;
              Print_It ;
              WriteLn
            END ;
          WriteLn ;
          WriteLn ;
          Write('Do you want to do another appraisal? (Y/N): ') ;
          Read(Kbd,Ch)    { Get the keyboard character. }
        END ;
    UNTIL Ch IN ['N','n'] ;  { END when the option entered is 'N' or 'n'. }
    Close(LST)                { Make sure the printer's buffer is emptied. }
END.
{ of the Appraisl program }
```

Chapter 19

The Break-Even Point

The break-even point is the point at which an enterprise's revenues and costs are exactly equal, and operating income is neither positive (gain) nor negative (loss). It can be assumed that, when operating below the break-even point, there is a loss. Conversely, when operating above the break-even point, there is a profit. A break-even point can be calculated for a company's entire operations or for a specific product or service.

Although reaching the break-even point is not the primary objective of a commercial enterprise, it is important for managers to be able to forecast and determine the factors that influence the operational position of the finite point known as break-even. The analysis of break-even point can be used in reviews of past history, but it is most useful when applied to future periods as a guide to business planning, pricing, and developing cost standards.

The break-even point can be computed by using certain minimum data, which include; (1) total estimated or actual fixed costs that will be or have been incurred, without regard for quantity or plant capacity, (2) total estimated or actual costs that vary with the quantity of units produced, (3) the number of units that have been sold or are forecasted to be sold, and (4) the unit selling price.

The assumption is that all costs and revenues are for the same period of time. It is then possible to estimate the sales volume and selling price required to yield a specific, targeted profit. Some managers prefer chart presentations for detailing break-even information. Tables of data with specific details and finite numbers can, however, provide a clearly defined profile of the facts essential to good planning.

Although break-even analysis is a very important problem-solving tool, it should be used with caution. You must certainly take into account the fact that market and competitive conditions can erode selling prices and decrease consumable quantities of units, and that costs of materials, labor, and overhead can rise through inflation. Also, any combination of these factors can change, with one item rising and another falling to upset the neatly planned break-even point. The prudent problem solver periodically updates his break-even analysis.

The purpose of the program BRKEVEN is to make the task of computing the break-even point for an endless series of costs and sales assumptions easy and rapid. Sample displays and printouts of the analyses that are accurately recalculated by entering changes in data assumptions can be generated in a few minutes.

EXECUTING THE BRKEVEN PROGRAM

A sample execution of the compiled code demonstrates the capabilities of the program in dealing with assumptions made in a hypothetical medium-sized project at a medium-sized company. After the automatic sign-on, the screen displays the banner heading for the program and requests a series of data inputs. The responses at the keyboard are shown underlined to the right of the screen's queries.

The first procedure called in the main part of the program is the SignOn, which clears the screen and displays the program's name and brief description. Next, the GetInfo procedure is called and the basic facts, the data on which the algorithms will operate, are collected.

Enter the TOTAL FIXED COST: <u>1000000</u>

Now the VARIABLE COSTS per unit: <u>12345.67</u>

Then the SELLING PRICE per unit: <u>23456.78</u>

Starting Quantity for the table: <u>10</u>

Ending Quantity for the table: <u>150</u>

Increments of Quantity to show: <u>10</u>

The screen clears, and the MakeReport procedure is called. First, titles for five columns of data are displayed at the top of the screen within a border of equal signs created by the BorderLine procedure:

```
:==============================================================:

QTY      TOTAL COST      TOTAL SALES      GAIN/LOSS       UNIT COST

:==============================================================:
```

The computed data is immediately displayed below the appropriate column headings. (These are shown in Fig. 19-1.) The screen then invites you to select an option:

Repeat the Display? (Y/N):

If you type any letter but <N>, the screen clears and the display is repeated on the screen. The option to repeat the display is displayed until you

```
=================================================================

                        BREAKEVEN TABLE

=================================================================
   QTY       TOTAL COST      TOTAL SALES       GAIN/LOSS      UNIT COST
=================================================================

     10      1123456.70       234567.80       -888888.90     112345.67
     20      1246913.40       469135.60       -777777.80      62345.67
     30      1370370.10       703703.40       -666666.70      45679.00
     40      1493826.80       938271.20       -555555.60      37345.67
     50      1617283.50      1172839.00       -444444.50      32345.67
     60      1740740.20      1407406.80       -333333.40      29012.34
     70      1864196.90      1641974.60       -222222.30      26631.38
     80      1987653.60      1876542.40       -111111.20      24845.67
     90      2111110.30      2111110.20            -0.10      23456.78
    100      2234567.00      2345678.00        111111.00      22345.67
    110      2358023.70      2580245.80        222222.10      21436.58
    120      2481480.40      2814813.60        333333.20      20679.00
    130      2604937.10      3049381.40        444444.30      20037.98
    140      2728393.80      3283949.20        555555.40      19488.53
    150      2851850.50      3518517.00        666666.50      19012.34

=================================================================
     90      2111110.41      2111110.41  =  BREAKEVEN POINT
=================================================================

    TOTAL FIXED COST:          1000000.00
    VARIABLE COSTS PER UNIT:     12345.67
    SELLING PRICE PER UNIT:      23456.78

=================================================================
```

Fig. 19-1. A sample printout from the Break-Even program.

144

type the letter <N>. Then, a new option is displayed.

For a printout, turn on the printer.

If "Yes," press 'Y.' (Any other key to quit):

If you select any key other than <Y>, the program ends. If you select <Y>, the printer duplicates the table of data that is displayed on the screen. When the printout is finished, a form feed is sent to the printer and you are invited to:

Do Another Printout? (Y/N)

You can repeat the printouts, as you were able to repeat the data at the screen, as long as you type the letter <Y>.

CODE LISTING FOR BRKEVEN

```
{ Determine the point in operations where total costs equal }
{ total revenues and there is neither profit nor loss.       }

PROGRAM BrkEven ;

  TYPE
    StringType = STRING[80] ;

  VAR
      { For the benefit of human eyes only, the program's }
      { variables are listed in alphabetic order.  The    }
      { compiler couldn't care less about the VAR order.  }
    BreakEven : Real ;
    Ch : Char ;
    CostBrkEven : Real ;
    EndQty : Integer ;
    FixedCost : Real ;
    IncrQty : Integer ;
    L : Integer ;
    ProfLoss : Real ;
    RevBrkEven : Real ;
    SellPrice : Real ;
    StartQty : Integer ;
    TotalCost : Real ;
    TotalSales : Real ;
    UnitCost : Real ;
    VariableCost : Real ;

      { FORWARD declarations are the procedures defined }
      { and listed in alphabetical order.              }
```

145

```
     { This method merely reduces the amount of planning }
     { required in ordering the PROCEDURES.              }

PROCEDURE BorderLine(VAR F:Text) ;
   FORWARD ;

PROCEDURE GetInfo ;
   FORWARD ;

PROCEDURE MakeReport(VAR F:Text) ;
   FORWARD ;

PROCEDURE SignOn ;
   FORWARD ;

PROCEDURE BorderLine ;       { Generate the "cosmetic" border line. }

   BEGIN
     { BorderLine }
     LowVideo ;
     Write(F,'   ') ;
     FOR L := 1 TO 68 DO
       BEGIN
         Write(F,'=')       { The "border" is a line of "=" }
         END ;              { signs.  It can be changed to  }
                            { any printable character of    }
                            { your choice.                  }
     WriteLn(F) ;
     HighVideo
   END ;
{ BorderLine }

PROCEDURE GetInfo ;       { Get the user's data from the keyboard. }

   BEGIN
     { GetInfo }
     GotoXY(0,5) ;
     HighVideo ;
     WriteLn('FIRST, THE BASIC FACTS ...') ;
     WriteLn ;
     LowVideo ;
     Write('  Enter the TOTAL FIXED COST:        ') ;
     HighVideo ;
     ReadLn(FixedCost) ;
     LowVideo ;
     Write('  Now the VARIABLE COSTS per unit:  ') ;
     HighVideo ;
     ReadLn(VariableCost) ;
     LowVideo ;
     Write('  Then the SELLING PRICE per unit:  ') ;
     HighVideo ;
```

```
      ReadLn(SellPrice) ;
      WriteLn ;
      WriteLn('THIS IS NEEDED FOR CALCULATIONS ...') ;
      WriteLn ;
      LowVideo ;
      Write('   Starting Quantity for the table?  ') ;
      HighVideo ;
      ReadLn(StartQty) ;
      LowVideo ;
      Write('   Ending Quantity for the table?    ') ;
      HighVideo ;
      ReadLn(EndQty) ;
      LowVideo ;
      Write('   Increments of Quantity to show?   ') ;
      HighVideo ;
      ReadLn(IncrQty) ;
      WriteLn ;
      WriteLn
    END ;
{ GetInfo }


PROCEDURE MakeReport ;    { Display and print the breakeven table. }

   VAR
      CurQuan : Integer ;

   BEGIN
      { MakeReport }
      ClrScr ;
      BorderLine(F) ;
      WriteLn(F) ;
      Write(F,'                          ') ;
      WriteLn(F,'BREAKEVEN TABLE') ;
      WriteLn(F) ;
      BorderLine(F) ;
      Write(F,'    QTY      TOTAL COST     TOTAL SALES') ;
      WriteLn(F,'     GAIN/LOSS      UNIT COST') ;
      BorderLine(F) ;
      WriteLn(F) ;
          { Assign values to the variables for the computations. }
      BreakEven := FixedCost / (SellPrice - VariableCost) ;
      RevBrkEven := SellPrice * BreakEven ;
      CostBrkEven := FixedCost + (VariableCost * BreakEven) ;
          { Now perform the computations and present the results. }
      CurQuan := StartQty ;
      WHILE (CurQuan <= EndQty) DO
        BEGIN
            { For simplicity, combine calculations and }
            { assign new names to the new values.       }
          TotalSales := SellPrice * CurQuan ;
          TotalCost := FixedCost + (VariableCost * CurQuan) ;
```

147

```
            UnitCost := TotalCost / CurQuan ;
            ProfLoss := TotalSales - TotalCost ;
            WriteLn(F,' ',CurQuan:7,'    ',TotalCost:12:2,'   ',
                    TotalSales:12:2,'    ',ProfLoss:12:2,'   ',
                    UnitCost:12:2) ;
          CurQuan := CurQuan + IncrQty
        END ;
      WriteLn(F) ;
      BorderLine(F) ;                  { Call the BorderLine PROCEDURE. }
      CurQuan := Trunc(BreakEven) ;    { Supress the decimal point.     }
      WriteLn(F,' ',CurQuan:7,'    ',CostBrkEven:12:2,'   ',
              RevBrkEven:12:2,' = BREAKEVEN POINT') ;
      BorderLine(F) ;                  { Call the BorderLine PROCEDURE. }
      WriteLn(F) ;                     { Write the last lines of data.  }
      WriteLn(F,'    TOTAL FIXED COST:          ',FixedCost:12:2) ;
      WriteLn(F,'    VARIABLE COSTS PER UNIT:   ',VariableCost:12:2) ;
      WriteLn(F,'    SELLING PRICE PER UNIT:    ',SellPrice:12:2) ;
      WriteLn(F) ;
      BorderLine(F)                    { Call the BorderLine PROCEDURE. }
    END ;
  { MakeReport }

PROCEDURE SignOn ;                     { Display the startup message.   }
                                       { Put the title in a fancy box.  }

  BEGIN
    { SignOn }
    ClrScr ;
    LowVideo ;
    GoToXY(12,8) ;                     { Set the cursor at column 12, row 9. }
    FOR L := 1 TO 56 DO                { Begin the FOR loop to draw a series }
      BEGIN                            { of 56 dollar-signs.                 }
        Write('$')                     { Draw the dollar-signs.              }
      END ;                            { End the FOR...DO loop.              }
    GotoXY(12,9) ;                     { Position $ signs for the borders.   }
    Write('$') ;
    GotoXY(67,9) ;
    Write('$') ;
    GotoXY(12,10) ;
    Write('$') ;
    GotoXY(15,10) ;
    HighVideo ;                        { Display the program's title.        }
    Write('BRKEVEN - QUANTITY/COST/SALES - BREAKEVEN ANALYSIS') ;
    LowVideo ;
    GotoXY(67,10) ;
    Write('$') ;
    GotoXY(12,11) ;
    Write('$') ;
    GotoXY(67,11) ;
    Write('$') ;
    GoToXY(12,12) ;
```

```pascal
      FOR L := 1 TO 56 DO                { Begin the FOR...DO loop, as above. }
        BEGIN
          Write('$')
        END ;
      Delay(1500) ;                      { Delay the next action by 1.5 seconds. }
      ClrScr
    END ;
{ SignOn }

BEGIN                                    { This is the main part of the program. }
  { BrkEven }
  SignOn ;
  GetInfo ;
  ClrScr ;
REPEAT
  MakeReport(CON) ;                      { Prepare and display the report. }
  WriteLn ;
  HighVideo ;
  Write('  Repeat the Display?  (Y/N): ') ;           { An option. }
  Read(Kbd,Ch)                           { Get the response from the keyboard. }
UNTIL Ch IN ['N','n'] ;       { This is a short-form response.       }
WriteLn ;
WriteLn ;
HighVideo ;
WriteLn('  For a printout, turn on the printer.') ;  { An option. }
Write('  If "Yes,"  press `Y.''  (Any other key to quit): ') ;
Read(Kbd,Ch) ;
WHILE Ch IN ['Y','y'] DO       { A short-form response. }
  BEGIN
    MakeReport(LST) ;                    { Print the report. }
    Write(LST,Chr(12)) ;        { Eject the paper to top of next form. }
    Write('  Do Another Printout?  (Y/N): ') ;  { An option. }
    Read(Kbd,Ch)
  END
END.
{ BrkEven }
```

Chapter 20

Commissions for Sales Representatives

Although the program in this chapter is for sales managers, everyone who wants to improve his or her Pascal programming skills can benefit from studying the code. Every person who is accountable for the sales activities of a group of manufacturers' representatives (or other independent sales agencies) knows the importance of having up-to-date records for each of his sales representatives or agents. At a minimum, the records must provide rapid access to data concerning sales volume, commission rates, amounts earned in commissions, portions of earned commissions that have been paid out, and portions of commissions that are still unpaid.

Such records are maintained in many ways. Frequently they are manual log books that depend on cross references to other internal records. The program in this chapter provides a workable solution to the problem of keeping records up-to-date and close-at-hand for immediate reference, review, and discussion. It is especially useful when a sales representative calls to gripe about the delay in his commission payment. REPCOMM provides a ready design for a sales and commission record that can be prepared and printed in a few minutes time.

After the automatic sign on is displayed, the four variables for Total_Sales, Total_Earned, Total_Paid, and Total_Owed are initialized to zero to prevent "garbage" in the calculations. The program asks for the date of the report and then prints it with a header for the printed page. Three lines of instructions are displayed:

Enter the sales volume for each rep when prompted.
When all entries are completed, type -1 in
response to the next request for "Sales Volume."

Your responses to a series of queries supply the data for the calculations:

Enter the sales volume for rep 1:   123542.76
What is the commission %-rate for rep 1: 10

At this point the screen fills in the data:

Commissions earned: 12354.28

Then another request follows:

What commissions have been paid to rep 1: 12000

The computer does a rapid calculation and displays:

Commissions still due: 354.28

The WriteReport procedure is called and sends the information just entered to the printer. In the main part of the program the totals are accumulated. The program moves on to the next Rep and asks the same series of questions:

Enter the sales volume for rep 2:   27555.50
What is the commission %-rate for rep 2:   7.5
Commissions earned: 2066.66
What commissions have been paid to rep 2: 2066.66
Commissions still due: 0.00

The above data is sent to the printer, and the totals are accumulated. The program continues:

Enter the sales volume for rep 3:   49500
What is the commission %-rate for rep 23   5

Commissions earned: 2475.00

What commissions have been paid to rep 3:   <u>1500</u>

Commissions still due: 975.00

```
*****************************************

   COMMISSIONS REPORT AS OF: 10/31/85

*****************************************


----------- Report for rep  1 -------------

Sales volume:                  123542.76
Commission rate: 10.00%
Commissions paid:               12000.00
Commissions unpaid:               354.28


----------- Report for rep  2 -------------

Sales volume:                   27555.50
Commission rate:  7.50%
Commissions paid:                2066.66
Commissions unpaid:                 0.00


----------- Report for rep  3 -------------

Sales volume:                   49500.00
Commission rate:  5.00%
Commissions paid:                1500.00
Commissions unpaid:               975.00

*****************************************
Total sales for all reps:      200598.26
Total commissions earned:       16895.94
Total commissions paid:         15566.66
Total commissions unpaid:        1329.28
*****************************************
```

Fig. 20-1. A sample printout from the Reps Commissions program.

To end the entries, you must enter -1 for the sales volume.

Enter the sales volume for rep 4:

The WrapUp procedure is called twice, once to display the totals on the screen and once to send the information to the printer, which completes the program's execution.

A SAMPLE REPCOMM PRINTOUT

Figure 20-1 shows the report generated by the printer for Reps 1 through 3 using the data from the example. The report could deal with as many as 25 representatives according to the CONSTant value assigned to MaxNumReps at the start of the code.

CODE LISTING FOR REPCOMM

```
{ Generate reports of reps' sales volume, commissions earned }
{ commissions paid, commissions still owed, and a summary.    }

PROGRAM RepComm ;

  CONST
    MaxNumReps = 25 ;   { Limit the number of reps to 25.      }
                        { Increase the MaxNumReps, if desired. }

  TYPE
    Rep_NumberType = 1..MaxNumReps ;
    StringType = STRING[80] ;

  VAR
    L : Integer ;
    Date : StringType ;
    Rep_Number : Rep_NumberType ;
    Commissions_Owed,Commissions_Earned,Commissions_Paid : Real ;
    Commission_Rate : Real ;
    Reps : ARRAY [Rep_NumberType] OF Real ;
    Sales_Volume : Real ;
    Total_Owed,Total_Earned,Total_Paid,Total_Sales : Real ;

  PROCEDURE SignOn ;       { Create and display the startup banner. }

    BEGIN
      { SignOn }
      ClrScr ;
      GotoXY(17,8) ;
      LowVideo ;
      FOR L := 1 TO 6 DO         { Do six iterations in }
```

```
          Write('REPCOMM') ;         { a row of 'REPCOMM'. }
      GotoXY(17,9) ;
      Write('R') ;                 { Start a column of letters }
      GotoXY(58,9) ;               { for the border design.    }
      Write('R') ;
      GotoXY(17,10) ;
      Write('E') ;
      GotoXY(58,10) ;
      Write('E') ;
      GotoXY(25,10) ;
      HighVideo ;
      Write('SALES COMMISSION REPORTER') ;         { Title. }
      LowVideo ;
      GotoXY(17,11) ;
      Write('P') ;
      GotoXY(58,11) ;
      Write('P') ;
    GotoXY(17,12) ;
    LowVideo ;
    FOR L := 1 TO 6 DO                    { Same as above. }
      Write('REPCOMM') ;
    Delay(1500) ;
    HighVideo ;
    ClrScr
  END ;
{ SignOn }


PROCEDURE Divider_Line(VAR Destination:Text) ;
  { Send a line of asterisks. }

  BEGIN
    { Divider_Line }
    FOR L := 1 TO 40 DO          { The quantity is 40 for a ... }
      BEGIN
        Write(Destination,'*') ; { ... line of asterisks or any }
      END                        { any printable character.     }
  END ;
{ Divider_Line }


PROCEDURE WrapUp(VAR Destination:Text) ;    { Do the summary. }

  BEGIN
    { WrapUp }
    Divider_Line(Destination) ;       { Execute the PROCEDURE. }
    WriteLn(Destination) ;
    WriteLn(Destination,'Total sales for all reps:    ',
                    Total_Sales:12:2) ;
    WriteLn(Destination,'Total commissions earned:    ',
                    Total_Earned:12:2) ;
    WriteLn(Destination,'Total commissions paid:      ',
                    Total_Paid:12:2) ;
```

```
          WriteLn(Destination,'Total commissions unpaid:    ',
                          Total_Owed:12:2) ;
        Divider_Line(Destination) ;
        WriteLn(Destination)
      END ;
{ WrapUp }

PROCEDURE WriteRepReport ;
    { Send reps' statistics to the printer. }

  BEGIN
    { WriteRepReport }
    WriteLn(LST) ;
    WriteLn(LST,'---------- Report for rep ',Rep_Number:2,' -------------') ;
    WriteLn(LST) ;
    WriteLn(LST,'Sales volume:                 ',Sales_Volume:12:2) ;
    WriteLn(LST,'Commission rate: ',Commission_Rate:5:2,'%') ;
    WriteLn(LST,'Commissions paid:             ',Commissions_Paid:12:2) ;
    WriteLn(LST,'Commissions unpaid:           ',Commissions_Owed:12:2) ;
    WriteLn(LST)
  END ;
{ WriteRepReport }

BEGIN
  { RepComm }
  SignOn ;
  Total_Sales  := 0 ;   { Initialize the Totals to start at zero. }
  Total_Earned := 0 ;
  Total_Paid   := 0 ;
  Total_Owed   := 0 ;
  LowVideo ;
  Write('Date of this Report  (MM/DD/YY): ') ;
  HighVideo ;
  ReadLn(Date) ;
  Divider_Line(LST) ;  { Execute the PROCEDURE. }
  WriteLn(LST) ;
  WriteLn(LST) ;
  WriteLn(LST,'  COMMISSIONS REPORT AS OF: ',Date) ;
  WriteLn(LST) ;
  Divider_Line(LST) ;  { Execute the PROCEDURE. }
  WriteLn(LST) ;
  WriteLn(LST) ;
  WriteLn ;
  WriteLn ;
  WriteLn('Enter the sales volume for each rep when prompted.') ;
  WriteLn('When all entries are completed, type -1 in ') ;
  WriteLn('response to the next request for "Sales Volume".') ;
  WriteLn ;
  WriteLn ;
  Rep_Number := 1 ;     { Set the value of Rep_Number to 1. }
```

```
REPEAT
   LowVideo ;
   Write('Enter the Sales Volume for rep ',Rep_Number,': ') ;
   HighVideo ;
   ReadLn(Sales_Volume) ;
   IF (Sales_Volume > - 1) THEN
         { Sales_Volume of -1 ends the input of data. }
         { If Sales_Volume is greater than -1, BEGIN. }
      BEGIN
      { Collect data, calculate, assign, and display values. }
         LowVideo ;
         Write('What is the commission %-rate for rep ',Rep_Number:2,': ') ;
         HighVideo ;
         ReadLn(Commission_Rate) ;
         Commissions_Earned := Sales_Volume * (Commission_Rate / 100.0) ;
         WriteLn('Commissions earned: ',Commissions_Earned:12:2) ;
         LowVideo ;
         Write('What commissions have been paid to rep ',Rep_Number:2,': ') ;
         HighVideo ;
         ReadLn(Commissions_Paid) ;
         Commissions_Owed := Commissions_Earned - Commissions_Paid ;
         WriteLn('Commissions still due: ',Commissions_Owed:12:2) ;
         WriteLn ;
         WriteRepReport ;
         Total_Sales  := Total_Sales + Sales_Volume ;
         Total_Earned := Total_Earned + Commissions_Earned ;
         Total_Paid   := Total_Paid + Commissions_Paid ;
         Total_Owed   := Total_Owed + Commissions_Owed ;
         Rep_Number   := Rep_Number + 1
      END
   UNTIL (Sales_Volume = - 1) ;       { REPEAT...UNTIL Sales_Volume is -1. }
   WriteLn ;
   WrapUp(CON) ;     { Execute the PROCEDURE; send to the video display. }
   WrapUp(LST)       { Execute the PROCEDURE; send to the printer.       }
END.
{ RepComm }
```

Chapter 21

Analyzing
Sales Performance

The program SALESRPT demonstrates the use of arrays and number crunching. At the same time it provides a program that can either be used in the form presented here or revised, customized, and modified to fit special needs.

The program is a "sales performance analyzer." It compares the performances of individuals against the average level, reports the number of dollars by which each is above or below average, and generates a printed, detailed report for further study. The program's name and purpose can easily be changed in the source code given here to refer to any kind of group and individual achievement in business, social, community, and sports events.

SALESRPT is highly versatile and extremely useful for the sales, marketing, financial, and senior managers of any enterprise. This program can be used to obtain a visual display and a hard-copy printout of sales data related to a variety of sources that you identify by your own confidential code number. The sources could be: (1) individual salespeople within a sales section; (2) sales districts; (3) sales regions and sales areas; (4) retailers, wholesalers, or dealers and distributors; (5) customers, users, national accounts, house accounts; (6) industries, markets, and products; (7) divisions and subsidiaries; (8) individual or groups of products and services.

Sounds like a lot of power—and it is. What's more, it all fits into a compact Turbo Pascal program. The program signs on, the screen clears, and the Starting__Values procedure asks you to enter date information.

Let's simulate a run with the bold type representing the display at the screen and the underlined type representing your responses:

WHAT PERIOD OF TIME DOES THIS ANALYSIS COVER?

(Please Enter All Dates In The Format MM/DD/YY):

Enter the Start Date:	10/01/85
Enter the End Date:	10/31/85
Enter Today's Date:	11/15/85

ENTER THE SALES AMOUNT FOR EACH ID NUMBER.

(To end the program, type −1 for 'Sales Dollars.)

Sales dollars for ID Number 1:	1301.36
Sales dollars for ID Number 2:	1333.52
Sales dollars for ID Number 3:	1344.57
Sales dollars for ID Number 4:	1355.89
Sales dollars for ID Number 5:	1426.50
Sales dollars for ID Number 6:	1223.35
Sales dollars for ID Number 7:	1223.01
Sales dollars for ID Number 8:	1546.58
Sales dollars for ID Number 9:	1555.58
Sales dollars for ID Number 10:	1565.68
Sales dollars for ID Number 11:	1213.24
Sales dollars for ID Number 12:	1267.89
Sales dollars for ID Number 13:	−1

After the − 1 is entered, the screen clears, the computations are made instantly by the computer, and the results appear on the screen, called by the

```
********************************************************************
                  SALES PERFORMANCE ANALYSIS

********************************************************************
 PERIOD COVERED BY THIS REPORT: 10/01/85 to 10/31/85
 DATE THIS REPORT WAS PREPARED: 11/15/85

 TOTAL SALES VOLUME:      16357.17
 AVERAGE SALES VOLUME:     1363.10
********************************************************************
 IDENTIFIER #         SALES $      $ ABOVE AVGE      $ BELOW AVGE
********************************************************************
         1            1301.36                            61.74
         2            1333.52                            29.58
         3            1344.57                            18.53
         4            1355.89                             7.21
         5            1426.50          63.40
         6            1223.35                           139.75
         7            1223.01                           140.09
         8            1546.58         183.48
         9            1555.58         192.48
        10            1565.68         202.58
        11            1213.24                           149.86
        12            1267.89                            95.21
********************************************************************
```

Fig. 21-1. A sample printout from the Sales Report program.

Make_Report procedure. At the bottom of the display you are asked:

Printout? Turn on the printer.

If YES, type 'Y' (Any other key to quit):

The printout is identical with the display, as shown in Fig. 21-1. Then you are asked whether or not you want to repeat the printout. Any response other than <Y> ends the program.

CODE LISTING FOR SALESRPT

```
{ Generate a report of individual and group sales performance. }
{ Calculate total, average, above, and below average levels.   }
{ The name and code may be revised to fit other than sales.    }

PROGRAM Sales_Rpt ;

   CONST
      { Establish the maximum number of entries }
```

```
            { at the desired number + 1.            }
    Max_Num_Ids = 51 ;

TYPE
    Id_Num_Type = 1..Max_Num_Ids ;
    String_Type = STRING[80] ;

VAR
    Avg_Sales : Real ;
    Ch : Char ;
    End_Date : String_Type ;
    Id_Number : Id_Num_Type ;
    Sales_Amt : ARRAY [Id_Num_Type] OF Real ;
    Start_Date,Today_Date : String_Type ;
    Total_Sales : Real ;

PROCEDURE Sign_On ;                          { Display the signon message. }

    BEGIN
      { Sign_On }
      ClrScr ;
      GotoXY(15,10) ;
      LowVideo ;
      Write('****************************************************') ;
      GotoXY(15,11) ;
      Write('*                                              *') ;
      GotoXY(15,12) ;
      HighVideo ;
      Write('*     SALESRPT -- Sales Performance Analyzer      *') ;
      GotoXY(15,13) ;
      LowVideo ;
      Write('*                                              *') ;
      GotoXY(15,14) ;
      Write('****************************************************') ;
      Delay(1500) ;
      ClrScr                        { Clear the screen; end this procedure }
                                    { and start the next procedure.        }
    END ;
{ Sign_On }

PROCEDURE Draw_A_Line(VAR F:Text) ;          { Draw a line of asterisks. }

    BEGIN
      { Draw_A_Line }
      LowVideo ;      { Note: the next two lines display and print as one. }
      Write(F,'  *********************************') ;
      WriteLn(F,'*********************************') ;
      HighVideo
    END ;
```

```
  { of Draw_A_Line }

PROCEDURE Starting_Values ;        { Collect data. Do initial calculations. }

   BEGIN
     { Starting_Values }
     GotoXY(1,5) ;
     LowVideo ;
     WriteLn(' WHAT PERIOD OF TIME DOES THIS ANALYSIS COVER?') ;
     WriteLn(' (Please Enter All Dates In The Format MM/DD/YY.)') ;
     GotoXY(1,8) ;
     Write('   Enter the Start Date: ') ;
     HighVideo ;
     ReadLn(Start_Date) ;
     LowVideo ;
     Write('   Enter the End Date:   ') ;
     HighVideo ;
     ReadLn(End_Date) ;
     LowVideo ;
     Write('   Enter Today''s Date:   ') ;
     HighVideo ;
     ReadLn(Today_Date) ;
     GotoXY(1,12) ;
     LowVideo ;
     Write(' ENTER THE SALES AMOUNT FOR EACH ID NUMBER.') ;
     GotoXY(1,13) ;
     Write(' (To end the program, type -1 for `Sales Dollars.'')') ;
     WriteLn ;
     WriteLn ;
     Id_Number := 1 ;          { Initialize the Id_Number count at 1.   }
     Total_Sales := 0 ;        { Initialize Total_Sales at zero dollars. }
     REPEAT
       Write('   Sales Dollars for ID Number ',Id_Number,':  ') ;
       HighVideo ;
       ReadLn(Sales_Amt[Id_Number]) ;
       LowVideo ;                { Restore LowVideo for the next query. }
       IF (Sales_Amt[Id_Number] > - 1) THEN
         BEGIN
           Total_Sales := Total_Sales + Sales_Amt[Id_Number] ;
           Id_Number := Id_Number + 1 ;
         END
     UNTIL ((Sales_Amt[Id_Number] = - 1) OR (Id_Number = Max_Num_Ids)) ;
     Id_Number := Id_Number - 1 ;
     Avg_Sales := Total_Sales / Id_Number ;      { Straightforward math. }
     ClrScr       { Clear the screen when -1 is the `Sales_Amt' entered. }
   END ;
{ Starting_Values }

PROCEDURE Make_Report(VAR F:Text) ;          { Create the sales report. }
```

```
VAR
  NumInRpt : Id_Num_Type ;

BEGIN
  { Make_Report }
  Draw_A_Line(F) ;
  WriteLn(F) ;
  WriteLn(F,'                    ','   SALES PERFORMANCE ANALYSIS') ;
  WriteLn(F) ;
  Draw_A_Line(F) ;
  WriteLn(F,'   PERIOD COVERED BY THIS REPORT: ',Start_Date,
          ' to ',End_Date) ;
  WriteLn(F,'   DATE THIS REPORT WAS PREPARED: ',Today_Date) ;
  WriteLn(F) ;
  WriteLn(F,'   TOTAL SALES VOLUME:   ',Total_Sales:10:2) ;
  WriteLn(F,'   AVERAGE SALES VOLUME: ',Avg_Sales:10:2) ;
  Draw_A_Line(F) ;
  WriteLn(F,'   IDENTIFIER #        SALES $       ',
          '$ ABOVE AVGE      $ BELOW AVGE') ;
  Draw_A_Line(F) ;
  FOR NumInRpt := 1 TO Id_Number DO
    BEGIN
      Write(F,'           ',NumInRpt:3,'           ',
          Sales_Amt[NumInRpt]:10:2) ;
      IF (Sales_Amt[NumInRpt] > Avg_Sales) THEN
        WriteLn(F,'        ',Sales_Amt[NumInRpt] - Avg_Sales:10:2)
      ELSE
        WriteLn(F,'                       ',
              Avg_Sales - Sales_Amt[NumInRpt]:10:2)
    END ;
  Draw_A_Line(F) ;
  END ;
{ Make_Report }

BEGIN
  { Sales_Rpt }
  Sign_On ;              { Execute the PROCEDURES in the order used. }
  Starting_Values ;
  Make_Report(CON) ;
  WriteLn ;
  WriteLn ;
  WriteLn('   Printout?  Turn on the printer.') ;
  Write('   If YES, type `Y'' (Any other key to quit): ') ;
  Read(Kbd,Ch) ;
  WHILE (Ch = 'Y') OR (Ch = 'y') DO
    BEGIN
      Make_Report(LST) ;                      { Print the final report. }
      Write(LST,Chr(12)) ; { Eject the paper to the next Top Of Form. }
      WriteLn ;
      WriteLn ;
```

```
        WriteLn('   Repeat the printout (`Y'' or `N'')','? ') ;
        Write('   If YES, Type `Y'' (Any other key to quit): ') ;
        Read(Kbd,Ch)
      END
END.
{ Sales_Rpt }
```

Chapter 22

A Four-
Function Calculator

This program, MINICALC, may never replace any of the handheld calculators you can buy for less than $5. I'm not, however, trying to replace anything, I'm just writing code to demonstrate how to get things done using Turbo Pascal.

MINICALC is a short program, but it demonstrates how simple it is to do basic calculations within a few dozen lines of code. The operators + (addition), – (subtraction) * (multiplication), and / (division) are used in this program within a group of IF . . . THEN statements that recognize the four operators.

The program signs on and displays one line of instructions, which tells you that you may use any of the four operators, + – * /. Then you are told to enter the first number followed by a <CR>, which is the Enter key. "A" is assigned the value of the first number. Next you enter the operator, followed by a <CR>. Finally, you enter the second number followed by a <CR>. "B" is assigned the value of the second number.

The IF . . . THEN clauses test for the operator you entered. The program drops through each of the clauses, but stops and takes the appropriate action when it reaches the appropriate operator, which is the one you had entered. "C" is assigned the value of the result of "A" and "B" after they have been affected by or acted upon by the operator.

A, B, and C have been declared to be variables of the type *real*. The statement "WriteLn (C:10:16)" causes the screen to display the calculated result, which is the value that has been assigned to "C" formatted as a real number with 10 integers to the left, and 16 places to the right of the decimal point.

Finally, the program asks "Do you want to do another calculation? Y)es or N)o." If you enter any character other than "N" (in either upper or lower-case), the program goes back to the line below the REPEAT statement and begins the process all over again. If you enter a lowercase "n," the statement "UpCase (Ch) = 'N'" converts it to the uppercase, and the program ends.

You can expand the utility of the MINICALC program by adding code for operators that use some of the mathematical functions that are built-into Turbo Pascal and are listed in Appendix D of this book.

CODE LISTING FOR MINICALC

```
(* A four-operator two-number calculator.  *)
(* Precision is real numbers to 16 places. *)

PROGRAM MiniCalc ;
 VAR
    A,B,C : Real ;
    Operator : Char ;
    Ch : Char ;

 BEGIN      { MiniCalc - This is the program; no separate procedures are used. }
   REPEAT                           { Keep going until the UNTIL condition is met. }
     ClrScr ;
     GotoXY(5,5) ;
     HighVideo ;
     Write('THIS PROGRAM TURNS YOUR EXPENSIVE COMPUTER') ;
     WriteLn(' INTO AN INEXPENSIVE CALCULATOR!') ;
     GotoXY(5,8) ;
     LowVideo ;
     Write('The operators you may use are:  ') ;  { Start the instructions. }
     HighVideo ;
     WriteLn('+  -  *  /') ;                  { End the instructions. }
     WriteLn ;
     LowVideo ;
     GotoXY(5,10) ;
     Write('Enter the first number followed by a <CR>:  ') ; { First data. }
     HighVideo ;
     Read(A) ;
     GotoXY(5,11) ;
     LowVideo ;
     Write('Now enter the operator followed by a <CR>: ') ;  { Operate on it. }
     HighVideo ;
     Read(Operator) ;
     GotoXY(5,12) ;
     LowVideo ;
     Write('Now the second number followed by a <CR>:  ') ;  { Second data. }
     HighVideo ;
     Read(B) ;
     IF Operator = '+' THEN
```

```
        C := A + B ;                              { Test forthe appropriate operator. }
    IF Operator = '-' THEN
        C := A - B ;                              { Assign values to C, the result.    }
    IF Operator = '*' THEN
      C := A * B ;
    IF Operator = '/' THEN
      C := A / B ;
    GotoXY(5,14) ;
    LowVideo ;
    Write('The calculated result:  ') ;
    HighVideo ;
    WriteLn(C:10:16) ;                      { Format the response to the 16th decimal. }
    GotoXY(5,16) ;
    LowVideo ;
    Write('Do you want to do another calculation? ') ;
    HighVideo ;
    Write('Y') ;                             { Highlight the Y. }
    LowVideo ;
    Write(')es or ') ;
    HighVideo ;
    Write('N') ;                             { Highlight the N. }
    LowVideo ;
    Write(')o: ') ;
    Read(Kbd,Ch) ;                          { Get the keyboard response. Do not echo. }
  UNTIL UpCase(Ch) = 'N' ;           { This is the condition for REPEAT or END. }
  WriteLn
END.
{ MiniCalc }
```

Chapter 23

Benchmarking and Testing Your Printer's Print-Quality

Ever thought of benchmarking the printing quality of your favorite printer? It's easy, if you have a program that puts the printer through its ASCII-character printing paces. This chapter offers two versions of a program that will do just that, and if your printer has the capability, the programs will print the extended character or graphics set of characters from ASCII 128 through 254 (decimal).

The first of the two versions, PRNTEST1, consists of a series of eight procedures. The first procedure, Headings, prints headings for the columns of sample printing. The other seven procedures are ASCII groups of printable characters that range from decimal 33 through decimal 126. The procedures are named to provide easy identification of the nature of the group of ASCII characters each procedure deals with. For example, it is obvious that the procedure Numbers prints the numbers in the ASCII table, and the procedure Upper Case Alpha deals with the capital or uppercase letters of the alphabet.

The constant, LineLen, is declared to be equal to 20. Each of the procedure's FOR . . . DO clauses contains the LineLen constant and therefore the length of each line printed is 20 characters. This is a good illustration of one utility of the CONST declaration. The line length could have been declared individually in each procedure; however, if you should want to adjust the length (or the width) of the character-printing line, you would have to change it in each of the seven procedures. By declaring as a constant at the start of the program, all you have to do is change the value (20 in this case) to whatever reasonable length you desire, and each procedure would be automatically ad-

```
ASCII      ASCII
NUMBER     CHARACTER
------------------------------------

48:  00000000000000000000
49:  11111111111111111111
50:  22222222222222222222
51:  33333333333333333333
52:  44444444444444444444
53:  55555555555555555555
54:  66666666666666666666
55:  77777777777777777777
56:  88888888888888888888
57:  99999999999999999999

65:  AAAAAAAAAAAAAAAAAAAA
66:  BBBBBBBBBBBBBBBBBBBB
67:  CCCCCCCCCCCCCCCCCCCC
68:  DDDDDDDDDDDDDDDDDDDD
69:  EEEEEEEEEEEEEEEEEEEE
70:  FFFFFFFFFFFFFFFFFFFF
71:  GGGGGGGGGGGGGGGGGGGG
72:  HHHHHHHHHHHHHHHHHHHH
73:  IIIIIIIIIIIIIIIIIIII
74:  JJJJJJJJJJJJJJJJJJJJ
75:  KKKKKKKKKKKKKKKKKKKK
76:  LLLLLLLLLLLLLLLLLLLL
77:  MMMMMMMMMMMMMMMMMMMM
78:  NNNNNNNNNNNNNNNNNNNN
79:  OOOOOOOOOOOOOOOOOOOO
80:  PPPPPPPPPPPPPPPPPPPP
81:  QQQQQQQQQQQQQQQQQQQQ
82:  RRRRRRRRRRRRRRRRRRRR
83:  SSSSSSSSSSSSSSSSSSSS
84:  TTTTTTTTTTTTTTTTTTTT
85:  UUUUUUUUUUUUUUUUUUUU
86:  VVVVVVVVVVVVVVVVVVVV
87:  WWWWWWWWWWWWWWWWWWWW
88:  XXXXXXXXXXXXXXXXXXXX
89:  YYYYYYYYYYYYYYYYYYYY
90:  ZZZZZZZZZZZZZZZZZZZZ

97:  aaaaaaaaaaaaaaaaaaaa
98:  bbbbbbbbbbbbbbbbbbbb
```

```
 99: cccccccccccccccccccc
100: dddddddddddddddddddd
101: eeeeeeeeeeeeeeeeeeee
102: ffffffffffffffffffff
103: gggggggggggggggggggg
104: hhhhhhhhhhhhhhhhhhhh
105: iiiiiiiiiiiiiiiiiiii
106: jjjjjjjjjjjjjjjjjjjj
107: kkkkkkkkkkkkkkkkkkkk
108: llllllllllllllllllll
109: mmmmmmmmmmmmmmmmmmmm
110: nnnnnnnnnnnnnnnnnnnn
```

Fig. 23-1. A sample printout from the Print Test program.

justed, adopting the value declared as the constant.

As Fig. 23-1, which is a sample printout produced by the program, demonstrates, each line is offset from the left column by the width of the tab character, ^I. Each line also has the decimal number in the ASCII collating sequence of the character that is being printed.

PRNTEST2, the second version of the print-test program consists of the main program without calls to separate procedures. The constant and the variables are the same in both programs and they serve the same purposes and are treated in the same manner.

From an operational standpoint, the programs produce identical results. Both programs start by clearing the screen. They display a one-line message announcing the start of the tests. The printer, which must be connected and turned on at the time, does its job. As soon as the printer is finished or the program's output to LST, the printer, has been dumped to the printer's buffer, the one-line message announcing that the tests are finished overwrites the starting message.

Look at the listings of the code for PRNTEST1 and PRNTEST2 and determine which approach you find easier for eyeball reading. Clearly, PRNTEST1 is easier. It also is easier to modify or maintain, which is one of the purposes of using groups of procedures in writing code in a structured language.

Figure 23-1 shows a sample of the printout generated by a NEC 7710 Spinwriter when the PRNTEST1 program was executed.

CODE LISTING FOR PRNTEST1

```
(*
    Printer testing ... this program prints the complete
    ASCII set of printable characters.  Procedures are
    used for each series of characters.  Output is directed
    to the printer to provide the ability to inspect the
    printer's character-quality.  The extended graphics
```

```
    procedure is especially for use with printers capable
    of printing those characters, of course.
*)

PROGRAM PrnTest1 ;

  CONST
    LineLen = 20 ;                       { Set the lengths of lines to print 20 chars. }

  VAR
    I,J : Integer ;

  PROCEDURE Headings ;                          { Print the column headings. }

    BEGIN
      WriteLn(LST,^I,'ASCII     ASCII') ;     { ^I = Ctrl I, the Horizontal Tab. }
      WriteLn(LST,^I,'NUMBER    CHARACTER') ;
      WriteLn(LST,^I,'-------------------------') ;
      WriteLn(LST)
    END ;
    { Headings }

  PROCEDURE Numbers ;                          { Print the numbers zero to nine. }

    BEGIN
      FOR I := 48 TO 57 DO                 { Assign numbers 48 through 57 to "I" }
        BEGIN
          Write(LST,^I,I,': ') ;     { Tab, and print the number assigned to "I" }
          FOR J := 1 TO LineLen DO
            Write(LST,Chr(I)) ;           { Print the ASCII character of value "I" }
          WriteLn(LST) ;                  { Print a CRLF to separate the groups. }
        END
    END ;
    { Numbers }

  PROCEDURE Upper_Case_Alpha ;             { Print the set of uppercase letters. }

    BEGIN
      FOR I := 65 TO 90 DO                      { Ditto for 65 through 90 }
        BEGIN
          Write(LST,^I,I,': ') ;
          FOR J := 1 TO LineLen DO
            Write(LST,Chr(I)) ;
          WriteLn(LST) ;
        END
    END ;
    { Upper_Case_Alpha }

  PROCEDURE Lower_Case_Alpha ;             { Print the set of lowercase letters. }

    BEGIN
```

```
          FOR I := 97 TO 122 DO
            BEGIN
              Write(LST,^I,I,': ') ;
              FOR J := 1 TO LineLen DO
                Write(LST,Chr(I)) ;
              WriteLn(LST) ;
            END
        END ;
        { Lower_Case_Alpha }

    PROCEDURE Punct1 ;                              { Print set 1: punctuation marks. }

      BEGIN
        FOR I := 33 TO 47 DO
          BEGIN
            Write(LST,^I,I,': ') ;
            FOR J := 1 TO LineLen DO
              Write(LST,Chr(I)) ;
            WriteLn(LST) ;
          END
      END ;
      { Punct1 }

    PROCEDURE Punct2 ;                              { Print set 2: punctuation marks. }

      BEGIN
        FOR I := 58 TO 64 DO
          BEGIN
            Write(LST,^I,I,': ') ;
            FOR J := 1 TO LineLen DO
              Write(LST,Chr(I)) ;
            WriteLn(LST) ;
          END
      END ;
      { Punct2 }

    PROCEDURE Punct3 ;                              { Print set 3: punctuation marks. }

  BEGIN
    FOR I := 91 TO 96 DO
      BEGIN
        Write(LST,^I,I,': ') ;
        FOR J := 1 TO LineLen DO
          Write(LST,Chr(I)) ;
        WriteLn(LST) ;
      END
  END ;
  { Punct3 }

    PROCEDURE Punct4 ;                              { Print set 4: punctuation marks. }
```

```
      BEGIN
        FOR I := 123 TO 126 DO
          BEGIN
            Write(LST,^I,I,': ') ;
            FOR J := 1 TO LineLen DO
              Write(LST,Chr(I)) ;
            WriteLn(LST) ;
          END
      END ;
      { Punct4 }


PROCEDURE Extended_Graphics ;     { Test the printer's extended character set. }

      BEGIN
        FOR I := 128 TO 254 DO
          BEGIN
            Write(LST,^I,I,': ') ;
            FOR J := 1 TO LineLen DO
              Write(LST,Chr(I)) ;
            WriteLn(LST) ;
          END
      END ;
      { Extended_Graphics }


BEGIN { PrnTest1 }
    ClrScr ;                              { Begin with a clear screen. }
    GotoXY(15,10) ;          { Display the START message at column 15, row 10. }
    WriteLn(CON,'>>>>>> S T A R T   T H E   T E S T S <<<<<<') ;
    Headings ;                            { Call the Procedure. }
    Numbers ;                             { Call the Procedure. }
    WriteLn(LST) ;                  { Move the paper one line as a separator. }
    Upper_Case_Alpha ;                    { Call the Procedure. }
    WriteLn(LST) ;                  { Move the paper one line as a separator. }
    Lower_Case_Alpha ;                    { Call the Procedure. }
    WriteLn(LST) ;                  { Move the paper one line as a separator. }
    Punct1 ;                              { Call the Procedure. }
    WriteLn(LST) ;                  { Move the paper one line as a separator. }
    Punct2 ;                              { Call the Procedure. }
    WriteLn(LST) ;                  { Move the paper one line as a separator. }
    Punct3 ;                              { Call the Procedure. }
    WriteLn(LST) ;                  { Move the paper one line as a separator. }
    Punct4 ;                              { Call the Procedure. }
    WriteLn(LST) ;                  { Move the paper one line as a separator. }
    Extended_Graphics ;                   { Call the Procedure. }
    GotoXY(10,10) ;  { Overwrite the START messgage with the FINISHED message. }
    WriteLn(CON,'>>>>> T H E   T E S T S   A R E   F I N I S H E D <<<<<') ;
    WriteLn(LST,Chr(12)) ;                { Send a form feed signal. }
    WriteLn(LST,Chr(7))                   { Sound the printer's bell. }
END.
{ PrnTest1 }
```

CODE LISTING FOR PRNTEST2

```
(*
    Printer testing ... this program prints the complete
    ASCII set of printable characters.  Procedures are
    used for each series of characters.  Output is directed
    to the printer to provide the ability to inspect the
    printer's character-quality.  The extended graphics
    procedure is especially for use with printers capable
    of printing those characters, of course.
*)
(*
    Note: This program differs from the PrnTest1 program which
    uses a series of Procedures.  PrnTest2, this program, uses
    one continuous series of statements as though it were a
    single Procedure.
*)

PROGRAM PrnTest2 ;

    CONST
        LineLen = 20 ;                      { Set the lengths of lines to print 20 chars. }

    VAR
        I,J : Integer ;

    BEGIN
        ClrScr ;                                        { Begin with a clear screen. }
        GotoXY(15,10) ;            { Display the START message at column 15, row 10. }
        WriteLn(CON,'>>>>>> S T A R T   T H E   T E S T S <<<<<<') ;
        { Print the column headings. }
        WriteLn(LST,^I,'ASCII     ASCII') ;        { ^I = Ctrl I, the Horizontal Tab. }
        WriteLn(LST,^I,'NUMBER    CHARACTER') ;
        WriteLn(LST,^I,'--------------------------') ;
        WriteLn(LST) ;
        FOR I := 48 TO 57 DO                     { Assign numbers 48 through 57 to "I" }
            BEGIN
                Write(LST,^I,I,': ') ;              { Tab; print the number assigned to "I" }
                FOR J := 1 TO LineLen DO
                    Write(LST,Chr(I)) ;             { Print the ASCII character of value "I" }
                WriteLn(LST)
            END ;
        WriteLn(LST) ;            { Print a CRLF to separate the complex statements. }
        FOR I := 65 TO 90 DO
            BEGIN
                Write(LST,^I,I,': ') ;
                FOR J := 1 TO LineLen DO
                    Write(LST,Chr(I)) ;
                WriteLn(LST)
            END ;
```

```
WriteLn(LST) ;
FOR I := 97 TO 122 DO
  BEGIN
    Write(LST,^I,I,': ') ;
    FOR J := 1 TO LineLen DO
      Write(LST,Chr(I)) ;
    WriteLn(LST)
  END ;
WriteLn(LST) ;
FOR I := 33 TO 47 DO
  BEGIN
    Write(LST,^I,I,': ') ;
    FOR J := 1 TO LineLen DO
      Write(LST,Chr(I)) ;
    WriteLn(LST)
  END ;
WriteLn(LST) ;
FOR I := 58 TO 64 DO
  BEGIN
    Write(LST,^I,I,': ') ;
    FOR J := 1 TO LineLen DO
      Write(LST,Chr(I)) ;
    WriteLn(LST)
  END ;
WriteLn(LST) ;
FOR I := 91 TO 96 DO
  BEGIN
    Write(LST,^I,I,': ') ;
    FOR J := 1 TO LineLen DO
      Write(LST,Chr(I)) ;
    WriteLn(LST)
  END ;
WriteLn(LST) ;
FOR I := 123 TO 126 DO
  BEGIN
    Write(LST,^I,I,': ') ;
    FOR J := 1 TO LineLen DO
      Write(LST,Chr(I)) ;
    WriteLn(LST)
  END ;
WriteLn(LST) ;
FOR I := 128 TO 254 DO
  BEGIN
    Write(LST,^I,I,': ') ;
    FOR J := 1 TO LineLen DO
      Write(LST,Chr(I)) ;
    WriteLn(LST)
  END ;
GotoXY(10,10) ; { Overwrite the START messgage with the FINISHED message. }
WriteLn(CON,'>>>>> T H E   T E S T S   A R E   F I N I S H E D <<<<<') ;
```

```
    WriteLn(LST,Chr(12)) ;                    { Send a form feed signal.  }
    WriteLn(LST,Chr(7))                       { Sound the printer's bell. }
END.      { This END matches the BEGIN at the top of the code. }
{ PrnTest2 }
```

Chapter 24

Copying
an ASCII File to a
Disk, Display, or Printer

Here is COPYIT, a short, versatile utility that enables you to make copies of a text file. You can copy the file to another file on the same disk while giving it a new name (as long as it follows the DOS naming-convention), copy the file to another disk and give the copy the same name as the original or assign it another file name, display it on the monitor's screen, or make a hard copy on your printer.

When you run COPYIT, the screen clears (you've noticed that I like to begin this way, although it isn't essential to the program's performance), and you are instructed by a message at column 5, row 5 on the monitor's screen: "Type the name of the file to be copied." You do so, and press the Enter key. The next instruction, at row 8 is: "Type the name of the file to be created." At rows 10, 11, and 12, the screen displays instructions:

`For a screen display, type CON:`

`To make a printout, type LST:`

`If you enter CON or LST, you must include the colon.`

At row 14, you see:

`Now ... type CON:, LST:, or a filename:`

176

You type your choice, which is echoed on the screen, and press the Enter key. After a 1.5 second (1500 milliseconds) delay or hold, the screen clears, and the action you entered takes place.

The EOF, End Of File, function is invoked, and while the end of the file is not sensed, the program reads the input file (Fi) a line at a time and writes it to the designated destination a line at a time. When the marker for the end of the file is read, the files are closed, the terminal's bell is sounded, and the program's run is at its end.

CODE LISTING FOR COPYIT

```
(*************************************************)
(* Name a source file, and make a copy of it    *)
(* under another name, or, if desired, send      *)
(* it to another drive, the screen, or printer. *)
(*************************************************)

PROGRAM CopyIt ;

  VAR
    InName : STRING [14] ;               { Name of the source file. }
    OutName : STRING [14] ;              { Name of the copy to be made. }
    Fi : Text ;                   { Symbol assigned to the input file. }
    Fo : Text ;                   { Symbol assigned to the output file. }
    Stuff : STRING [80] ;               { The length of "stuff" in a line. }

  BEGIN  { CopyIt }
    ClrScr ;
    LowVideo ;
    GotoXy(5,5) ;
    Write('Type the name of the file to be copied:  ') ;
    NormVideo ;
    ReadLn(InName) ;
    Assign(Fi,InName) ;
    LowVideo ;
    GotoXY(5,8) ;
    WriteLn('Type the name of the file to be created.') ;
    GotoXY(5,10) ;
    WriteLn('For a screen display, type CON:') ;
    GotoXY(5,11) ;
    WriteLn('To make a printout, type LST:') ;
    GotoXY(5,12) ;
    WriteLn('If you enter CON or LST, you must include the colon.') ;
    GotoXY(5,14) ;
    Write('Now ... type CON:, LST:, or a filename:  ') ;
    NormVideo ;
    ReadLn(OutName) ;
    Delay(1500) ;          { Hold for 1.5 seconds so the response can be seen. }
    ClrScr ;                            { Clear the screen and continue. }
```

```
      Assign(Fo,OutName) ;
      Reset(Fi) ;
      ReWrite(Fo) ;
      WHILE NOT EOF(Fi) DO          { While not at the end of the input file ... }
        BEGIN                        { Loop for reading and writing the files. }
          ReadLn(Fi,Stuff) ;            { Read a line. }
          WriteLn(Fo,Stuff)            { Copy a line. }
        END ;                          { End the loop on EOF. }
      Close(Fo) ;              { The task is finished.  Close the output file. }
      Close(Fi) ;                    { Also, close the input file.   }
      Write(Chr(7))                  { Signal that the files are closed. }
END.
{ CopyIt }
```

Chapter 25

Print it with PRINTIT

People always seem to need a utility program that allows them to make a hard copy printout of a file. If you do any programming at all, you must have such a program on hand, a program that is accurate, relatively compact, and fast running. This chapter offers two variations of a short and very effective program designed only to make printouts of ASCII text files such as the FILENAME.PAS source-code files that are created with the Turbo Pascal editor.

The files are named PRINTIT1 and PRINTIT2, but of course, you can give them other names within the naming conventions of DOS. The differences will be explored as we "walk through" a run of the compiled source code for each of the two.

A WALK THROUGH PRINTIT1

After the screen is cleared, the following instruction is displayed on the monitor's screen:

Type the name of the ASCII file you want to print:

In accordance with filename conventions, if the file you want to print is on a drive other than the one on which you have placed the executable version of PRINTIT1, you can precede the name of the file you want to print with the "other" disk drive's identifying letter and a colon. Otherwise PRINTIT1

179

expects to find the file in the directory of the same disk on which PRINTIT1 is located.

The file name you enter is assigned to the string variable called NameIt. The PRINTIT variable is assigned the value of NAMEIT, which it carries to the end of the program. If the file cannot be found, a two-line error message is displayed:

Sorry ... but I can't find the <NameIt>.

Check the name and the drive and try again.

The program is exited, and the DOS prompt is displayed. The program must be started all over again. (You will see how this "fatal error" is averted with the addition of more comprehensive error-handling code in PrintIt2.)

If the file's name is in the disk's directory, the program passes the test for an I/O error. It then goes directly to the BEGIN . . . END loop that follows the ELSE directive. A form feed is sent to the printer, and WHILE NOT at the end of the file that is being read, each line that is read is sent to LST, which is the printer.

When the program reads the end-of-file marker, the file being read, PrintIt, is closed. The printer's bell is sounded. (If your printer doesn't have a "bell," you can ignore or omit the "WriteLn (LST,Chr(7));" statement, or change LST to CON to sound the computer's bell instead of the printer's. Or enter WriteLn's for both the CON and the LST.)

Then the screen displays:

>>>>>> That's it for now! <<<<<<

A carriage return and line feed, WriteLn (LST), are sent to ensure that the printer's buffer has been emptied. The program's run and the printout have been completed.

A WALK THROUGH PRINTIT2

The PRINTIT2 version has a few additional lines of code you may find worthwhile. Note that IOerr has been declared as a VAR of the type Boolean. The {$I – } switch appears at the start of the program's operation, immediately following the ClrScr function. Error handling is now within a REPEAT . . . UNTIL loop. The effect is important.

In PRINTIT1 if an I/O error occurs, such as would be caused by the entry of an invalid or inaccessible filename, the program is exited immediately after the error message is displayed. With the I/O error-handling code of PRINTIT2, the same error message as is generated by PRINTIT1 is displayed when an I/O error occurs. The program, however, doesn't quit at that point. Instead, the program goes back to column 5, row 10, and again displays the initial request:

Type the name of the ASCII file you want to print:

This continues until one of two things happen: one, a valid filename is entered, or two, the program is deliberately aborted by entering a Ctrl-C or, under MS-DOS or PC-DOS, a Ctrl-Break.

There are two other relatively minor variations in the PRINTIT2 code and operation when compared with PRINTIT1. First, when printing begins, the program displays the message:

>>>>>> Now Printing <NameIt> <<<<<<

And second, the form feed is sent to the printer after the sign off message is displayed, instead of at the start of the actual printout. Some of you may prefer it that way.

CODE LISTING FOR PRINTIT1

```
(***********************************************)
(* PrintIt1 reads an ASCII file and prints it.  *)
(* Make sure the printer is on and ready to go. *)
(***********************************************)

PROGRAM PrintIt1 ;

  VAR
    PrintIt : Text ;
    NameIt : STRING [128] ;

  BEGIN  { PrintIt1 }
    ClrScr ;
    LowVideo ;
    GotoXY(10,10) ;                          { Display the request for a name }
    Write('Type the name of the ASCII file you want to print: ') ;
    HighVideo ;
    Read(NameIt) ;                           { Wait for the name to be typed in }
    Assign(PrintIt,NameIt) ;                 { Look for and open the file }
    {$I-}                                     { I/O Error handling switch }
    ReSet(PrintIt) ;
    {$I+}
    IF IOresult <> 0 THEN                     { If there's an error in the name ... }
      BEGIN                                  { Error Statement }
        Write(Chr(7)) ;                      { Sound the computer's bell }
        GotoXY(10,12) ;                      { Advise the user }
        WriteLn('Sorry ... but I can''t find ',Nameit,'.') ;
        GotoXY(10,14) ;
        WriteLn('Check the name and the drive and try again.') ;
      END                                    { Error Statement ... Exit the program }
    ELSE
```

```
        BEGIN                           { ELSE ... if no error, continue the program }
          WriteLn(LST,Chr(12)) ;              { Send a formfeed to the printer }
          WHILE NOT EOF(PrintIt) DO        { While we are still in the file ... }
            BEGIN                         { Read and print }
              ReadLn(PrintIt,NameIt) ;      { ... read the next line }
              WriteLn(LST,NameIt)           { ... and print the line }
            END ;                        { Read and print to End Of File }
          Close(PrintIt ) ;                { Close the file }
          WriteLn(LST,Chr(7)) ;            { Sound the printer's bell }
          GotoXY(20,16) ;
          WriteLn('>>>>>> That''s it for now! <<<<<<') ;
          WriteLn(LST)                     { Empty the buffer's contents }
        END                            { ELSE }
END.
{ PrintIt1 }
```

CODE LISTING FOR PRINTIT2

```
(*************************************************)
(* PrintIt2 reads an ASCII file and prints it.  *)
(* It differs from PrintIt1 in error checking.  *)
(* Make sure the printer is on and ready to go. *)
(*************************************************)

PROGRAM PrintIt2 ;

  VAR
    IOerr : Boolean ;
    PrintIt : Text ;
    NameIt : STRING [128] ;

  BEGIN  {PrintIt2 }
    ClrScr ;
    {$I-}             { Turn off the IO error handling.  We'll do it with code. }
    REPEAT
      LowVideo ;
      GotoXY(5,10) ;                          { Display the request for a name }
      Write('Type the name of the ASCII file you want to print: ') ;
      NormVideo ;
      Read(NameIt) ;                        { Wait for the name to be typed in }
      Assign(PrintIt,NameIt) ;              { Look for and open the file }
      ReSet(PrintIt) ;
      IOerr := (IOresult <> 0) ;
      IF IOerr THEN                         { If there's an error in the name ... }
        BEGIN
          Write(Chr(7)) ;                      { Sound the computer's bell }
          GotoXY(10,12) ;                      { Advise the user there's an error }
          WriteLn('Sorry ... but I can''t find ',Nameit,'.') ;
          GotoXY(10,14) ;
          WriteLn('Check the name and the drive and try again.') ;
```

```
            Delay(1500) ;                        { Hold for 1.5 seconds,  then ... }
            ClrScr ;
         END
      UNTIL NOT IOerr ;
      {$I+}                                       { Restore the default condition }
      BEGIN                                 { There's no error.  Continue the program }
         ClrScr ;                                 { Clear the screen of old stuff }
         GotoXY(20,10) ;                          { Advise the user, things are okay now }
         WriteLn('>>>>>> Now Printing: ',NameIt,' <<<<<<') ;
         WHILE NOT EOF(PrintIt) DO                { While we are still in the file ... }
            BEGIN                                 { Read and print }
               ReadLn(PrintIt,NameIt) ;          { ... read the next line }
               WriteLn(LST,^I,NameIt)            { ... tab in and print the line }
            END ;                                 { Read and print to End Of File }
         Close(PrintIt) ;                         { Close the file }
         GotoXY(23,12) ;
         WriteLn('>>>>>> That''s it for now! <<<<<<') ;   { Sign off message }
         WriteLn(LST,Chr(12)) ;                   { Do a final form feed }
         WriteLn(LST,Chr(7))                      { Sound the printer's bell }
      END
   END.
   { PrintIt2 }
```

Chapter 26

Elements of a Three-Part Database Program

Turbo Pascal offers a capability for creating programs for files that handle text and data effectively. The documentation supplied with Turbo Pascal provides three skeletons for segments of a usable and useful database program. In this chapter I will expand the segments and make three individual, but related, programs out of them: START, UPDATE, and LISTALL.

Each of the three segments, or programs, declares the same labels, assignments, and values in the CONST and in the TYPE blocks. If however, there is the slightest difference or an error is entered in writing the code, it will cause a problem. You will note, too, that each of the programs has only a main block and does not make calls to individual procedures.

THE START PROGRAM

The first of the three programs is appropriately named START. The value declared for the label MaxNumRecords in the CONST block provides for a maximum number of 100 individual records. Of course, the number of records can be increased or decreased merely by changing the value assigned to the CONSTant MaxNumRecords.

The TYPEs can be given labels or identifiers that best suit the application of the program. I chose to apply the same labels as those used in the example provided in the Turbo Pascal documentation, which appears to be a minimal inventory program. Obviously, with an understanding of the simple principles involved, you can create other identifiers of your own choosing. Whatever the relevance of the labels' names might be, the structure of the program remains essentially the same as that given here.

START requests the entry of the name of the data file to be operated on. After you type the name of the data file (DataFile) and press the Enter key, the program asks whether or not this is a new file, (Yes or No?). If you respond by pressing the <N> key, for No, this specific program ends and you are returned to the DOS prompt. Obviously, the START program is used only when a new file is to be named and created. If you respond <Y> for Yes, this is a new file, you are advised or alerted by the message:

If the file exists, its contents will be erased.

If you want to create a NEW file

with the same name, press <Y>.

Or, to continue without creating a

NEW data file, press any other key.

Pressing any key other than <Y> has the same effect as pressing the <N> key did in response to the very first query. The program is exited, and you are returned to the DOS prompt. If you do press the <Y> key, you are informed that the file (DataFile) is now being created.

"DataFile" is assigned the identifier "ItemFile" with a capacity of 100 records, which is the value of MaxNumRecords, as assigned in the CONST block. An examination of the DOS directory will reveal the existence of a new file identified by the name you entered in response to the initial query. When the START program ends it displays the message:

****** DONE ******

CODE LISTING FOR START

```
PROGRAM Start ;

  CONST
    MaxNumRecords = 100 ; { Assign 100 as the maximum number of records }

  TYPE
    ItemName = STRING[20] ;    { Each type can store 20 characters }
    InStk = STRING[20] ;
    Supp = STRING[20] ;
    Data = STRING[20] ;
    Item = RECORD
            Name : ItemName ;
            ItemNumber : Integer ;
```

```
          InStock : InStk ;
          Supplier : Supp ;
        END ;


VAR
   Ch : Char ;
   DataFile : Data ;
   ItemFile : FILE OF Item ;
   ItemRec : Item ;
   I : Integer ;

BEGIN                                         { Start }
   ClrScr ;
   GotoXY(1,5) ;
   LowVideo ;
   Write('Enter the name of the data file: ') ;
   HighVideo ;
   ReadLn(DataFile) ;
   WriteLn ;
   LowVideo ;
   Write('Is this a new file? (Y/N): ') ;
   HighVideo ;
   Read(Ch) ;
   IF UpCase(Ch) IN ['Y'] THEN
     BEGIN
       WriteLn ;
       WriteLn ;
       WriteLn('If the File exists, its contents willbe erased.') ;
       WriteLn ;
       WriteLn('If you want to create a NEW file') ;
       WriteLn('with the same name, press <Y>.') ;
       WriteLn ;
       WriteLn('Or, to continue without creating a') ;
       Write('NEW data file, press any other key: ') ;
       Read(Kbd,Ch) ;
   IF UpCase(Ch) IN ['Y'] THEN
     BEGIN
       WriteLn ;
       WriteLn ;
       WriteLn(DataFile,' is now being created.') ;
       WriteLn ;
       Assign(ItemFile,DataFile) ;
       ReWrite(ItemFile) ;
       WITH ItemRec DO
         BEGIN
           Name := '' ;
           FOR I := 1 TO MaxNumRecords DO
             BEGIN
               ItemNumber := I ;
               Write(ItemFile,ItemRec)
```

```
                END ;
          END ;
        Close(ItemFile)
      END ;
    WriteLn ;
    WriteLn ;
    WriteLn('      ****** DONE ******')
  END
ELSE
END.
{ Start }
```

START creates the file in which the records are stored, or if a file already exists with the same name, it is overwritten. If the file exists, overwriting it will erase, delete, or otherwise make any of the data that may have been stored in its records unretrievable. So, obviously, if the file already exists and you do not intend to change its name or erase its contents, you can skip over the START program for the moment and go directly to the second of the three programs, UPDATE.

THE UPDATE PROGRAM

UPDATE is the maintenance program. With it you can add information to a specific record and delete or overwrite the information already stored in any of the records. As in START, the maximum number of records is determined by the value assigned to MaxNumRecords in the CONST block.

Notice that the CONST and the TYPE blocks are the same in both the START and the UPDATE programs. There are, however, minor but important differences in the VAR block. The variables "Ch" has been dropped, and the variable "Counter" has been added. The program itself uses no PROCEDURE calls; it is an entity or single block.

The program instructs you to:

Enter the name of the data file to update:

After you do so and press the Enter key, the program attempts to find a data file with that name; if it fails to find the name as you entered it in the directory, this error message is displayed:

I can't find that file!

The program then ends, and the DOS prompt is displayed. On the other hand, if the data file you named does exist, the program jumps to ELSE and instructs you to:

Enter the record number (0 = Stop):

At this point in the program, the program seeks the record number, finds it, and begins to display the four ReadLn statements to which you must respond with the appropriate data. After you have entered your response to the fourth query (which, in this case, is the supplier's ID) and pressed the Enter key, the screen instantly clears and you are instructed again to "Enter the record number." You can repeat the procedure as often as you wish, and type the number zero when you want to quit.

When you do type a zero, the file you have been working with is closed and the program is exited.

CODE LISTING FOR UPDATE

```
PROGRAM UpDate ;

  CONST
    MaxNumRecords = 100 ;

  TYPE
    ItemName = STRING[20] ;
    InStk = STRING[20] ;
    Supp = STRING[20] ;
    Data = STRING[20] ;
    Item = RECORD
               Name : ItemName ;
               ItemNumber : Integer ;
               InStock : InStk ;
               Supplier : Supp ;
           END ;

  VAR
    DataFile : Data ;
    ItemFile : FILE OF Item ;
    ItemRec : Item ;
    I,Counter : Integer ;

  BEGIN
    ClrScr ;
    GotoXY(1,5) ;
    WriteLn('---------------------- UPDATE ---------------------------') ;
    WriteLn ;
    LowVideo ;
    Write('Enter the name of the data file to update: ') ;
    HighVideo ;
    Read(DataFile) ;
    Assign(ItemFile,DataFile) ;
    {$I-}
    ReSet(ItemFile) ;
    {$I+}
    IF IOresult <> 0 THEN
```

```
      BEGIN
        WriteLn ;
        WriteLn ;
        WriteLn('I can''t find that file!')
      END
    ELSE
      BEGIN
        WriteLn ;
        WriteLn ;
        LowVideo ;
        Write('Enter the record number (0 = Stop): ') ;
        HighVideo ;
        ReadLn(Counter) ;
        WHILE Counter IN [1..MaxNumRecords] DO
          BEGIN
            Seek(ItemFile,Counter - 1) ;
            Read(ItemFile,ItemRec) ;
            WITH ItemRec DO
              BEGIN
                LowVideo ;
                Write('Enter the item''s name:  ') ;
                HighVideo ;
                ReadLn(Name) ;
                LowVideo ;
                Write('Enter the qty in stock:  ') ;
                HighVideo ;
                ReadLn(InStock) ;
                LowVideo ;
                Write('Enter the supplier''s ID:  ') ;
                HighVideo ;
                ReadLn(Supplier) ;
                ItemNumber := Counter ;
              END ;
            Seek(ItemFile,Counter - 1) ;
            Write(ItemFile,ItemRec) ;
            ClrScr ;
            WriteLn ;
            LowVideo ;
            Write('Enter the item number (0 = Stop): ') ;
            HighVideo ;
            ReadLn(Counter) ;
          END ;
      END ;
    Close(ItemFile)
  END.
{ UpDate }
```

THE LISTALL PROGRAM

Now that you have created a data file and entered data, you must have a way to retrieve that data. This is the purpose of the program LISTALL. As with the other two programs in this set of three, the labels and the values of the CONST and the TYPE blocks are retained. The contents of the VAR block are the same as those of the START program.

LISTALL instructs you to:

Enter the name of the data file to list:

If the file's name doesn't exist, the error message "I can't find that file" is displayed, and the program is exited. If the file's name is correct and does exist as you entered it, the program asks:

Printout or Screen? (S or P):

If you should type any character other than <P> or <S>, the query will be repeated UNTIL you enter one of the two characters. <S> causes a rapid retrieval and display of all the records in the file. <P> does the same rapid retrieval, but sends the information to the display (defaults to CON) and to LST, the printer, which should be on and ready. If the printer is not on or ready, the record appears only at CON, the video display, and the program appears to lock up at the keyboard. The moment the printer is turned on, connected, and ready, however, the printout is made. The program then continues, closes the data file, and displays the message:

****** DONE ******

CODE LISTING FOR LISTALL

```
PROGRAM ListAll ;

  CONST
    MaxNumRecords = 100 ;

  TYPE
    Data = STRING[20] ;
    ItemName = STRING[20] ;
    InStk = STRING[20] ;
    Supp = STRING[20] ;
    Item = RECORD
             Name : ItemName ;
             ItemNumber : Integer ;
             InStock : InStk ;
             Supplier : Supp ;
           END ;

  VAR
    DataFile : Data ;
    Ch : Char ;
```

```pascal
    ItemFile : FILE OF Item ;
    ItemRec : Item ;
    I : Integer ;


BEGIN
  ClrScr ;
  GotoXY(1,5) ;
  WriteLn('--------------- DISPLAY & PRINT --------------------') ;
  WriteLn ;
  LowVideo ;
  Write('Enter the name of the data file to list: ') ;
  HighVideo ;
  Read(DataFile) ;
  WriteLn ;
  Assign(ItemFile,DataFile) ;
  {$I-}
  ReSet(ItemFile) ;
  {$I+}
  IF IOresult <> 0 THEN
    BEGIN
      WriteLn ;
      WriteLn ;
      WriteLn('I can''t find that file!')
    END
  ELSE
    BEGIN
      REPEAT
        WriteLn ;
        LowVideo ;
        Write('Printout or Screen? (S or P): ') ;
        HighVideo ;
        ReadLn(Ch) ;
      UNTIL UpCase(Ch) IN ['S','P'] ;
      FOR I := 1 TO MaxNumRecords DO
        BEGIN
          Read(ItemFile,ItemRec) ;
          WITH ItemRec DO
            BEGIN
              IF Name <> '' THEN
                BEGIN
                  WriteLn ;
                  WriteLn(' * Item #:      ',ItemNumber:20,' ') ;
                  WriteLn(' * Item Name: ',Name:20) ;
                  WriteLn(' * In stock:   ',InStock:20) ;
                  WriteLn(' * Supplier:   ',Supplier:20) ;
                  WriteLn ;
                END ;
              IF UpCase(Ch) IN ['P'] THEN
                BEGIN
                  IF Name <> '' THEN
```

```
                BEGIN
                  WriteLn(LST) ;
                  WriteLn(LST,' # Item #: ',ItemNumber:5,' ') ;
                  WriteLn(LST,' # Item Name: ',Name:20) ;
                  WriteLn(LST,' # In stock: ',InStock:20) ;
                  WriteLn(LST,' # Supplier: ',Supplier:20) ;
                  WriteLn(LST)
                END ;
              END ;
            END ;
          END ;
      Close(ItemFile) ;
      WriteLn ;
      WriteLn('       ****** DONE ******') ;
    END
END.
{ ListAll }
```

Chapter 27

A Database
Program with Enhanced
I/O Error Handling

This chapter is based on the lessons learned from Chapter 26. Therefore, it follows naturally, that it would be valuable to read Chapter 26 first. The three separate programs presented in Chapter 26, START, UPDATE, and LISTALL, are converted to procedures, thereby integrating them into a single program.

The procedures are called from the main block of a new program now named DATAFILE. This program contains more comprehensive I/O error handling than the error handling in the code listings for START, UPDATE, and LISTALL in Chapter 26. Although there are important improvements in I/O error handling, the differences in operation between the two approaches are essentially transparent to the user—until a human error or a typo is made, or an incorrect data file name is introduced.

As you look at the listings, note that the labels, the assignments, and the values are the same in the CONST and the TYPE blocks. The VAR block has been expanded to include all the variables that are used in START, UP-DATE, and LISTALL, plus a new declaration, which declares the variable "IOerr" to be of the type Boolean.

The program begins with a REPEAT . . . UNTIL loop that repeats the sequential calls to the Procedures and built-in Functions until you deliberately enter the character <Q> to quit the program. Start is the first procedure called. Except for the fact it cannot stand alone, Procedure Start is identical in content to Program START.

The completion of Procedure Start is delayed for one second before the call is made to Procedure Update. The only purpose for the delay is to display the contents of the screen for the length of the delay. If this delay were to be omitted, the completed display of data would go by so fast as to be virtually invisible. The use of this delay is not essential to the operation of the program. It was included as an embellishment of the visual presentation, and therefore, can be eliminated without having any apparent effect on the program's ability to store and retrieve information. On the other hand, if the one-second delay appears to be too short, it can be extended by increasing the Delay value of 1000, which is the length of the delay in milliseconds.

The Procedure UpDate is significantly different from the Program UPDATE. The Procedure UpDate asks for the same entries as does the Program UPDATE; however, note that a REPEAT . . . UNTIL segment encloses the first statement in which the name of the data file is requested, and the error message (if appropriate) is signaled. The difference is apparent in the program's operation. Whereas an I/O error in the Program UPDATE would, in effect, cause the program to abort, making it necessary to restart the Program UPDATE, the error handling method in the Procedure UpDate prevents such an abort, or as it is woefully but popularly called by programmers, a "fatal error."

Thus, in case of an I/O error, such as one caused by a typo or the entering of a nonexistent or misspelled filename, the REPEAT . . . UNTIL segment of code returns the program to the Write statement that immediately follows the REPEAT instruction. If you do not succeed in identifying the name of an appropriate data file, you can deliberately and gracefully exit the DataFile program by following the instruction to:

Press <Q> to Quit, or any other key to continue:

If the name of the data file you have entered passes the test made inside the REPEAT . . . UNTIL segment, the program continues with code that is identical with the section of code following the ELSE clause listed in the Program UPDATE. When you have finished updating, you press <0> instead of a record number. The Procedure UpDate is exited, and the Procedure ListAll is called.

As with the Procedure UpDate, a REPEAT . . . UNTIL segment encloses the I/O error handling and error message statements. In this way, as before, a fatal error is eliminated, and the program persistently repeats the instructions until you make a valid response or deliberately press <Q> to quite. If you do press <Q>, the HALT statement gracefully brings you out of the DataFile program and returns you to the DOS prompt. The options to display or print the contents of the data file are the same in both the procedure and the program.

When you successfully complete and deliberately exit the REPEAT . . . UNTIL segment of code given at the end of the main block of code, the data file you have been working with is closed, and a final message tells you:

****** ALL DONE ******

CODE LISTING FOR DATAFILE

```
(* DataFile converts three separate procedures *)
(*        Start, UpDate, and ListAll            *)
(* into a single integrated database manager.  *)

PROGRAM DataFile ;

   CONST
      MaxNumRecords = 100 ;           { The max of 100 records can be changed here. }

   TYPE
      ItemName = STRING[20] ;
      InStk = STRING[20] ;
      Supp = STRING[20] ;
      Data = STRING[20] ;
      Item = RECORD
                 Name : ItemName ;
                 RecordNumber : Integer ;
                 InStock : InStk ;
                 Supplier : Supp ;
             END ;

   VAR
      Ch : Char ;
      DataFile : Data ;
      ItemFile : FILE OF Item ;
      ItemRec : Item ;
      I,Counter : Integer ;
      IOerr : Boolean ;

   PROCEDURE Start ;

      BEGIN  { Start }
        ClrScr ;
        { Position the opening message on the screen at column 1, row 5. }
        GotoXY(1,5) ;
        WriteLn('------------------ START --------------------') ;
        WriteLn ;
        LowVideo ;
        Write('Enter the name of the data file: ') ;
        HighVideo ;
        ReadLn(DataFile) ;
        WriteLn ;
        LowVideo ;
        Write('Is this a new file?  Y)es or N)o: ') ;
        HighVideo ;
        Read(Ch) ;
   IF UpCase(Ch) IN ['Y'] THEN                  { Accept upper or lower case <Y>. }
```

```
      BEGIN                              { If (Ch) is a <Y>, begin this part. }
        WriteLn ;
        WriteLn ;                               { Read carefully. }
        WriteLn('If the file exists, its contents will be erased.') ;
        WriteLn ;
        WriteLn('If you want to create a new file') ;
        WriteLn('with the same name, press the <Y> key: ') ;
        WriteLn ;
        WriteLn('To continue without creating a') ;
        Write('new data file, press any other key.') ;
        Read(Kbd,Ch) ;
        IF UpCase(Ch) IN ['Y'] THEN          { Accept upper or lower case <Y>. }
          BEGIN                          { If (Ch) is a <Y>, begin this part. }
            WriteLn ;
            WriteLn ;
            WriteLn(DataFile,' is now being created.') ;
            WriteLn ;
            Assign(ItemFile,DataFile) ;
            ReWrite(ItemFile) ;        { Open the file. Delete any data in it. }
            WITH ItemRec DO
              BEGIN                          { Reserve space for the data. }
                NAME := '' ;
                FOR I := 1 TO MaxNumRecords DO
                  BEGIN
                    RecordNumber := I ;
                    Write(ItemFile,ItemRec)
                  END ;
              END ;
          END ;
        WriteLn ;
        Close(ItemFile) ;                     { Close the file. }
        WriteLn ;
        WriteLn('     ****** DONE ******') ;
      END
    ELSE
  END ;
{ Start }


PROCEDURE UpDate ;

  BEGIN  { UpDate }
    ClrScr ;
    GotoXY(1,5) ;
    WriteLn('-------------------- UPDATE ----------------------') ;
    {$I-}                     { Turn off automatic abort in case of I/O error. }
    REPEAT
      WriteLn ;
      LowVideo ;
      Write('Enter the name of the data file to update: ') ;
      HighVideo ;
```

196

```
      Read(DataFile) ;
      Assign(ItemFile,DataFile) ;
      ReSet(ItemFile) ;
      IOerr := (IOresult <> 0) ;              { Assign a True value to IOerr. }
      IF IOerr THEN
        { IF IOerr is True ... display a message. }
        BEGIN
          WriteLn ;
          WriteLn ;
          WriteLn('I can''t find that file!') ;
          WriteLn ;
          Write('Press <Q> to Quit, or any other key to continue: ') ;
          Read(Kbd,Ch) ;
          WriteLn ;
          IF UpCase(Ch) IN ['Q'] THEN
            HALT
        END ;
UNTIL NOT IOerr ;
{$I+}
{ Continue if there's no error in the data file's name. }
BEGIN
  WriteLn ;
  WriteLn ;
  LowVideo ;
  Write('Enter the record number (0 = Stop): ') ;
  HighVideo ;
  ReadLn(Counter) ;
  WHILE Counter IN [1..MaxNumRecords] DO
    { While the count is >= 1 and <= 100 ... }
    BEGIN
      Seek(ItemFile,Counter - 1) ;
      Read(ItemFile,ItemRec) ;
      WITH ItemRec DO
        BEGIN                          { Collect data for the file's records. }
          LowVideo ;
          Write('Enter the item''s name:  ') ;
          HighVideo ;
          ReadLn(Name) ;
          LowVideo ;
          Write('Enter the qty in stock:  ') ;
          HighVideo ;
          ReadLn(InStock) ;
          LowVideo ;
          Write('Enter the supplier''s ID:  ') ;
          HighVideo ;
          ReadLn(Supplier) ;
          RecordNumber := Counter ;
        END ;
      Seek(ItemFile,Counter - 1) ;
      Write(ItemFile,ItemRec) ;
      ClrScr ;
```

```
        GotoXY(1,7) ;
        WriteLn ;
        LowVideo ;
        { Press <0> to quit the data collection. }
        Write('Enter the item number (0 = Quit): ') ;
        HighVideo ;
        ReadLn(Counter) ;
      END ;
    END ;
    Close(ItemFile)
  END ;
{ UpDate }

PROCEDURE Listall ;

  BEGIN  { ListAll }
    ClrScr ;
    GotoXY(1,5) ;
    WriteLn('--------------- DISPLAY & PRINT --------------------') ;
    WriteLn ;
    {$I-}                          { See ... Procedure UpDate ... for comments. }
    REPEAT
      WriteLn ;
      LowVideo ;
      Write('Enter the name of the data file to list: ') ;
      HighVideo ;
      Read(DataFile) ;
      Assign(ItemFile,DataFile) ;
      ReSet(ItemFile) ;
      IOerr := (IOresult <> 0) ;
      IF IOerr THEN
        BEGIN
          WriteLn ;
          WriteLn ;
          WriteLn('I can''t find that file!') ;
          WriteLn ;
          Write('Press <Q> to Quit, or any other key to continue: ') ;
          Read(Kbd,Ch) ;
          WriteLn ;
          IF UpCase(Ch) IN ['Q'] THEN
            HALT
        END ;
    UNTIL NOT IOerr ;
    {$I+}
    { Continue if there's no error in the datafile's name. }
    BEGIN
      REPEAT
        WriteLn ;
        LowVideo ;
        Write('Printout or Screen? (S or P): ') ;
        HighVideo ;
```

198

```
            ReadLn(Ch) ;
        UNTIL UpCase(Ch) IN ['S','P'] ;          { Accept only <S> or <P>. }
        FOR I := 1 TO MaxNumRecords DO
          BEGIN
            Read(ItemFile,ItemRec) ;
            WITH ItemRec DO
              BEGIN
                IF Name <> '' THEN
                  { If the record has a name entered... }
                  BEGIN
                    { Send the record to the video display. }
                    WriteLn ;
                    WriteLn(' * Record Number: ',RecordNumber:3,' ') ;
                    WriteLn(' * Item Name: ',Name:20) ;
                    WriteLn(' * In stock:  ',InStock:20) ;
                    WriteLn(' * Supplier:  ',Supplier:20) ;
                    WriteLn ;
                  END ;
                IF UpCase(Ch) IN ['P'] THEN
                  { If the printer has been selected... }
                  BEGIN
                    { And if the record has a name entered... }
                    IF Name <> '' THEN
                      BEGIN
                        { Send the record to the printer. }
                        WriteLn(LST) ;
                        WriteLn(LST,' * Record Number: ',RecordNumber:3,' ') ;
                        WriteLn(LST,' * Item Name: ',Name:20) ;
                        WriteLn(LST,' * In stock: ',InStock:20) ;
                        WriteLn(LST,' * Supplier: ',Supplier:20) ;
                        WriteLn(LST)
                      END ;
                  END ;
              END ;
          END ;
        Close(ItemFile) ;                        { Close the file that was opened. }
        WriteLn ;
        WriteLn('        ****** DONE ******') ;
      END
  END ;
{ ListAll }

BEGIN  { main block of DataFile }
  REPEAT
    Start ;                                { Call the Procedure. }
    Delay(1000) ;          { Delay 1-second to display the  "done" message. }
    UpDate ;                               { Call the Procedure. }
    Delay(1000) ;          { Delay 1-second to display the  "done" message. }
    ListAll ;                              { Call the Procedure. }
    WriteLn ;
    { Offer an option at the end of the last procedure. }
```

199

```
        WriteLn('Press <Q> to Quit.  Any other key to continue: ') ;
        Read(Kbd,Ch) ;
        { Keep the program going until <Q> is pressed in response. }
    UNTIL UpCase(Ch) IN ['Q'] ;
    WriteLn ;
    WriteLn ;
    WriteLn ;
    WriteLn('      ****** ALL DONE ******') ;  { That's it. }
    Close(ItemFile) ;                          { Close the file. }
    WriteLn(Chr(7))                            { Ring the terminal's bell. }
END.
{ This is the "real" END of the DataFile program }
```

Chapter 28

Further Enhancements to the Database Manager

A database manager program provides many opportunities for customization, practice with writing code, and/or play. I combine all three in this version of the DATAFILE program presented in Chapter 27. The name I chose is DATAFIL1; however, you can rename it to suit your own preferences, of course. I will point out the most significant differences in code between DATAFILE and DATAFIL1. The listing of the code for DATAFIL1 is given at the end of this chapter.

How have I "customized" the program? The START, UPDATE, and LISTALL programs in Chapter 26, and the conversions to procedures in the DATAFILE program in Chapter 27 concerned themselves with a very limited number of fields for a pseudo-inventory program. DATAFIL1 has more general applications in that it is a file of records of names, street addresses, cities, states, zip codes, and phone numbers. True, some of us prefer to use our pocket or briefcase-size directories; however, the point of this chapter's exercise is to present you with the "fleshed-out skeleton" of a database program whose personal usefulness as an application program depends on your own ingenuity in modifying the code.

THE DATAFIL1 PROGRAM

The DATAFIL1 program creates, updates, and lists up to 100 records (this number can be changed) in a data file to which you assign an unambiguous name. The listing can be sent to the screen or to the screen and to the printer simultaneously.

The primary operational limitation in the DATAFILE program is that you must always go sequentially through the three procedures, even if you merely want to update a file or list the contents of a data file. DATAFIL1 overcomes that limitation by presenting a menu in the first procedure, Start, from which you can choose <C> to create a new data file of records, <U> to update an existing file or any of its records, <L> to list the records in an existing data file, or <Q> to quit the program and return to DOS without operating on a data file.

The maximum number of records is, as before, declared as a constant with the value of 100 and can be changed to suit your needs. The TYPE declarations have been significantly changed to establish an array of strings of varying length, each with a name for a field that closely resembles the nature of the string. Lengths are also assigned to each of the strings. These lengths can be changed to fit specific types of strings. For example, I assigned a length of 25 characters to the string for the field identified as PersonName, while I assigned a length of 2 to the string for St, the state, and 5 to the string for Z, the ZIP code, and 14 to the string for Ph, the phone number.

The labels assigned in the TYPE block are made part of the array Item. They are assigned plain English names, which they carry throughout the program. The names and the assignments in the VAR block are the same as in the DATAFILE program.

Note that PROCEDURE ListAll and PROCEDURE UpDate must be declared at the start of the program as "Forward." This is because both are called from within the first procedure, Start. The Procedure Start is called from the main block of code (at the end of the code's listing). It clears the screen and presents the menu with four choices: <C> to create a new data file, <U> to update an existing file, <L> to list an existing data file, and <Q> to quit the program immediately.

The response is read from the keyboard, assigned to the character (Ch), and tested by a series of IF . . . THEN statements. If the character read at the keyboard passes the tests (that is, if it has been assigned the value of one of the four allowable characters), appropriate action is taken as designated by the BEGIN . . . END groups that follow each IF . . . THEN statement.

If <U> is the response, Procedure UpDate is called and the action then is very much the same as in the DATAFILE program, complete with I/O error handling. "L" calls the Procedure ListAll. "C," of course, falls through each of the IF . . . THEN tests, keeps the program in the Procedure UpDate, and activates the "WriteLn ('Enter the name of the data file:')" statement. "Q" brings the program to Turbo Pascal's built-in Halt function, which ends the program and returns you to the DOS prompt. Data files are opened and closed within each of the procedures. Note the brevity of the main BEGIN . . . END block. It's purpose, under the rules of Pascal, is to get the whole thing started.

CODE LISTING FOR DATAFIL1

```
(* DataFil1 converts and embellishes the three      *)
(* separate procedures: Start, UpDate, and ListAll *)
```

```
(* into a single integrated database manager.        *)

PROGRAM DataFil1 ;

  CONST
    MaxNumRecords = 100 ;           { The max of 100 records can be changed here. }

  TYPE
    PersonName = STRING[25] ;
    Addr = STRING[25] ;
    Cit = STRING[20] ;
    St = STRING[2] ;
    Z = STRING[5] ;
    Ph = STRING[14] ;
    Data = STRING[128] ;
    Item = RECORD
              RecordNumber : Integer ;
              Name : PersonName ;
              Address : Addr ;
              City : Cit ;
              State : St ;
              ZIP : Z ;
              Phone : Ph ;
           END ;

  VAR
    Ch : Char ;
    DataFile : Data ;
    ItemFile : FILE OF Item ;
    ItemRec : Item ;
    I,Counter : Integer ;
    IOerr : Boolean ;

  PROCEDURE ListAll ;
    FORWARD ;

  PROCEDURE UpDate ;
    FORWARD ;

  PROCEDURE Start ;

    BEGIN  { Start }
      REPEAT
        ClrScr ;
        { Position the opening message on the screen at column 1, row 5. }
        GotoXY(1,5) ;
        WriteLn('------------------- START -------------------') ;
        WriteLn ;
        LowVideo ;
        WriteLn('Enter <C> to Create a new data file.') ;
        WriteLn('Enter <U> to UpDate an existing data file.') ;
```

```
WriteLn('Enter <L> to List an existing data file.') ;
Write('Enter <Q> to Quit this program now: ') ;
HighVideo ;
Read(Ch) ;
IF UpCase(Ch) IN ['U'] THEN
  BEGIN
    UpDate ;
    ListAll
  END ;
IF UpCase(Ch) IN ['L'] THEN
  BEGIN
    ListAll ;
    Halt
  END ;
IF UpCase(Ch) IN ['Q'] THEN
  BEGIN
    Halt
  END ;
WriteLn ;
WriteLn ;
LowVideo ;
Write('Enter the name of the data file: ') ;
HighVideo ;
ReadLn(DataFile) ;
WriteLn ;
LowVideo ;
Write('Is this a new file?  Y)es or N)o: ') ;
HighVideo ;
Read(Ch) ;
IF UpCase(Ch) IN ['Y'] THEN          { Accept upper or lower case <Y>. }
  BEGIN                              { If (Ch) is a <Y>, begin this part. }
    WriteLn ;
    WriteLn ;                        { Read carefully. }
    WriteLn('If the file exists, its contents will be erased.') ;
    WriteLn ;
    WriteLn('If you want to create a new file') ;
    WriteLn('with the same name, press the <Y> key: ') ;
    WriteLn ;
    WriteLn('To continue without creating a') ;
    Write('new data file, press any other key.') ;
    Read(Kbd,Ch) ;
    IF UpCase(Ch) IN ['Y'] THEN       { Accept upper or lower case <Y>. }
      BEGIN                           { If (Ch) is a <Y>, begin this part. }
        WriteLn ;
        WriteLn ;
        WriteLn(DataFile,' is now being created.') ;
        WriteLn ;
        Assign(ItemFile,DataFile) ;
        ReWrite(ItemFile) ;    { Open the file. Delete any data in it. }
        WITH ItemRec DO
          BEGIN                       { Reserve space for the data. }
```

```
                    NAME := '' ;
                    FOR I := 1 TO MaxNumRecords DO
                      BEGIN
                        RecordNumber := I ;
                        Write(ItemFile,ItemRec)
                      END
                END
            END ;
          WriteLn ;
          Close(ItemFile) ;              { Close the file. }
          WriteLn ;
          WriteLn('     ****** DONE ******')
        END ;
    UNTIL UpCase(Ch) IN ['Q'] ;
    IF UpCase(Ch) IN ['Q'] THEN
      HALT
  END ;
{ Start }


PROCEDURE UpDate ;

  BEGIN   { UpDate }
    ClrScr ;
    GotoXY(1,5) ;
    WriteLn('-------------------- UPDATE --------------------') ;
    {$I-}                       { Turn off automatic abort in case of I/O error. }
    REPEAT
      WriteLn ;
      LowVideo ;
      Write('Enter the name of a data file to update: ') ;
      HighVideo ;
      Read(DataFile) ;
      Assign(ItemFile,DataFile) ;
      ReSet(ItemFile) ;
      IOerr := (IOresult <> 0) ;          { Assign a True value to IOerr. }
      IF IOerr THEN
        { IF IOerr is True ... display a message. }
        BEGIN
          WriteLn ;
          WriteLn ;
          WriteLn('I can''t find that file!') ;
          WriteLn ;
          Write('Press <Q> to Quit, or any other key to continue: ') ;
          Read(Kbd,Ch) ;
          WriteLn ;
          IF UpCase(Ch) IN ['Q'] THEN
            HALT
        END ;
    UNTIL NOT IOerr ;
    {$I+}
    { Continue if there's no error in the data file's name. }
```

```
BEGIN
  WriteLn ;
  WriteLn ;
  LowVideo ;
  Write('Enter the record number (0 = Stop): ') ;
  HighVideo ;
  ReadLn(Counter) ;
  WHILE Counter IN [1..MaxNumRecords] DO
    { While the count is >= 1 and <= 100 ... }
    BEGIN
      Seek(ItemFile,Counter - 1) ;
      Read(ItemFile,ItemRec) ;
      WITH ItemRec DO
        BEGIN                          { Collect data for the file's records. }
          WriteLn ;
          LowVideo ;
          Write('Enter the person''s name:  ') ;
          HighVideo ;
          ReadLn(Name) ;
          LowVideo ;
          Write('Address:      ') ;
          HighVideo ;
          ReadLn(Address) ;
          LowVideo ;
          Write('City:        ') ;
          HighVideo ;
          ReadLn(City) ;
          LowVideo ;
          Write('State:        ') ;
          HighVideo ;
          ReadLn(State) ;
          LowVideo ;
          Write('ZIP number:   ') ;
          HighVideo ;
          ReadLn(ZIP) ;
          LowVideo ;
          Write('Phone number: ') ;
          HighVideo ;
          ReadLn(Phone) ;
          RecordNumber := Counter ;
        END ;
      Seek(ItemFile,Counter - 1) ;
      Write(ItemFile,ItemRec) ;
      ClrScr ;
      GotoXY(1,7) ;
      WriteLn ;
      LowVideo ;
      { Press <0> to quit the data collection. }
      Write('Enter the item number (0 = Quit): ') ;
      HighVideo ;
      ReadLn(Counter) ;
```

```
            END ;
        END ;
        Close(ItemFile) ;
        Delay(1000)
    END ;
{ UpDate }


PROCEDURE Listall ;

  BEGIN  { ListAll }
    ClrScr ;
    GotoXY(1,5) ;
    WriteLn('--------------- DISPLAY & PRINT -------------------') ;
    WriteLn ;
    {$I-}                        { See ... Procedure UpDate ... for comments. }
    REPEAT
      WriteLn ;
      LowVideo ;
      Write('Enter the name of the data file to list: ') ;
      HighVideo ;
      Read(DataFile) ;
      Assign(ItemFile,DataFile) ;
      ReSet(ItemFile) ;
      IOerr := (IOresult <> 0) ;
      IF IOerr THEN
        BEGIN
          WriteLn ;
          WriteLn ;
          WriteLn('I can''t find that file!') ;
          WriteLn ;
          Write('Press <Q> to Quit, or any other key to continue: ') ;
          Read(Kbd,Ch) ;
          WriteLn ;
          IF UpCase(Ch) IN ['Q'] THEN
            HALT
        END ;
    UNTIL NOT IOerr ;
    {$I+}
    { Continue if there's no error in the datafile's name. }
    BEGIN
      REPEAT
        WriteLn ;
        WriteLn ;
        LowVideo ;
        Write('Printout or Screen? (S or P): ') ;
        HighVideo ;
        ReadLn(Ch) ;
    UNTIL UpCase(Ch) IN ['S','P'] ;        { Accept only <S> or <P>. }
    FOR I := 1 TO MaxNumRecords DO
      BEGIN
```

```pascal
            Read(ItemFile,ItemRec) ;
            WITH ItemRec DO
              BEGIN
                IF Name <> '' THEN
                  { If the record has a name entered... }
                  BEGIN
                    { Send the record to the video display. }
                    WriteLn ;
                    WriteLn(' * Record Number:  ',RecordNumber:3,' ') ;
                    WriteLn('     ------------------------------------------') ;
                    WriteLn(' * Person''s Name:   ',Name:25) ;
                    WriteLn(' * Address:         ',Address:25) ;
                    WriteLn(' * City:            ',City:20) ;
                    WriteLn(' * State:           ',State:2) ;
                    WriteLn(' * ZIP:             ',ZIP:5) ;
                    WriteLn(' * Phone Number:    ',Phone:14) ;
                    WriteLn ;
                  END ;
                IF UpCase(Ch) IN ['P'] THEN
                  { If the printer has been selected... }
                  BEGIN
                    { And if the record has a name entered... }
                    IF Name <> '' THEN
                      BEGIN
                        { Send the record to the printer. }
                        WriteLn(LST) ;
                        WriteLn(LST,' * Record Number:  ',RecordNumber:3,' ') ;
                        WriteLn(LST,
                                '     ------------------------------------------')
                            ;
                        WriteLn(LST,' * Person''s Name:   ',Name:25) ;
                        WriteLn(LST,' * Address:         ',Address:25) ;
                        WriteLn(LST,' * City:            ',City:20) ;
                        WriteLn(LST,' * State:           ',State:2) ;
                        WriteLn(LST,' * ZIP:             ',ZIP:5) ;
                        WriteLn(LST,' * Phone Number:    ',Phone:14) ;
                        WriteLn(LST)
                      END ;
                  END ;
              END ;
          END ;
        Close(ItemFile) ;                       { Close the file that was opened. }
        WriteLn ;
        WriteLn('        ****** DONE ******') ;
      END ;
      Halt
    END ;
  { ListAll }

BEGIN  { main block of DataFil1 }
```

208

```
   Start ;                                    { Call the Procedure. }
   WriteLn(Chr(7))                            { Ring the terminal's bell. }
END.
{ This is the "real" END of the DataFil1 program }
```

Appendices

Turbo-87 and TurboBCD Pascal

The interest in Turbo Pascal as a language/compiler for serious applications programs is growing rapidly. To enhance the desirability and utility of its extraordinary compiler, Borland International introduced two additional versions of its compiler: 1) Turbo-87, which supports the Intel 8087 microprocessor and gains a significant increase in the speed of calculations using real number arithmetic, and 2) TurboBCD, which uses binary coded decimal (BCD) real numbers to obtain higher accuracy.

Turbo-87 is ideally suited as a compiler for Turbo Pascal code that involves complex multistep computations such as those often required for calculating lengthy and sophisticated engineering and scientific data. TurboBCD has special features that make it very well suited to business applications programs.

Turbo-87 compiles Turbo Pascal code and provides support for the 8087 math coprocessor. The distinctions are in real number processing and formatting. Programs compiled with Turbo-87 will not run on a computer that does not have the 8087 chip installed. Programs processed with the Turbo Pascal compiler, however, will run on a computer with or without the 8087 chip. The 8087 supports the long-real data type. This delivers an accuracy of 16 digits within the range of 4.19E-307 to 1.67E+308.

TurboBCD compiles code written in Turbo Pascal. As with Turbo-87, the distinctions are in real number processing and formatting, and the omission of several built-in functions: sin, cos, arctan, ln, exp, sqrt, and pi. BCD reals in TurboBCD have a range of 1E-63 through 1E+63 with an 18-digit precision. Although not included in the code for the programs in this book, TurboBCD offers a special formatting function, Form, that can be of interest to those writing business programs in Turbo Pascal.

Fundamentally, the Form function is to Turbo Pascal what the PRINT USING statement is to BASIC. It provides a means for specifying the formats for numeric and string fields so that data is sent to a program's output (either to a monitor or a printer) in a style best suited to the appearance of business documents.

As an example, here is the code for BCDsampl, a program that demonstrates some of the capabilities of TurboBCD in formatting numeric and string fields.

CODE LISTING FOR BCDSAMPL

```
(* Demonstration of TURBO-BCD formatting. *)

PROGRAM BCDsampl ;

  VAR
    Ch : Char ;
    Number1 : Real ;
    Number2 : Real ;
    Number3 : Real ;

  BEGIN
    ClrScr ;
    LowVideo ;
    Write('Enter a real number:  ') ;
    HighVideo ;
    ReadLn(Number1) ;
    WriteLn ;
    LowVideo ;
    Write('You entered (displayed before formatting): ') ;
    HighVideo ;
    WriteLn(Number1) ;
    WriteLn ;
    LowVideo ;
    WriteLn('         TURBO-BCD can reformat the number.') ;
    WriteLn ;
    WriteLn('         It can right justify, fill with asterisks, ') ;
    WriteLn('         align the decimal points, add dollar signs, ') ;
    WriteLn('         and, where necessary, insert commas before ') ;
    WriteLn('         every third digit.') ;
    Delay(3000) ;
    WriteLn ;
    HighVideo ;
    WriteLn(Form('*$##,###,###.##',Number1)) ;
    WriteLn ;
    LowVideo ;
```

```
      WriteLn('Try another number as large as 999,999,999.99') ;
      Write('(Don''t bother to enter the $-sign or the commas.): ') ;
      HighVideo ;
      ReadLn(Number2) ;
      HighVideo ;
      WriteLn ;
      WriteLn(Form('*$##,###,###.##',Number2)) ;
      LowVideo ;
      WriteLn ;
      Write('And another, please: ') ;
      HighVideo ;
      ReadLn(Number3) ;
      WriteLn ;
      WriteLn(Form('*$##,###,###.##',Number3)) ;
      WriteLn ;
      WriteLn ;
      WriteLn('Press any key to display all three numbers ...') ;
      Read(Kbd,Ch) ;
      ClrScr ;
      GotoXY(10,5) ;
      WriteLn(Form('*$##,###,###.##',Number1)) ;
      GotoXY(10,6) ;
      WriteLn(Form('*$##,###,###.##',Number2)) ;
      GotoXY(10,7) ;
      WriteLn(Form('*$##,###,###.##',Number3)) ;
      GotoXY(10,9) ;
      LowVideo ;
      WriteLn('Note the decimal points are aligned one above the other.') ;
      GotoXY(1,12) ;
      HighVideo ;
      WriteLn(Form('@#######################','String fields')) ;
      WriteLn(Form('@#######################','can be')) ;
      WriteLn(Form('@#######################','right-justified.')) ;
      GotoXY(1,17) ;
      LowVideo ;
      Write('Complete instructions are in Chapter 23 ') ;
      WriteLn('of the TURBO Pascal documentation. ') ;
      GotoXY(1,19) ;
      HighVideo ;
      WriteLn(Form('@#######################','Thanks for reading.')) ;
      GotoXY(1,21) ;
      Write(Form('@#######################','THIS IS THE END!'))
END.
```

Details of the arguments and field specifiers for Turbo-87 and TurboBCD are adequately detailed in the documentation for Turbo Pascal, making descriptions in this book quite superfluous. Adding the formatting syntax to the Write and WriteLn functions of the code contained in this book can augment your personal pleasure and your knowledge. At the same time, it can enhance the appearance of the screen displays and of the printed reports the programs generate. As presented in this book, the programs will compile and execute with any of three versions, Turbo Pascal, Turbo-87, and TurboBCD. I chose the generic or neutral ground for the code in this book, writing it for the more universal version, Turbo Pascal.

It is suggested that, if you are involved with financial and business ventures, you would do well to obtain the TurboBCD version of Turbo Pascal. And, if you are involved with engineering and scientific programming, obtain the Turbo-87 version, and of course, install the 8087 chip. You'll certainly see the improvements when doing lengthy and complex calculations.

Appendix B

Turbo Pascal Operators

The Turbo Pascal operators are one type of Turbo expressions that specify rules for computing values. Here, operators are listed in order of precedence:

1. Unary minus, which is the minus sign (–) with only one operand.
2. NOT operator.
3. Multiplying operators, which are the asterisk character (*), the division character (/), and these words: div, mod, and, shl, shr.
4. Summing characters, which are the plus sign (+), the minus sign (–), or, xor.
5. Relational operators, which are expressed by these symbols: =, < >, <, >, < =, > =.

   Operators of equal precedence are recognized from the left to the right sequence in which they appear. Enclosing expressions and the operators within parentheses changes the actual order of computation. The parentheses give the expression they enclose an independence and a precedence over other operators within the same statement.

   If the operands of a multiplying and an adding operator are of the Integer type, the result is of the Integer type. If, however, one or both of the operands is of the type Real, the result is of the Real type.

UNARY MINUS

   The unary minus denotes a negation of its operand, which may be of the Real or Integer type.

THE NOT OPERATOR

The NOT operator inverses or negates the logical value (1 becomes 0, or 0 becomes 1) of its Boolean operand; fore example, NOT True = False, and NOT False = True.

Turbo Pascal also allows the NOT operator to be applied to an Integer operand. In this case, bitwise, negation occurs, as in these examples:

```
NOT 0      = -1
NOT -15    = 14
NOT $2345  = $DCBA
```

MULTIPLYING OPERATORS

Operator	Operation	Operand Type	Result Type
*	multiplication	Real	Real
*	multiplication	Integer	Integer
*	multiplication	Real, Integer	Real
/	division	Real	Real
/	division	Integer	Real
/	division	Real, Integer	Real
div	integer division	Integer	Integer
mod	modulus	Integer	Integer
and	arithmetic *and*	Integer	Integer
and	logical *and*	Boolean	Boolean
shl	shift left	Integer	Integer
shr	shift right	Integer	Integer

ADDITION OPERATORS

Operator	Operation	Operand Type	Result Type
+	addition	Real	Real
+	addition	Integer	Integer
+	addition	Real, Integer	Real
−	subtraction	Real	Real
−	subtraction	Integer	Integer
−	subtraction	Real, Integer	Real

Operator	Operation	Operand Type	Result Type
or	arithmetic *or*	Integer	Integer
or	logical *or*	Boolean	Boolean
xor	arithmetic *or*	Integer	Integer
xor	logical *or*	Boolean	Boolean

RELATIONAL OPERATORS

Operator	Use
=	equal to
< >	not equal to
>	greater than
<	less than
> =	greater than or equal to
< =	less than or equal to

Appendix C

Program
Headings and Blocks

Pascal programs must have program headings and program blocks. The blocks are divided into declarations and statements.

PROGRAM HEADINGS

In Turbo Pascal, the program heading is optional. It is good practice to include the name of the program in the heading, ending with a semicolon, which indicates the end of the statement. For example, if the program's name is TopScore, the program heading would as:

```
Program TopScore ;
```

The so-called standard Pascal requires a listing of the parameters through which the program communicates with the environment. The parameters are surrounded by parentheses and each parameter is separated from the next by a comma, as in this example:

```
Program TopScore(Input,Output) ;
```

In Turbo, "Input" is assumed to be the keyboard. "Output" is assumed to be the video display, or CON. If these assumptions are the desired defaults, the words "Input" and "Output" may be omitted from the program heading.

PROGRAM BLOCKS

Immediately following the program heading is a program "block" divided into several parts:

1. Label declaration
2. Constant definition
3. Type definition
4. Variable declaration
5. Procedures and functions

Label Declarations

A label declaration is a label-name followed by a colon. It enables the program to branch directly to a statement preceded by the label. The labels must be declared and each must be separated from other labels in a list by a comma. A semicolon terminates the list of labels. Standard Pascal limits labels to numbers with a maximum of four digits. In Turbo Pascal, numbers and digits can be used as labels. "Label" is a reserved word.

Constant Definitions

A constant definition allows "synonyms" to be used as identifiers for constant values. Const, a reserved word, heads this list of definitions in the program block. It is followed by a list of constant assignments, each of which is separated from the other by a semicolon. Each constant name-assignment is separated from its assigned value by an equal sign. Turbo Pascal predefines the following values, which can be referenced within a program without having to be listed as a constant:

```
Name        Type and Value

Pi          Real (3.1415926536E+00).

False       Boolean (the truth value is false).

True        Boolean (the truth value is true).

Maxint      Integer (32767).
```

Type Assignments

The reserved word "type" heads the type section of the program block. It is followed by one or more type assignments separated by semicolons. An equal sign is used to separate each type identifier from its defined type; as in:

```
Quantity = Integer ;
```

```
Place = (office,lobby,foyer,hall,elevator) ;

Series = array[1..15] of Real ;
```

Variable Declarations

Variables must be declared before they can be used. The compiler reports as an error any use of a variable that has not been declared. The reserved word "var" heads the list of variables, each of which is separated from its identifier by a colon. Each line ends with a semicolon. Identifiers of the same type may be listed in sequence and separated from each other by commas. An example is shown below:

```
VAR

    Outward,Inward,Distance : Real ;

    I,N,Q : Integer ;

    Okay, NotOkay : Boolean ;

    Buffer : array[0..127] of Byte ;
```

User-Defined Procedures

The user-defined procedure consists of a procedure heading followed by a block which consists of a declaration and a statement. The procedure heading contains the reserved word "procedure" followed by the name of the procedure, which may then be followed by a formal parameter list; the whole heading is terminated by a semicolon. The statements to be performed by the procedure follow the heading, and if used, the parameter list.

Functions

"Function" is a reserved word and defines a part of a program that computes and returns a value.

The Statement Part

Every Pascal program has a statement part, which is always the last part of any block. The statement part consists of a series of statements followed by a semicolon. A compound statement or series of statements starts with the reserved word BEGIN and is followed by the list of individual statements. The reserved word END followed by a semicolon terminates the statement part. At the very end of a program, a period follows the final use of the reserved word END.

Identifiers: Reserved Words, Constants, Variables, and Expressions

---

Identifiers are the names assigned to items such as constants and variables. In standard Pascal, an identifier must start with a letter. It may be followed by additional letters and digits, within the limitations of the specific compiler used by the programmer. As with several other compilers, Turbo Pascal has a capability that can be very helpful in writing or inventing identifier-labels that are easily read by the unaided human eye. With Turbo Pascal you are able to use the underline character (_) anywhere a letter can be used. For example, here's an identifier—an unusual and deliberately long one that emphasizes the point—as it might appear in standard Pascal:

Fetchandfindtherightdigit

Of course this is rather hard to read and does slow us down a bit. With Turbo Pascal we can write the same identifier as:

```
Fetch_and_find_the_right_digit
```

The improvement is obvious. Many programmers choose to write long identifiers in a combination of uppercase and lowercase letters. Using the same set of words as in our previous example, this is illustrated here:

```
FetchAndFindTheRightDigit
```

In Turbo Pascal the same identifier might be written as:

```
Fetch_And_Find_The_Right_Digit
```

Turbo Pascal identifiers are not case sensitive. Capital and small letters can be intermixed within a word or a sentence without confusing the compiler. For example, as far as the compiler is concerned, these four identifiers are identical:

NICEGOING
NiceGoing
nicegoing
nIcEgOiNg

The maximum length for an identifier name in Turbo Pascal is 127 characters, counting letters, numbers, and underscores. Frankly, an identifier 127 characters long has to be ranked with the rarest occurrences in nature and science.

RESERVED WORDS

All versions and variations of Pascal use special identifiers called *reserved* or *key* words. These special identifiers are part of the syntax of the Pascal programming language. This means they cannot be used for any purpose within the source code of a program other than the one for which they are intended. They cannot be used to name programs, constants, or data types.

You have encountered many of them in the programs in this book. For example, the word PROGRAM is used at the absolute start of every program's source code, not just in this book, but in the entire universal of Pascal syntax. PROGRAM cannot be used as an identifier anywhere else in a Pascal program. It can, however, be used as part of a string of characters that is to be sent to the console for viewing or to a printer, for example. In such cases, PROGRAM and all the string's characters must be surrounded by single quotation marks.

Here is a list of RESERVED or KEY words for the standard Pascal:

AND	ARRAY	BEGIN	CASE	CONST	DIV
DO	DOWNTO	ELSE	END	FILE	FOR
FUNCTION	GOTO	IF	IN	LABEL	MOD
ALL	NOT	OF	OR	PACKED	PROCEDURE
PROGRAM	RECORD	REPEAT	SET	THEN	TO
TYPE	UNTIL	VAR	WHILE	WITH	

No doubt, if you've keyed in the source code provided in this book, you recognize many of the words in the above list. And here are some that Turbo Pascal has added to the list of RESERVED words:

ABSOLUTE   EXTERNAL   INLINE
SHL   SHR   STRING
XOR

CONSTANTS

Certain words have been given or have acquired standard values that cannot be changed. For example, Pi, the mathematical term has one value (see Appendix C) and is referred to as a *constant*.

When we want to change the value of an identifier, it is declared to be a *variable*, which is the opposite of a *constant*. Turbo Pascal predefines three constants, Real, Boolean, and Integer. These may be referenced in a program or a procedure without requiring that they be previously defined.

TYPE and VALUE: NAME:

Real (3.145926536E + 00)   Pi
Boolean   False/True
Integer (32767)   Maxint

VARIABLES

At times it is necessary to work with an identifier whose value is either unknown or might be changed during the program's operation. The process is to create a name as an identifier and declare it to be one of the types listed above. The *variable* identifiers are called *variables* simply because the values assigned to them can be made to vary (new values can be assigned to them) inside a program.

EXPRESSIONS

An *expression* is sometimes compared with a mathematical formula. It may consist of a number of assorted identifiers of compatible types connected by operators or symbols. The program works rapidly to evaluate the relationships of the identifiers, and on the basis of the operators, combine the values assigned to the identifiers, and assign a single value to the combination.

To illustrate the point, assume there are three variable identifiers: A, B, C. They have been declared to be of the integer type. Within the program, each has been assigned a value, A : = 5, B : = 3, and C : = 1. The program is using an expression:

$$A + B - C * 7 ;$$

The program evaluates the above expression as:

```
5 + 3 - 1 * 7 ;
```

Of course, the result of this calculation is 49. The value of the entire expression can be assigned to another variable of the same type as A, B, and C. It can be assigned to D, for example, which then acquires the value of 49. Its value can also be assigned to any one of the declared variables A, B, or C, which changes the variable's value accordingly, as in these two examples:

```
B := A + B - C * 7 ;
D := A + B - C * 7 ;
```

Perhaps it becomes more clear why, in Pascal, an *expression* is sometimes associated with the word *formula*.

Predefined Procedures and Functions

To simplify the task of programming, virtually all programming languages have predefined procedures and functions (or their equivalents) built into the language. The compiler recognizes them by name and takes the necessary actions. This significantly relieves the programmer of the requirement to write formulas or detailed, often-complex lines of code each time an often-repeated action or calculation is called by the program's code.

Turbo Pascal provides an excellent set of predefined procedures and functions that can be called by name from within the source code written by the programmer.

PREDEFINED PROCEDURES

Assign(F,N)	Assign file F to the file whose name is N.
BDos(R)	Make a BDOS call with register R (CP/M-86)
BDos(F,P)	Make a BDOS call to F with P (CP/M)
BIOS(F,P)	Make a BIOS call to F with P (CP/M)
BlockRead(F,D,N)	Read N blocks from D to file F
BlockWrite(F,D,N)	Write N blocks from D to file F
Chain(F)	Chain to file F
Close(F)	Close file F
ClrEol	Clean the screen to the end of the line on which the cursor is positioned

ClrScr	Clear the entire screen (same as CLS in MSDOS)
CrtExt	Send the terminal reset string
CrtInit	Send the terminal initialization sequence
Delay(M)	Delay M milliseconds before the next call
Delete(S,P,L)	Delete section of string S
DelLine	Delete the line on which the cursor is positioned
Dispose(P)	Recover memory used by P^5
Erase(F)	Delete file F from the directory
Execute(F)	Execute file F
FillChar(V,L,D)	Fill V with data D for L bytes
GetMem(P,I)	Allocate I bytes of RAM for P^5
Goto(X,Y)	Move the cursor to column X, row Y (1,1 is the upper left corner position)
Halt	Stop the program and return to the system
HighVideo	Set the video display to high intensity
Insert(S,D,P)	Insert string D into S
InsLine	Insert a line on the video display
LongSeek(F,P)	A special seek routine for MSDOS
LowVideo	Set the video display to dimmed intensity
Mark(P)	Mark the heap pointer at P^5
Move(S,D,L)	Move L bytes from S to D
MSDos(R)	Make a call to MSDOS with register R
New(P)	Create or reserve memory for P^5
NormVideo	Switch form dim to normal video intensity
Randomize	Initialize a random seed
Read(Pl,. . .)	Read items in from the keyboard
Read(F,Pl,. . .)	Read items in form the file F
ReadLn((Pl,. . .)	Same as Read(Pl,. . .) above, but move to a new line at the end of the list of items
ReadLn(F,Pl,. . .)	Same as Read(F,Pl,. . .) above, but move to a new line at the end of the list of items (for a textfile in ASCII only)
Release(P)	Reset the heap pointer to P^5
Rename(F)	Rename file F
Reset(F)	Open file F for input
Rewrite(F)	Open file F for output
Seek(F,P)	Move to record P in file F
Str(N,S)	Convert number N to string S
Val(S,N,P)	Convert string S to number N (error at P)
Write(Pl,. . .)	Write items out to the screen
Write(F,Pl,. . .)	Write items out for file F
WritelN(Pl,. . .)	Same as Write(Pl,. . .), but starts a new line after the Write expression is completed
WriteLn(F,Pl,. . .)	Same as WriteLn(F,Pl,. . .), but starts a new

line after the WriteLn expression is completed
(for a textfile in ASCII only)

PREDEFINED FUNCTIONS

Abs(A)	Absolute value of A (Real, Integer)
Addr(V)	Address of variable V (Pointer)
Addr(SubP)	Address of subprogram SubP (Pointer)
ArcTan(X)	Arctangent of X (Real)
BDos(F,P)	Performs a BDOS call, and returns register A (CP/M)
BDosHL(F,P)	Same as above, but returns the HL pair (CP/M)
Bios(F,P)	Performs a BIOS call, and returns the HL pair (CP/M)
Chr(I)	Character with the ASCII value of I (Char)
Concat(S,. .,S)	Concatenate the strings (String)
Copy(S,P,L)	Substring of P length L (String)
Cos(X)	Cosine of X (Real)
EOF(F)	Test file F for End-Of-File (Boolean)
EOLn(F)	Test file F for End-Of-Line (Boolean)
Exp(X)	Exponential of X (Real)
FilePos(F)	Current record in file F (Integer)
FileSize(F)	Total records in file F (Integer)
Frac(X)	Fractional portion of X (Real)
Hi(I)	Upper byte of I (Integer)
Int(X)	Integer portion of X (Real)
KeyPressed	Keyboard status flag (Boolean)
Length(S)	Length of string S (Integer)
Ln(X)	Natural logarithm of X (Real)
Lo(I)	Lower byte of I (Integer)
MemAvail	Bytes/paragraphs available (Integer)
Pos(P,S)	Position of string P in string S (Integer)
Ptr(I)	Pointer to address I (Pointer)
Odd(I)	Odd/even test of I (Boolean)
Ord(Sc)	Ordinal value of scalar variable (Integer)
Pred(Sc)	Predecessor of scalar value (same type)
Random	Random value from 0.0 to 0.999 . . . (Real)
Random(I)	Random value of from 0 to I-1 (Integer)
Round(X)	Rounded-off value of Real (Integer)
ShL(I)	Shift left (Integer)
ShR(I)	Shift right (Integer)
Sin(X)	Sine of X (Real)
SizeOf(V)	Size in bytes of variable V (Integer)
SizeOf(T)	Size in bytes of data type T (Integer)
Sqr(A)	Square of A (A * A) (Real, Integer)

Sqrt(A)	Square root of A (Real)
Succ(Sc)	Successor of scalar value (same type)
Swap(I)	Swap upper with lower bytes of I (Integer)
Trunc(X)	Truncated value of X (Integer)
UpCase(C)	C converted to upper case (Char)

Keyboard Input

The predefined, Boolean function KeyPressed is unique to Turbo Pascal. It makes it possible to continuously check the status of the Kbd device while a series of actions continues. If any key is pressed, TRUE is returned; otherwise FALSE is returned. The Turbo TUTOR, a book and diskette combination published by Borland International, provides an excellent example of the KeyPressed function operating from within a procedure, which is appropriately named CheckCommand:

```
Procedure CheckCommand ;

VAR

     Cmd          : Char ;

BEGIN

     IF KeyPressed THEN

     BEGIN

     Read(Kbd,Cmd) ;              { read key w/out echo }

     Cmd := UpCase(Cmd) ;         { force to upper case }
```

```
    case Cmd of

        •

        •

        •        { handle commands }


    ELSE

        Write(Chr(7)) ;        { beep at illegal cmd }

    END

  END

END ;   { of Procedure CheckCommand }
```

As Borland points out, by scattering calls to this procedure through your program (with commands written into the case statement), you can give the illusion of real-time commands, with swift response to any user input at any point. There is, however, an important restriction on the use of this procedure: make sure you don't call CheckCommand at a point where any of the commands could have side effects on what's being currently done. For example, don't call it if the program is updating the display and CheckCommand can change that display. Instead, call CheckCommand just before or just after that section of code.

I/O Error Handling

Several of the programs in this book make use of I/O error handling in the way Borland recommends. If you want to use I/O error handling more frequently than in the examples or if you want to expand and increase its use, the following examples can provide some guidance.

For example, assume that a program queries you for the name of a file, and you type in a name, but you misspell it, make a typo, or enter the name of a file that doesn't exist in the disk's directory. Without I/O error handling, the program would abort and return you to DOS; you would then have to restart the program. If you've entered data, it might not be saved, or it might be scrambled. Turbo Pascal solves this problem with compiler directives.

You can disable the "abort on I/O error" message and its action in sections of code or for the entire program by turning off the I/O error handling feature. You do this by inserting the switch {$I–} (which looks like a comment but the dollar sign makes the difference) into your program at the point at which you want to defeat the automatic aborting process. You turn the I/O error handling with its automatic abort-on-error process back on by inserting another switch that cancels the first. Type {$I+}, and press the Enter key again. Here is an example:

```
{$I-}

REPEAT
```

```
      Write('Type the name of the file: ') ;

      ReadLn(Name_It) ;

      Assign(In_File,Name_It) ;

      Reset(In_File) ;

      IOerr := (IOresult <> 0) ;

      IF IOresult > 0 THEN

            WriteLn('I can''t find that file.  Try it again.')
UNTIL NOT IOerr ;

{$I+}
```

Note again, for emphasis, that it is the $ sign that makes the I– and I+ behave as compiler directives rather than as comments to be ignored by the compiler. The default value for I/O error handling is {$I+}.

With the above section of code inserted in your program, if for any reason you type the name of a file that is not in the disk's directory, the program would not abort but would display the advice:

```
I can't find that file.  Try it again.
```

IOerr is declared as VAR of the type Boolean. Therefore, IOerr remembers that was an I/O error, even after IOresult has been reset to 0.

With this information, try revising some of the programs that ask for filename inputs. Include the above code sample. Chapters 25 through 28 provide examples from which you can learn and which you may want to use in your own program code.

Index

Edited by Marilyn L. Johnson

Other Bestsellers From TAB

Turbo Pascal
Programming with Applications

SOFTWARE AVAILABLE

If you are intrigued with the possibilities of the programs included in *Turbo Pascal Programming with Applications* (TAB Book No. 2627), you should definitely consider having the ready-to-run disk containing the software applications. This software is guaranteed free of manufacturer's defects. (If you have any problems, return the disk within 30 days, and we'll send you a new one.) Not only will you save the time and effort of typing the programs, the disk eliminates the possibility of errors that can prevent the programs from functioning. Interested?

Available on disk for IBM PC, 128K or greater (requires Turbo Pascal/3.0 or later) at $24.95 for each disk plus $1.00 shipping and handling.